VINDICATIONS

VINDICATIONS

Essays on Romantic Music

by DERYCK COOKE

With a memoir of the author by Bryan Magee

CAMBRIDGE UNIVERSITY PRESS
Cambridge
London   New York   New Rochelle   Melbourne   Sydney

First published in Great Britain in 1982
Published in the USA and Canada by the Press Syndicate
of the University of Cambridge
32 East 57th Street, New York, NY 10022 USA

Library of Congress Catalog Number: 82–4295

ISBN 0 521 24765 9 hard covers
ISBN 0 521 28947 5 paperback

Printed in Great Britain

Editorial Preface

Shortly before he died, I suggested to Deryck Cooke in a letter that he might collect together into a book those of his published articles he thought worth reprinting. He replied, with characteristic self-deprecation, that 'apart from the Beethoven article ['The Unity of Beethoven's Late Quartets'] ... and one or two salvoes on the Mahler Ten warfront—which wouldn't make any sort of book—there aren't any!' After Cooke's death in October 1976, Hazel Smalley, my brother Colin and I assembled all of his articles we could find and soon discovered that, as we had suspected, there was copious material for a book: indeed, the task of selection was a difficult one, but we had the generous assistance of Berthold Goldschmidt, who read through all the available material and concurred in our final choice. Our omissions are, for the most part, of the shorter, more straightforward pieces; all Cooke's major articles will be found here, including essays on the four composers he cared about most passionately—Wagner, Bruckner, Mahler and Delius. The essay on Beethoven's late quartets presents an important and cogent theory which challenges most accepted views of these works. To make the selection as comprehensive as possible, we have included his justification of the Lennon–McCartney songs—a superb piece of no-nonsense analysis—and, as a sample of his flair for writing about literature as well as music, a BBC talk on *Wuthering Heights*, which, as Bryan Magee notes in his Memoir, was Deryck Cooke's favourite novel.

'The Musical Symbolism of Wagner's Music Dramas' first appeared in *The Musical Times*, June 1952, pp.258–62; 'Wagner's Operatic Apprenticeship' in *The Musical Times*, February 1965, pp.103–5; 'The Bruckner Problem Simplified' in four articles in *The Musical Times*—January 1969, pp.20–22, February 1969,

pp.142–4, April 1969, pp.362–5 and May 1969, pp.479–82—which
were later reprinted in a revised version as a booklet by *The
Musical Newsletter* in association with Novello & Co. Ltd.; 'The
Facts Concerning Mahler's Tenth Symphony' in *Chord and
Discord*, Vol. 2 No.10, 1963, pp.3–27; 'The Word and the Deed' in
The Listener, 2 July 1964, pp.22–3; 'Delius: A Centenary Evalua-
tion' in *The Listener*, 25 January 1962, pp.195–6; 'Delius and Form'
in *The Musical Times*, June 1962, pp.392–3 and July 1962, pp.460–
5; 'The Unity of Beethoven's Late Quartets' in *The Music Review*,
Vol. 24 No.1, February 1963, pp.30–49; 'Strauss, Stravinsky and
Mozart' in *The Listener*, 9 November 1961, p.789; 'Shakespeare
into Music' in *The Listener*, 23 April 1964, pp.665–7; 'Reactionary'
in *The Listener*, 2 November 1967, p.582; 'The Lennon–
McCartney Songs' in *The Listener*, 1 February 1968, pp.157–8;
'The Futility of Music Criticism' in *The Musical Newsletter* (New
York), January 1972, pp.7–9. Thanks are due to the various editors
and publishers of the journals in which these articles appeared for
their kind permission to reprint. 'Mahler's Melodic Thinking',
'Reading and Re-reading *Wuthering Heights*' and 'The Future of
The Language of Music' were originally given as BBC broadcast
talks, and have been edited for publication. 'The Future of Musical
Language' was originally intended as the final chapter of Deryck
Cooke's first book, *The Language of Music*, and is published here
for the first time.

David Matthews

Contents

Deryck Cooke: a Memoir

Bryan Magee

One day, towards the end of the First World War, Mabel Cooke was shovelling coals in the back yard of her home in Leicester. Suddenly she dropped the coal bucket and rushed into the house crying: 'Something's happened to Vic!' At about that time on the same day her husband Vic, a soldier on active service in France, upset a kerosene lamp over himself and was horribly burnt. He was sent home severely disabled, and died only three or four years later. In the meantime the couple had a child, their only one, Deryck, who was born on 14 September 1919.

Deryck could never remember his father, but one of his most pungent early recollections was of the atmosphere of death and dying in the house. All his life he felt a closeness to death, and it could be that this was one of the causes. The fact that his father died when he did had other consequences which certainly influenced Deryck's personality. One was that he grew up poor. Another was that he was brought up entirely by women—his widowed mother and grandmother—in a home in which he was the centre of love and attention.

It was typical of the situation that his mother made shift to have him taught the piano but could not afford to buy him much music. However, he borrowed from the Leicester public library, and became adept at mastering difficult works in the permitted two weeks. He also spent many hours with friends playing four-handed arrangements of symphonies and chamber music, and it was in this form that he first made the acquaintance of a good deal of the standard orchestral repertory. The fact that he did so from inside the music, so to speak, as a performer and not just a listener, left its mark.

As with so many other bright children who grow up in a working class environment, it never entered his head that there was anything antithetical between popular culture and art. He knew all the popular songs of the day, and went hungrily to the cinema, especially to musicals and thrillers. He devoured thrillers in book form too, and comics, and strip cartoons—mixed up with more and more novels and poetry as he got older. All these interests were to stay with him throughout life: the man who constructed the performing version of Mahler's Tenth Symphony followed 'Peanuts' every day while doing so, and relaxed with the thrillers of Simenon, Eric Ambler and John Le Carré. As a child his highest ambition had been to play cricket for Leicester (or even, in moments of more secret, more reckless fantasy, for England). In 1970, when an article he had written about Freddie Trueman was reprinted in a book of *Great Cricketers*, he was more elated than any reception for an article on music could have made him.

His friends at Wyggeston Grammar School in Leicester remember him as an equable boy, open faced, warm and outgoing. A group of them used to go for walks in the countryside—walks which by some arcane rule were never allowed to be shorter than twenty-three miles—during which they would talk the talk of intelligent adolescents, most of it about whatever it was they were reading at the time. As a group they were mildly interested in politics, but more in music, and most of all in literature. However, by the time Deryck went into the sixth form his most obviously outstanding gift was for piano playing, and it was as an organ scholar that he went up to Selwyn College, Cambridge. At around this time, in his late teens, it came to be taken for granted that his professional future would be something to do with music. His family and most of his friends assumed it would centre on the piano. Good judges still recall confidently that he was the finest undergraduate pianist in the Cambridge of his day—indeed, of both his days, for he belonged to that generation of students whose university careers were split into two by the Second World War.

He was still at school, however, and only just old enough to stand on his own feet, when his mother died. For him, coming as it did at the awkward turn between adolescence and adulthood, everything about this event combined to make it a traumatic experience. Having grown up without a father, and as an only child, his most powerful affections were heavily concentrated on his mother, and her death itself was a lingering and painful one from cancer of the oesophagus. There was a part of him that never got over it. As a middle-aged man he would react with disconcerting vehemence against the smell of boiled fish, or the smell of disinfectant, because they reminded him with unbearable vividness of his mother's dying.

When the Second World War began he was a pacifist at first, and went before a tribunal. But two things eventually made him change his mind. One was the realization that only force was going to stop Hitler from plunging Europe back into the Dark Ages; the other was the news photographs of people wounded in the fight against him. He joined the Royal Engineers, and was plunged into his full share of action—among other things, he was on a troopship that was torpedoed in the Mediterranean, and he took part in the invasion of the Italian mainland at Salerno beachhead. By sunny contrast, when the point was reached towards the end of the war when it became obvious that the fighting was over as far as his unit was concerned, he and some of his colleagues formed a dance band. Their standard was high, and their reputation spread, and such was the demand for their services that Deryck in effect spent his last year in uniform, most of it after the war, travelling around Austria as a dance band pianist. A tape recording survives from later years of a breath-stopping performance by him of 'Tiger Rag'.

One characteristic aspect of Deryck's army service was that he refused to become an officer. In the social atmosphere of England at the time when he joined up it was taken for granted that recruits from Oxbridge would become officers, but Deryck declined to be one. He had a sense of class identification which he retained all his life, both positively and negatively: he felt himself very much at home among the ordinary soldiers, and he did not feel himself to be a member of the officer class. In later years, when I knew him, I found this outlook partly admirable and partly unadmirable, and we had one or two heated arguments about it. The admirable part was not just that he was unimpressed by status or rank or social position: it was something rarer and more remarkable than that, especially in so gifted a man. It was that he could be drawn to another individual by things that had nothing whatever to do with that person's intelligence or abilities or interests or education, but rested on quite other human attributes. He could form as intimate and real a friendship with an unintelligent, inarticulate person as he could with someone who shared his musical and other interests. I am in no doubt that this deep-lying, sub-verbal, intuitive sensitivity and responsiveness to otherwise inexpressible human feeling was also at the heart of his unique musical insight, and profoundly conditioned his view of what music was, or ought to be.

On the other hand there was also, unmistakably, an element of class prejudice added to this. To the end of his life Deryck was put off at first by an upper middle class accent. He was able to overcome this and form just as close friendships with upper middle class people as with anyone else, and he did so with a great many; nevertheless it was always, at the very beginning, a barrier that had to be surmounted. This led him into an unfair dislike and dismissal of people who did not rouse his interest sufficiently for him to make the effort. As a result, perfectly ordinary, unremarkable people were liable to encounter from him a hostility which they could not but find unjustified and therefore objectionable. The bureaucratic hierarchy of the BBC, in which he worked for most of his adult life, abounded in such people for twenty or thirty years after the war, and the fact that they owed their power and influence not to merit but to the accident of privilege kept him inexhaustably supplied with fuel for his anger. That some of them should have come to dislike him in return was inevitable, but there was nevertheless something properly enraging about the fact that broadcasting in general, and the music on it in particular, tended to be run by mediocrities.

After the war, Deryck returned to Cambridge to complete his studies. This second spell at Cambridge held particular significance for his life as a whole. His compositions, which were in a late romantic, post-Wolf, post-Strauss idiom, had real quality, and were publicly performed to impressed audiences. He fell deeply, passionately in love with someone who, he felt sure, was the life partner for him. But after his affair with her had been going for a long time and seemed to have become unshakably established she was bowled over by a complete stranger, and without warning she left Deryck and went off to America and got married. The effect on Deryck was shattering. It destroyed something dangerously near to the heart of his self-confidence: he went into a serious depression, during which he tore up all the music he had composed, and he never composed again. (One or two manuscripts survive which happened to be in the possession of friends. The best of these compositions, it seems to be agreed, is a setting of Rilke's *Sonnets to*

Orpheus, and a setting of a sequence of Shakespeare sonnets also has serious merit.)

In 1947 he left Cambridge and joined the BBC as assistant to Harold Rutland in the script-writing unit of the music department. This involved going to live in London for the first time, and London was to be his home for the rest of his life. At first he lodged in a house in South Kensington belonging to William Mann, a friend from Cambridge. (John Warrack was another inhabitant.) Then when Deryck met his Belgian wife Jacqueline he moved to Hampstead, and after that with her to Chalk Farm. Perhaps to his regret, they never had any children.

Deryck worked for the BBC for nearly thirty years, from 1947 until his death in 1976. It is true that he left the staff in 1959 in order to freelance, but even as a freelance most of his work continued to be for the BBC, and he returned to the staff in 1965 as head of the script-writing unit he had worked in as a junior before. This unit's task is to produce the millions of words a year which are read out over the air by BBC announcers in introducing and supplementing music. The historical and musical accuracy needs to be scrupulous, the critical understanding catholic and cogent, the writing economical yet clear, and easy both to speak and to listen to. For many years much of it was written by Deryck. His standards were always of the highest; but the job was of its nature a faceless one, and the work itself, however good, characterless and ephemeral. It was his outside activities—his books and articles, his lectures, his performing version of Mahler's Tenth Symphony—that brought him fame and, much more important than that, a sense of personal fulfilment. In the course of time it became a source of almost intolerable frustration to him that he was financially unable to free himself from an office job in order to devote himself fully to the work he loved and was best at. The fact that this has been the standard problem of the writer down the generations was no consolation to him.

His first full-length book, *The Language of Music,* was published by Oxford University Press in 1959. He once told me that it was written primarily *against* the long held and still fashionable Stravinskian view that music is not expressive of emotion—is not, indeed, expressive of anything. He set out to show that throughout the history of Western music the same, or similar, musical configurations had been used to express the same, or similar, feelings or states of mind or dramatic situations, and therefore, although no one would dream of postulating a dictionary-like set of equivalencies, there simply were, as a matter of fact, perennial associations—be they rooted in any mixture one cares to assume of convention, human psychology and the physics of music—which enabled music to function as some sort of language of the emotions, albeit one which was for the most part untranslatable into words. One of his subsidiary theses was that ever since the sixteenth century a deliberate departure from tonal moorings had been used to express 'emotions of the most painful type', which meant that we had now in the twentieth century developed a whole musical language whose powers of expression were limited to such emotions: 'it does not express the simple fundamental sense of being at one with nature and life.'

Deryck was hostile to modernism right across the board—not only in music but in the other performing arts, the visual arts, and literature as well—and always for the same basic reason: he thought that when an art self-consciously makes its own techniques the chief object of its interest, thereby transmogrifying a means into an end, it forfeits its real end and true nature, namely, the expression of human feeling. But far from his anti-modernism being philistine, facile or smug, for most of his life it was deeply troubled: he hated being out of what seemed to him the mainstream of his time, and he had recurrent doubts that it might be he, after all, who was missing the point of a valid artistic approach. So he would often come back for a fresh try at some acknowledged modernist masterpiece. However, towards the end of his life he came to the conclusion that it really was modernism, and not his response to it, that was defective.

A year after the publication of *The Language of Music* the BBC published a booklet by Deryck on Mahler to mark the centenary of the composer's birth in 1860. The chief significance of this little work was that the writing of it set him in search of something worthwhile to say about the composer's last, unfinished symphony, and thus drew him into a study of the sketches for it which was to absorb him for the rest of his life, culminating in the publication in 1976 of a performing version in full orchestral score. There is no need for me to tell the detailed story: Deryck tells it himself in his published introduction to the score. He was always the first to say that what he published was not what Mahler would have published. Mahler, in accordance with his normal practice, would have changed innumerable things and then again have had second, third and fourth thoughts; he would have cut, inserted, expanded, reduced, in all the unforeseeable ways of genius. What Deryck saw himself as doing was something quite different. Here was this continuous sketch by Mahler for a symphony on the largest scale, written at the height of his powers and full of superb music. Was no one ever to hear any of it, or even be allowed to get any idea of what it was like? To give that question the answer No would be to carry musical puritanism to an absurd degree of self-denial, and to consign some very great music to oblivion. Surely what was needed was for the sketch to be rendered performable, so that the material could at least be heard, and people could begin to get some idea of what Mahler had in mind for his last symphony. This Deryck set himself modestly to do.

It is absolutely essential to stress the completeness of Mahler's sketch. Deryck had to orchestrate, to fill out the harmony, and to make decisions about tempo and a great many other things, but he did not have to *compose* anything in the free sense of the word compose, as Süssmayr had to do in finishing Mozart's *Requiem*, or Alfano in finishing Puccini's *Turandot*. The prejudice that still exists against Deryck's version rests almost entirely on a misunderstanding of this. As he wrote in his Introduction, 'the thematic line throughout, and something like 90% of the counterpoint and harmony, are pure Mahler, and vintage Mahler at that.' Having said this, however, there remains for the rest of us something awesome about the quality of Deryck's achievement. For the orchestration is not only magnificent, it is magnificent *Mahlerian* orchestration of the finest subtlety, insight and imagination. It is as if Deryck's musical personality has been completely dissolved into Mahler's material. The unique empathy displayed here by one musician for another is beyond the power of words to describe. But the result, which now stands before us, is a great symphony—one of the greatest by Mahler or anybody else—which the world would not otherwise have had. To refuse then to perform it, as some conductors do, on the ground that its attribution is ambiguous, is to put musicological considerations above musical ones. In my opinion the right attitude, expressed with deliberate crudity, is: 'This is a great symphony: what better justification than that could we have for performing *any* symphony?'

Mahler's widow came round eventually to something like this view. She had been persuaded by Bruno Walter to put a ban on any further performances of Deryck's performing version after its first (incomplete) broadcast in 1960, but in 1963 she was induced to listen to a tape of it, whereupon she sat down the same day and wrote to him: 'I was so moved by this performance that I immediately asked Mr. Byrns [the conductor Harold Byrns] to play the work a second time. I then realized that the time had come when I must reconsider my previous decision not to permit the performance of this work. I have now decided once and for all to give you full permission to go ahead with performances in any part of the world.' If I may permit myself the impertinence of adding my view to this, I feel inwardly certain that this score will sooner or later be absorbed into the repertory as the accepted performing version of Mahler's Tenth Symphony, and that it will enshrine Deryck's name, rightly, in the history of music.

It was in connection with this work that I first met him. As a Mahler lover I attended the Promenade Concert of 13 August 1964 at which the full length score was given its first public performance, again in the version to be later superseded, by the London Symphony Orchestra conducted by Berthold Goldschmidt (who had provided advice and encouragement throughout the work on it). So impressed was I by the achievement, and fascinated by the story behind it, that, when shortly afterwards I acquired a television series called 'This Week in the Arts', I wanted to make a documentary programme about it. I telephoned Deryck to discuss it, and thus we met for the first time.

We had lunch at the Savile Club, so it was there that I saw for the first time this great warm bear of a man in a baggy grey suit, his movements a little lumbering, a touch of the Midlands still in his voice, and his football-shaped head so big that it made him appear slightly moon faced. Only two or three times in my life have I felt such an immediate and powerful rapport with someone I had never met before. Not only did we come to realize during the lunch that we shared some of our most deeply felt interests, we seemed also to be in immediate and hyperstimulating communication about them. Our lunch became excited and noisy, not least because of the plentiful musical illustrations, but we were oblivious of the people at the surrounding tables: we each knew we had found a fellow spirit. We became close friends on the instant, and remained such for the rest of Deryck's life. I have known few men of whom I could say plainly and simply that I loved them, but Deryck was one.

My proposed documentary with him was never made, because my series was on ITV whereas the BBC had contractual rights not only over Deryck's services but over all the performances that had so far taken place of the musical material. However, from that time onwards he and I met frequently, mostly for evenings of drink, food and argument, though sometimes we would go to a public performance together; and there is one uproarious evening I remember, of more than Wagnerian length, which was entirely devoted to our shared repertory of popular songs from the interwar years, sung by the two of us in raucous unison to a piano accompaniment (by Deryck) of a higher standard than our singing could unridiculously be heard with. The quantities we drank together on some of these evenings were gargantuan, and quite unmatched in my experience with anyone else. The occasion on which I drank more than on any other of my life started with aperitive spirits in Deryck's flat, then moved to a pub where we downed more spirits and chased them with glassfuls of beer, and ended in a restaurant where the two of us did justice to a very nice dinner accompanied by six bottles of wine. At the end of that we were still arguing at least coherently about music, and when we came to leave the restaurant we did so in an impeccably dignified, if over-carefully controlled manner. In any other company half that amount of drink would have had me either slurring my words or bumping into the furniture, and probably both.

Our discussions always seemed to become arguments, whether what we were talking about was music, literature, politics, social questions, our personal lives, or anything else. This was nothing to do with alcohol, for it happened just as frequently when we did not drink at all. These arguments often became heated and sometimes almost violent: one of them ended with him physically bundling me out of his flat. Our behaviour in this respect used to upset our accompanying women friends much more than it did us. We were always on the best of terms the next day, and did not even bother with explanations or apologies. The odd thing, though, is that neither of us behaved in this way with anyone else. The reason, I believe, is that the same things were closest to our hearts, and in our general attitudes to them we were strikingly similar, yet some of our most passionately held views were, though almost, not quite

the same. The most deeply felt differences are notoriously between
people who are close.

I remember my exhilarated sense of discovery at our very first
meeting when I realized that, although I was supposed to be something of a Wagner expert, this man's knowledge of Wagner out-
stripped mine on every front. He carried an accurate and almost
month-by-month biography of Wagner in his head, and he knew
the scores better than anyone has ever known them, including
maybe Wagner himself: his retention of them extended down into
the smallest print of the inner parts, and he had a startling ability to
perceive relationships between configurations of notes at widely
different points in a work. His understanding of, and insight into,
The Ring was founded on just such a detailed perception of the
metamorphosis of the musical material, together with an awareness of its psychological and dramatic import at every point.
Throughout the time I knew him he regarded the book he was
planning to write on this as his life's work: once, at the bottom of a
trough of suicidal depression, he remarked to me that it was only
the unwrittenness of this book that kept him in the world. It was to
have been a multi-volume work in two main parts, the first an
analysis of the dramatic text of *The Ring,* the second an analysis of
the score. When he died, only the first half of the first part had been
completed; but even this constituted a book of 353 pages, which has
been published posthumously by Oxford University Press as *I Saw
the World End.* As far as my knowledge goes, the fact that Deryck
never wrote the second half of the whole work is as big a loss to
Wagner studies as there has ever been. Others might have made as
good a fist as he at the textual analysis, but his understanding of the
music was unique and irrecoverable. He talked to me about it
enough to leave me with a permanently painful sense of the riches
of insight which that part of the book would have contained. His
recorded 3-disc lecture on *The Ring,* justly renowned though it is, is
a mere drop from that ocean.

Deryck regarded Wagner's art as uniquely marvellous, in that it
compassed a range of experience equalled only by Shakespeare,
plumbed depths of emotion reached by no other artist, and was
beautiful beyond anything else imaginable. His attitude to it was
idolatrous—he often said things like 'Wagner is God', or 'Wagner
is my God'—but whereas other Wagnerolaters merely rhapsodize
and worship, he was a hard headed, sharp eyed, perennial student

of the detailed 'what' and 'how'. Furthermore, he was not narrowed by his adoration of Wagner: it certainly did not preclude a total empathy with Mahler for purposes of his work on the Tenth Symphony, nor did it prevent his writing some of the best essays that have ever been published on certain other composers, for instance on Bruckner and Delius.

In fact Deryck, like Wagner, although phenomenally gifted musically, was insatiably interested in all sorts of things unconnected with music. He devoured novels—Sterne, Dickens, Melville, Dostoevsky, Zola, Hardy, Conrad, Kafka. His special favourite was *Wuthering Heights,* and his most notable blind spots Jane Austen, Trollope and Henry James. The political writer to whom he felt most closely akin was George Orwell—a cornery, awkward yet idealistic critic of the Left from within the Left, like himself. He loved Shakespeare and a range of poets from the Elizabethans to Rilke. He once remarked that if he were given another life he would want to devote it to the study of language and languages. This was a fascination which showed itself in all sorts of ways, from a love of translation to an enthusiasm for crossword puzzles, or the invention of persuasive names for non-existent composers, broadcasts from the Continent of whose ingeniously titled works he would inveigle the *Radio Times* into announcing. (His accomplice in this trick, Robert Layton, was one of his three closest friends at the BBC, the other two being Hans Keller and Robert Simpson.) Unconnected again with all these things, he was an enthusiastic follower of sport, especially cricket and football. And he loved with a special edge, even more than most of us, the evenings spent in pubs with friends, the lunches in Soho restaurants, the hours of exhilarating talk. He was an enjoyer, in a spirit not of superficial hedonism but of gut involvement, and in all his pursuits he was therefore much more interested in avoiding what he did not like than in criticizing it. In everything he was before all else a man of feeling. It was in a level of feeling deeper than words—always authentic, never affected or self-conscious—that his intellectual work was firmly rooted.

For all his other interests, though, he was a musician first and foremost. I have heard several professional musicians, including well known composers, describe him as the most musical person they have ever known. As one of these, the composer Robert Simpson, put it, 'music seemed simply to flow out of him'. Perhaps the odd thing is that this unique musicality went not into composing or performing music but into writing about it. Even so, his personality and approach partook more of the creative artist than they did of the scholar, though they certainly contained sizable elements of both. As a conceptual thinker, in the academic sense, he was competent but unremarkable, though he kept himself up to scratch by a painstaking insistence on professional standards in all things down to the humblest sleeve note or station announcement. However, his real gifts were those of flair, intuition, insight, imaginative empathy—and for these, in his fields of special interest, there was no one to touch him. He could see or hear in a score what nobody else could see or hear until he pointed it out to them. To take one of innumerable examples—the Delius Violin Concerto: this work had always been so taken for granted as being rhapsodic and formless that even people who found it beautiful tended to say that they liked it in spite of its being formless; yet along came Deryck and pointed out an unmistakable (once he had put his finger on it) form in all its full and ungainsayable detail. (See p. 123)

He never looked on himself as a music critic, and he turned down invitations to accept one of the established and prestigious critical posts. Although he wrote a lot of freelance criticism the general run of music criticism nevertheless represented an activity he despised. He once wrote (see p. 204): 'The great composers, whatever else they may or may not have been, were the supreme musical minds in history. As such, they deserve nothing but our gratitude and admiration for what they have bequeathed us. The spectacle of a far lesser musical mind censuring one of them for supposed "weaknesses", which are in fact illusions produced by blind spots, is quite ludicrous. And when, as so often, the censure is put forward in an arrogant, self-regarding, self-advertising way, the result is enough to make the angels weep.' Typically, he went on immediately: 'We have all been guilty of this, to some extent. I remember one article of my own—a wholesale attempt to write off Stravinsky's *Rake's Progress*—the thought of which now makes me shudder.' And he concluded, in a sentence which comes close to embodying the heart of his approach: 'Humility—the realistic recognition of one's own musical littleness, compared with the masters, is the very first requisite of any writer on music.'

Perhaps his recognition of his own musical littleness went too far. I found in him a strange combination of towering gifts, of which he was aware, with a self-effacing diffidence about exercising them. In fact he had, it seemed to me, a fear of self-assertion in any form, artistic or otherwise. In the last ten years or so of his life the recurrent depressions, the heavy drinking, the outbursts of aggression, all seemed to point to some deep-seated sense of frustration, and I could not help wondering whether he was beginning to be aware of a lack of self-fulfilment. That so prodigiously musical a person, with a mastery of large-scale orchestration, should write no music of his own always seemed to me to require more explanation than the one I have given. But perhaps this is a blind spot of mine. There was certainly some great inner unhappiness in those later years, but it may have had other causes—for instance, possibly the circumstances surrounding the break-up of his marriage, or the ill health which finally overtook him.

In 1971 he had an operation to remove pressure on the optic nerve of his right eye. Before the operation the doctors thought, and so did he, that he probably had a tumour on the brain. It turned out to be an enlarged blood vessel that was causing the trouble, but I am not sure that Deryck was wholly confident that in being told this he was being told the truth. Some years after the operation, and only just before he died, he joked about having got through a Beethoven and Smetana complex (the reference was to the deafness that had crept up on him in adult life) and a Mahler complex (he had at one time felt an intuition that he was going to die at the same age as Mahler had) only now to fall victim to a George Gershwin complex. Gershwin died of a tumour on the brain.

There was no tumour, but the very real circulatory troubles that Deryck had were exacerbated for a long time by his excessive smoking and drinking. The symptoms included not only pains in the legs, and breathlessness, but also headaches, and giddiness, and it could only too well be that these fed unspoken suspicions in his mind. Eventually he managed to reduce both his smoking and his drinking, but by then it was too late: his circulatory system was unable to recover. Even so, the end, when it came, was unexpected and shocking.

Between midnight and one on the morning of 27 October 1976 a conversation I was having with a guest in my home turned to Mahler, and she asked about Deryck—whom she had never met— and the Tenth Symphony. I told her the story, and got out one of the recordings, which I had not played for a good long while. Because of the lateness of the hour I made no attempt to play it all through, but picked out snippets in illustration of what I had been saying. Finally I put on the beginning of the last movement, and over the sequence of huge, single blows on the big military drum that keep bringing the music to a dead stop before it can get properly started I heard myself, to my own surprise, saying: 'This expresses something that almost never is expressed in music: a sense of real catastrophe. It's as if the bottom is dropping out of everything. It's disaster, and on a timeless, hopeless, final scale. It's the end, if such a thing is conceivable.' Later that morning, towards noon, someone telephoned me to tell me that Deryck had had a stroke the previous day and been rushed into hospital, where he had died between midnight and one that morning.

The Musical Symbolism of Wagner's Music-Dramas

The man who sets out to write about music undertakes one of the most difficult and treacherous tasks in the world. So long as he confines himself to musicology, and deals only with matters of historical fact, he can attain to the unimpeachable accuracy of science; but when he ventures into the realm of interpretation, and attempts to clarify the ideas and emotions which lie within the actual notes, he lapses into mere speculation and guesswork. The date of composition of a Mozart symphony is a matter susceptible of proof; but the meaning of the symphony, as matters stand at present, is open to debate. Opinions conflict, and one man's is as good (or as bad) as another's.

This is, of course, partly due to the inherent imprecision of language as a means for discussing the subtle and precise shades of feeling which music alone can convey. We need a more accurate terminology, with the various meanings of 'meaning' clearly defined and classified, before we can begin to investigate the meaning, or meanings, of any piece of music. But even if we can create such a precision instrument, a much larger stumbling-block awaits us: the fact that *music is a language which has no dictionary*. When a composer uses a certain phrase, we may feel that he is expressing by means of it a particular idea or group of ideas, and we may say so; but what rational justification have we for making such a statement? In what sense does a certain succession of notes 'express' a particular idea or emotion? What is the emotional connotation of this chord or that rhythm?

No valid answer has been found to these questions: there is here an almost uncharted territory, awaiting the most careful research. Albert Schweitzer alone has done pioneer work in this field: in his monumental book on J. S. Bach, he undertook a classification of that composer's musical vocabulary, showing how he used certain musical phrases over and over again to express similar ideas contained in the various texts he set, and explaining exactly how these phrases could be considered as expressions of the ideas concerned. And his classification is of the utmost value for a proper understanding of Bach's music. For instance, when listening to the aria in the St. Matthew Passion, 'Come, healing cross' ('Komm, süsses Kreuz'), we do not receive the full meaning of the music unless we are aware that the viola da gamba obbligato, with its quadruple stopping and dotted rhythm, is a pictorial representation of Simon of Cyrene staggering beneath the weight of the cross and, by implication, a symbol of a human experience—the painful business of 'taking up one's cross'. To ignore this is to appreciate the music merely as an example of a da capo aria with a virtuoso obbligato of a somewhat *recherché* character. Here, as almost everywhere, Bach uses music as a language for expressing his (Christian) conception of the nature of things: and he is able to do this by reason of the natural symbolism of music itself. The laboured sound of quadruple stopping on a bass stringed instrument, caused by drawing the bow across the four strings from the lowest to the highest, is a natural way of representing in music the intense effort involved in heaving a cross forward on one's shoulders, and the jerky rhythm of dotted notes a no less natural symbol for an unsteady gait.

Now there is no doubt that, from earliest times to the present day, many composers have used the natural symbolism of music as a language in this way, to a greater or lesser degree. Some of the terms of the language are universal: a particular instance is the phrase of two notes, the second a semitone lower than the first, which is used, usually in a minor key, to render with acute realism the sound of a moan of grief or pain. A commonplace of the madrigalists in their canzonets of hopeless love, it is to be found in Bach's Crucifixus from the B minor Mass, in the simpleton's song in Mussorgsky's *Boris Godunov*, in the *Miserere* in Verdi's *Il Trovatore*, and it has turned up recently in Schoenberg's *A Survivor from Warsaw*; there are, of course, innumerable other instances. Some of the terms, on the other hand, are the property of a single composer or a group of composers. The dissonance of the dominant minor ninth, for example, which was used so often to underline moments of terror and anguish in nineteenth-century music, appeared hardly at all before Beethoven, who may be regarded as having 'coined' this word in the musical vocabulary;

and the chord formed like a first inversion of the dominant minor ninth plus eleventh is practically the sole property of Wagner.

The meaning of such terms of musical language derives from their association with words; and when they occur without words the same general meaning still attaches to them. It should, then, be possible to build up a dictionary of musical symbols, based on a close study of the vocal works of the great composers, the symbols being classified as (*a*) those which are universal to all composers, and (*b*) those which form the phraseology of a group or of a single man; and (*c*) according to the ideas they represent. Such a dictionary would, of course, be no more infallible for the purpose of 'translating' music into words than a foreign dictionary is for translating from another language into one's own: translation is not a science, but an art, and a delicate one at that. The resulting 'translations', again, will be of no greater value than translations of literature from one language into another. There will still be various versions, each of them to some degree inadequate; but they will approximate more closely to the original, and consequently to one another, than do the present hit-or-miss attempts that one reads daily. And they will then be as much of a help to the listener as, for example, a translation of Goethe's *Faust* is to the non-German reader with a reasonable knowledge of the language: a helpful guide to the proper understanding of the original work.

Until that happy day arrives we must be content to do as best we can: that is, before discussing the meaning of a particular composer's music, we must, as Schweitzer did for Bach, make a glossary of the terms of his musical language. (It is perhaps in this way that the much-needed dictionary will come into being: many writers working each on an individual composer, and later comparing and collating results.) The composer whose music forms the subject of this essay, Richard Wagner, is one whose subtle meanings will never be elucidated by the prevailing hit-or-miss methods, as the existing commentaries on his music show. The conflicting opinions as to the significance of this or that motive are the product of an extremely superficial acquaintance with the elements of his musical speech; and the commentators' failure to give any justification for providing the motives with their various names has led to a widespread belief that Wagner's use of leitmotif is based on an intellectually manufactured system, whereby he identifies the characters, ideas and emotions of his dramas with arbitrary successions of notes, and naively expects us to follow suit. In actual fact it is nothing of the sort, but a perfectly legitimate extension of the already existing musical language for his own purposes, as can be easily proved.

Let us take, as an example, the Siegfried motive from *The Ring*:

Ex. 1

Wagner identifies this motive quite patently with Siegfried himself, and in consequence it must be supposed to represent all that the word 'hero' meant to Wagner. Now we see that it begins by progressing melodically from the lower dominant up through the tonic to the minor mediant; why should there be anything particularly symbolic of heroism in that succession of notes? Before attempting to answer this question, let us consider other themes which begin with this formula, and see if we can prove a general tendency to equate it with ideas of heroism. We can find three more in *The Ring* itself: the motives associated with, the heroic race of the Volsungs (which of course includes Siegfried) (Ex. 2a), with the half-human half-divine Valkyries (Ex. 2b), and with the Valkyrie's annunciation of death to the hero (Siegmund) (Ex. 2c).

Ex. 2

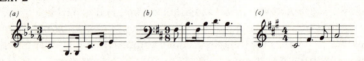

Heroic enough ideas; let us agree that, for some reason or other, Wagner chose to identify this melodic formula with the heroic element in human life.

And now, if we turn to another composer who was attracted by the idea of heroism—Beethoven—we shall find confirmation for Wagner's choice. In the symphony which he himself entitled the Eroica, Beethoven used the formula as the beginning of the opening theme of the funeral march, a theme too well known to need quotation. (This may have been another of Beethoven's coinages, but a great amount of research would be needed to prove it.) Need we be surprised then to find that it forms the skeleton of the theme of Schumann's song 'The Two Grenadiers' ('Die beiden Grenadiere') (Ex. 3a), and of a song by Schubert from *Die Winterreise* entitled, significantly enough, 'Mut' (spirit or courage'?

Ex. 3

Could we take a step further and include the finale of Brahms's First Piano Concerto and the opening of his Piano Quintet, neither of which has words to confirm our surmise? This question takes us too far afield at this stage, but at least we have seen four composers agreeing on the meaning of a particular melodic progression.

But can one give any reason why this formula of three notes should be regarded by composers as the musical root-word 'hero'? None, perhaps, any more than we can say why the sound of the actual word should convey the sense it does. Yet, whereas the word clearly possesses its meaning only by virtue of long association, the musical sound is felt by many to express the quintessential idea: is there no reason for this feeling? All one can say is that, in the first place, the phrase is based on the minor triad, which in classical tonality is the time-honoured, axiomatic musical symbol for tragedy; secondly, that to take a step melodically from the dominant to the tonic is to perform one of the most decisive actions in music, and to make it an upward step is to employ the symbolism we acknowledge to be inherent in music whenever we speak of high and low notes or upward and downward progressions; thirdly, the minor mediant is the note which gives the minor key its essentially tragic character, being a depression of the natural major third of the harmonic series. Consequently to step up melodically from dominant to tonic in the minor key, and then further up to the mediant, is equivalent to taking a decisive step towards the heights in a tragic context and to proceed on upwards into the very heart of tragedy itself. Which, after all, is a description of the action of a hero.

Of course, the basic significance of the phrase is modified by the special meaning which each composer gives it by factors of speed, rhythm, harmony and particularly by whatever follows after. The indomitable character of Siegfried's theme is to be found in these factors. Its tempo is swift but majestic, its rhythm buoyant, and the tonic is harmonized by the *major* chord, giving a confident start. In consequence the following minor mediant has an even more tragic implication than it would have had otherwise: the melody moves, as it were, into the thick of trouble. This sets in high relief its triumphant continuation, which recoils two steps to leap right over the minor mediant, above the upper dominant to the sub-mediant (A flat) which is harmonized in the natural way by the *major* chord. Again, the deep sense of grief conveyed by the opening of the Eroica funeral march is to be found in the extreme slowness of its speed, the dragging, dotted rhythm, the unchanged C minor harmony which accompanies its first phrase and the drooping of the melody from the third back to the tonic. Other examples of the modification of the essential formula by contributory factors are the galloping rhythm of the Valkyries' motive and its ever-upward melodic drive, the slow measure of the Volsungs' theme, which rises only to fall, the plodding march-rhythm of Schumann's Grenadiers, and the jog-trot bravado of Schubert's death-doomed winter-journeyer. Another consideration is that Siegfried and the Valkyries leap straight from tonic to mediant; the other versions, representing ideas of a more sombre character, arrive at the mediant less impetuously, by means of the intermediate note. (It begins to look as though our dictionary, like all the best foreign dictionaries, will be a bulky affair, with several columns or pages for the various uses of each of the really fundamental words!)

We have seen how Wagner has employed a current term of musical phraseology as part of his own musical language. Let us now take an example of a formula peculiar to himself, which he uses to express an idea of frequent occurrence in his music-dramas. The second act of *Tristan und Isolde* begins as follows:

Ex. 4

This phrase permeates much of the music of the second act and is, the commentaries tell us, the 'Day' motive. It is said to represent the 'false daylight' of everyday life, in which Tristan stood by his honour as a knight, friend and servant of King Mark, winning for him the woman he loved himself; the inimical daylight as opposed to the friendly night, in which he will be united with his beloved in death. (The interpretation is based faithfully on ideas expressed in the text.) But this is too much for adherents of the 'music is only music' school: heroism may possibly be 'suggested' by a few notes in the minor key, but how can such abstract ideas as these be represented by any musical formula? As before, we shall not answer the question immediately, but first seek other examples of the use of this formula in Wagner's works.

Wagner maintained that, in laying down *The Ring* after Act II of *Siegfried*, and taking up *Tristan*, he was not making a break in his ideas, but continuing them; that there was a close connection between the characters of Siegfried and Tristan, each of whom was led by a false sense of honour into winning his love not for himself, but for a friend whom he served; and that *Tristan* was the concentrated expression of the idea of love represented by Siegfried and Brünnhilde, which could not be set forth within the framework of *The Ring* without unbalancing it. Now, in *Götterdämmerung*, Gutrune, who leads Siegfried into his false action, seducing him by means of the potion of forgetfulness, is represented by a variant of the same formula as the 'Day' in *Tristan*:

Ex. 5

The connection is obvious. Day is the false ideal which formed a barrier between Tristan and Isolde, Gutrune the false ideal which formed a barrier between Siegfried and Brünnhilde. But Gutrune's motive is itself a variant of that associated with Fricka in *Die Walküre*, when she opposes the love of Siegmund and Sieglinde:

Ex. 6

This, in turn, is derived from the phrase which Wotan sings in *Das Rheingold*, when he conceives the idea of an invincible sword wielded by a hero to preserve the honour of the gods (Ex. 7a), a phrase which Siegmund takes up in Act I of *Die Walküre* when he calls for the promised sword (Ex. 7b) and sings over and over again as he approaches the sword, to draw it from the tree (Ex. 7c).

Ex. 7

(a) So greet I the fort, safe from dis-may and dread!

(b) A sword, my fa-ther fore-told me, I'd find in my dir - est need.

(c) In dir - - est need, this I should find,

Again the connection is obvious. Siegmund's wooing of Sieglinde is undertaken unwittingly in the service of Wotan, and the sword which he regards as the means of winning his love is actually the weapon created by Wotan to regain the ring and preserve his own honour; Siegmund's unconscious attachment to this false ideal stands between him and Sieglinde, hence the hitherto unexplained entry of the Renunciation of Love motive when he actually lays hand on the sword. In the text, Fricka points this out to Wotan, and her remarks are naturally punctuated by this 'barrier' motive (Ex. 6): actually it is not merely Fricka who stands between the two lovers, but the inherent falsity of their position, unknown to them (although Sieglinde senses it later). The link with Gutrune is clear, if we remember that Siegfried's wooing of Brünnhilde in *Götterdämmerung* is also undertaken in ignorance of the true state of affairs, in the service of Gunther; he too is unwittingly regaining the ring for another (Hagen), and he actually lays the sword (the same sword), in the name of honour, between himself and his true love, Brünnhilde, so that he may remain faithful to Gutrune, the false ideal to which he is pledged.

Wagner had used this melodic formula before in *Lohengrin*; it begins the well-known Forbidden Question motive, sung by

Lohengrin when he warns Elsa that she must never ask his name, if she wishes to keep him as her husband (Ex. 8a). The reason for its use here is obvious: he cannot woo Elsa in his own character, but only as an anonymous servant of the Grail; hence he is in a false position as a human lover. But its use is equivocal, and this fact goes far to explain why *Lohengrin* is generally felt to be Wagner's least satisfactory conception. The Grail, which should be a symbol of all that is most holy, is here put in a false light, as the motive clearly shows, for it allows its servants to try and make the best of both worlds. One feels sympathy for Elsa: Lohengrin should be either her divine champion or her human lover; he cannot, in the nature of things, be both. (It is significant that Wagner at one time wished to give the opera a happy ending, but could not see a way out of the problem.) So again we find the formula attached to a false allegiance forming a barrier between two lovers, and again, as in *Die Walküre*, an inimical third party (Ortrud) seizes on it in Act II as an essential flaw in their relationship which must lead to their downfall (Ex. 8b).

Ex. 8

Ne - ver as thou dost love me,   Shall aught to ques-tion move thee,

This was the first time in Wagner's music that the phrase had been elevated to the status of a leitmotif, but it occurs once in the preceding opera, when Venus curses Tannhäuser for his treachery in leaving her after swearing eternal fidelity: she prophesies that he shall never find happiness in the world of men now that he has broken his oath to her. Once more, attachment to a false ideal (carnal love) forms a barrier between the hero and his true love (Elisabeth):

Ex. 9

Hence   to   the   cheer - less   haunts   of __ men,

Wagner was to make his final use of this phrase in *Parsifal*; it is introduced in the opening bars of the prelude:

Ex. 10

Throughout the opera, the opening two bars of this theme are associated with the Grail itself, the cup from which Christ drank at the last supper; they are nearly always followed, as here, by the 'barrier' motive, attached now to the spear which pierced Christ's side on the cross, and filled the same cup, the Grail, with blood. It is this spear which Klingsor used to pierce Amfortas, when he was seduced by Kundry into letting it out of his grasp, giving him a wound that could not be healed. Amfortas, as guardian of the Grail, was bound by laws of chastity; when he lay with Kundry, no doubt he swore fidelity to her, as Tannhäuser did to Venus, and in consequence, like Tannhäuser, raised the barrier of carnal love between himself and his true love, in this case the love of God. The unhealable spear-wound, then, represents sin, the attachment to the flesh which forms a permanent barrier between man and God. The whole symbolism is made quite clear in the opening and closing bars of the opera. In the Prelude, the opening phrase, symbolizing the Grail, or man's hope of salvation though the power of God's love, instead of continuing its ascent to the heights, falls back into the 'barrier' motive, which represents, as we have said, attachment to the flesh (Ex. 10a): towards the end of the opera, when Amfortas's wound has been healed by the Redeemer, Parsifal, the 'barrier' motive disappears, and the motive attached to the Grail floats serenely upwards, finding its resolution in the final chord:

(Here the 'barrier' motive is placed rightly in direct opposition to the idea of the Grail, annulling the false alliance of the two in *Lohengrin*.)

It is now evident that Wagner used this motive to express man's attachment to false ideals, which erect a barrier between himself and his true ideal; and now we must answer the question 'What is there in the actual notes to convey such an idea?' It is, of course, significant that the motive is a kind of 'falsification' of the 'hero' motive (Ex. 11).

Ex. 11

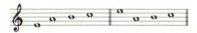

It conforms to the same 'tragic' pattern of the minor triad, with dominant, tonic and mediant; but the initial step, from dominant to tonic, is a downward one, and the rise from tonic to mediant, as in the more sombre variants of the 'hero' motive, is made by means of the intermediate step of the supertonic. When it reaches the mediant, it is already lower than when it began, and it has a tendency to repeat itself, driving further and further downwards (Exx. 5, 6 and 10); in any case it never rises above the dominant on which it began. This gives it that quality of sadness which is inherent in all 'falling' motives. With the entry of the hero motive the music becomes invigorated and presses upwards, with the 'barrier' motive it loses power and slips downwards. Another significant point is that its character is usually thrown into high relief, by its habit of falling like a threat or a shadow into an essentially major context. In Act I of *Lohengrin* (Ex. 8a), it follows immediately after the serene major motive of the Grail itself, and at the beginning of Act II (Ex. 8b) it comes straight after the joyous major ending of Act I. At the beginning of Act II of *Tristan* (Ex. 4), it again follows an Act I which had ended brightly in the major, and in addition it gives a false start (in G minor) to a prelude which is essentially in B flat major. In *Parsifal* (Ex. 10) it opposes suddenly to the tranquil A flat opening the sadness of C minor, and checks the ascent of the music by its falling motion. In the mouths of Wotan and Siegmund (Ex. 7), it is contrasted with the rising C major motive of the sword; with Fricka (Ex. 6) it settles into a predominantly minor context (it is harmonized in C minor), portending Siegmund's death. Only for Gutrune (Ex. 5) is it used in the major, and she, after all, is an unwitting agent, used by Hagen to throw dust in Siegfried's eyes: seduction and deception are the keynotes here, as in many other places in *Götterdämmerung*.

It is perhaps necessary to add one thing, in conclusion. It is quite impossible to ascertain how far Wagner was *conscious* of his persistent use of this or any other formula, or how far his use of music as an expressive language was the product of rational thought. Wagner, who wrote so much on so many subjects, hardly ever referred to his actual processes of musical composition. The only clue we have is a paragraph on the development of the Rhine-maidens' original cry of 'Rhinegold' throughout the whole of *The Ring*: in it he expressed surprise at the way in which the phrase evolved into ever new harmonic forms, as the idea it represented became modified by subsequent events in the drama. This implies that direct inspiration played a very large part. Whatever the truth in this matter, there can be no doubt that his use of music as a language was always coherent and consistent, and a detailed analysis of his procedure rules out the element of coincidence. Despite all the excellent books written about Wagner, we still await the most necessary of all, the one which will bring out the true significance of his works by getting to grips with the stuff of the music itself.

[1952]

Wagner's Operatic Apprenticeship

When examining, in *Opera and Drama,* the various attempts to elevate opera from a naive entertainment into a serious dramatic art-form, Wagner was realistic enough to glance at Rossini, and note that his success showed what opera-lovers really wanted: tunes. Nevertheless, he persevered with his own blueprint for music-drama, and realized it so magnificently in *The Ring, Tristan, Die Meistersinger* and *Parsifal,* that by the time of his death it seemed that he had killed the old-style opera stone dead. But during the present century, that strange creature, the opera-lover (as opposed to the lover of great musical stage-works), has proved resilient enough to live down again to Wagner's estimate of him. He may now go to music-dramas, but what he really enjoys is an old 'tuney' set-number opera, however musico-dramatically inept. Hence the revival of the ostensibly serious operas of Handel, Rossini, Bellini, Donizetti, and the early Verdi.[1] And the intellectual opera-lover rather defiantly justifies his (not always openly avowed) preference by discussing such operas quite seriously, treating them as genuine musical dramas like Wagner's.

Since I personally regard Wagner's musical dramas as being self-evidently on the artistic level of Shakespeare's poetic dramas, and the works mentioned above as belonging to an altogether inferior category, I find all this incomprehensible. Nevertheless, *chacun à son gout;* and since tuney set-number operas are back again, it may be time to reconsider Wagner's own apprentice operatic works, which were regarded as something to be hushed up during the total ascendancy of music-drama, to see if anything can be salvaged from them, to delight opera-lovers.

[1] Comic opera lies outside this discussion, being a legitimate entertainment-genre of a consciously artificial kind.

I did actually reconsider them in 1963, Wagner's 150th anniversary year, when introducing two BBC Third Programme concerts of extracts from them. But since these attracted little attention, it may be useful to summarize my conclusions here. As I see it, the still-surviving notions (1) that Wagner was a freak genius, an amateur who triumphed despite a lack of normal professional training, and (2) that his early operatic works are utterly jejune, giving no hint of his later powers, are both untenable: despite the music's evident immaturity, it is thoroughly professional, and at times clearly foreshadows the later Wagner.

The professionalism might seem inexplicable, since Wagner's only tuition was a six-months' course in counterpoint and form, at the age of eighteen, with Theodor Weinlig, Cantor of St Thomas's, Leipzig. But his previous study of a harmony-book, and of many scores, must have taught him much already: even while studying with Weinlig he composed a quite powerful overture (still extant) and incidental music (lost), for a production of Raupach's tragedy *King Enzio* at the Leipzig Theatre. And he soon picked up operatic experience. As a nineteen-year-old repetiteur at the Würzburg Opera he wrote a new barn-storming final section for the aria 'Wie ein schöner Frühlingsmorgen' in Marschner's *Vampyr,* for his brother Albert, who was singing the tenor role. Meanwhile he had completed Act I of his first opera *Die Feen* (*The Fairies,* with text— after Gozzi—by himself, as ever afterwards) and he finished the whole work within the year. Two numbers from it were given at a Würzburg concert, but the Leipzig Opera rejected it as too advanced (!), and Wagner was never to hear it. He then became conductor to a seedy theatrical troupe in Magdeburg, and so entered on five years' professional purgatory in third-rate provincial opera-houses. It was at Magdeburg, at the age of 21, that he completed his second opera, *Das Liebesverbot* (*The Ban on Love,* after Shakespeare's *Measure for Measure*), and conducted its disastrous premiere just as the bankrupt company was breaking up in general acrimony. He never heard it again in his lifetime. Four years later came *Rienzi,* and success.

These facts speak for themselves as to Wagner's strictly professional initiation; and the prophetic element in his early operas— despite the influence of Weber and Marschner on *Die Feen,* of Bellini and Donizetti on *Das Liebesverbot,* and some of Spontini and Meyerbeer on *Rienzi*—is equally undeniable. They reveal

Wagner aready building scenes on a grand scale, and forging that uniquely expressive motivic language which was to develop, but not change, throughout his career. The Wagnerian large-scale sweep can only be experienced from performances, unfortunately, but concerning the emergence of Wagner's musical language I offer a few music quotations in support of my view.

Even in the fragmentary opening scene for a projected opera, *Die Hochzeit,* which was all that preceded *Die Feen,* the first recitative is unified by three separate statements of an expressive phrase (three descending steps and a leap up—Ex. 1) which was to

Ex. 1

become a fingerprint: especially in *Die Walküre*—see Brünnhilde's 'War es so schmählich', as developed by the orchestra during her altercation with Wotan, her 'Der dieser Liebe' (motive on the orchestra), and a cell of the Siegfried motive. In the *Vampyr* interpolation, the second theme (Ex. 2) uses sequences of a four-note figure (bracketed) which were to become pervasive in

Ex. 2

Wagner's later music: dubbed ineptly by comentators the 'Flight' motive in *Das Rheingold,* the complex is actually Wagner's ubiquitous love-motive (happy, sad, agitated or content, according to major, minor, fast or slow contexts). It is attached to Freia as goddess of love, to Siegmund and Sieglinde, Siegfried and Brünnhilde, and, outside *The Ring,* to Isolde, for example, in her invocation to 'Frau Minne' (another goddess of love), and to Eva in her cajoling of Hans Sachs. Here it is agitated, and in fact it expresses love in distress.

In *Die Feen,* there are foreshadowings of Wagner's later exteme chromaticism: no doubt it was 'modernisms' like Ex. 3 that shocked the Leipzig Opera officials! Perhaps it is mere coincidence that the first motive in this first Wagner opera (Ex. 4—the 'magic' motive, presented in the overture after four preliminary bars) is exactly the same melodic pattern as the first motive of the last music-drama,

Ex. 3

Ex. 4

Parsifal, where it also begins the prelude; but an expressive phrase much dwelt on shortly afterwards (Ex. 5a—not used as a motive in the opera) is the embryo of another basic term of Wagner's musical language—a leap down and three ascending steps. It appears in *Rienzi* as Ex. 5c, again only in the overture, but in the intervening *Liebesverbot* it occurs not only in the overture but throughout the opera, as the 'ban on love' motive itself (Ex. 5b). And it reappears, in various forms, in all Wagner's works, always standing between lovers; as Fricka's fury against Siegmund and Sieglinde, for example, or the Gibichungs' scheming against Siegfried and Brunnhilde, or 'Day' in *Tristan*. Also, for *Das Liebesverbot,* Wagner conceived a theme for the nuns' *Salve Regina* in the convent scene (Ex. 6—not used as a motive), which a decade later

Ex. 5

Ex. 6

he lifted *notatim* for the 'Feast of Grace' motive of *Tannhäuser*
(this itself having connections with the 'Dresden Amen' Grail
motive in *Parsifal*).

So far, so Wagnerian. Yet Wagner's early progress shows a
curious uncertainty of purpose; the general style changes from work
to work, despite the enduring thread indicated above. Ex. 1, 2, 3, 4
and 5a faithfully typify his first natural progress along his true path,
as the future consummator of the new German opera established
by Weber and Marschner. But the rejection of *Die Feen,* together
with the German public's preference for French and Italian
composers to even Weber and Marschner, convinced him that
German opera had no future; and this conviction, as well as his
irritation with the lack of sensuousness in the German operatic
style (plus his ambition to launch himself with a great popular

Ex. 7

success), led him to imitate French and Italian models in *Das
Liebesverbot* and *Rienzi,* until he rediscovered his German self in
Der fliegende Holländer. Ex. 5b, 5c and 6 only reflect the
indestructible Wagnerian thread running through works which are
very largely uncharacteristic; the entirely Italianate Ex.7, from
Das Liebesverbot, with its quaint curtailing of the opening
orchestral theme before its final tonic, followed by a pause before
the voice takes up the theme (a procedure familiar to us from 'La
donna è mobile'), is entirely typical of the work, and even of parts
of the more Meyerbeerian *Rienzi.*

But this Italianateness—to return to my opening remarks—may make the work acceptable today, as it could not be during Wagner's full maturity. A world which takes seriously Verdi's *Oberto* and *Un Giorno di Regno* should find much to enjoy in *Das Liebesverbot* (and certainly, if *Attila* can take the stage, *Rienzi* can—judiciously cut!). *Das Liebesverbot* is certainly worth the occasional performance, not only for its one or two embryonic Wagnerisms, and its all-pervading Italianate tuniness, but also because it shows how Wagner acquired that sensuousness which was later to leaven his innate German sobriety. And there need be no fear of ineffectiveness. Even Wagner's least characteristic early operatic music has, to my ears at least, a force of utterance which suggests an intense personality behind the pastiche; certainly the big dramatic choruses have plenty of punch. Moreover, the libretto is adequately constructed—though there is no point in a painstaking comparison with the original play, since Shakespeare's great theme of Christian forgiveness is transformed into the raw young Wagner's defiant exaltation of unbridled sensuality over puritannical strictness. At the time, Wagner belonged to a group known as 'Young Europe' which, like our own 'angries', reviled the hypocritical respectability of their national tradition. Hence the interesting fact that the scene is transferred from Vienna to Sicily, and Angelo becomes a German viceroy who tries to stamp out the Italian people's natural sexual vitality. Wagner was a natural symbolist, even at the start, and even in disguise.

[1965]

The Bruckner Problem Simplified

The textual problem presented by the different versions of Bruckner's symphonies is one of the most vexatious in all musicology, and the person ultimately responsible was Bruckner himself. Had he only possessed the normal self-confidence of the great composer, he would have produced, like Beethoven or Dvořák, a single definitive score of each of his nine symphonies; and we should have had a simple list of works and dates[1] as follows:

No. 1 (1866)	No. 4 (1880)	No. 7 (1883)
No. 2 (1872)	No. 5 (1876)	No. 8 (1887)
No. 3 (1877)	No. 6 (1881)	No. 9 (unfinished, 1896)

This would have been an absolutely straightforward situation, with the single exception that nos. 3 and 4 did not reach their definitive forms until after no. 5 had been completed.

We can only regret that Bruckner did not stick to these first definitive forms (no. 8 excepted). If he had, we should have been perfectly happy to accept them as what they were, without any idea that they stood in need of drastic revision. But it was not to be. After the premiere of no. 2 in 1873, Johann Herbeck persuaded Bruckner to make considerable alterations for the next performance in 1876; and so began that sorry business of the composer's revising his symphonies under the influence of well-meaning colleagues who wanted to make them more easily accessible to the public. In 1883, Josef Schalk and Ferdinand Löwe persuaded him to revise the orchestration of no. 7, even making certain changes themselves; and in 1887 Hermann Levi's adverse reaction to no. 8 induced him to revise the work altogether (which he did in collaboration with Josef Schalk). After that, Bruckner himself became

---

[1] Each date indicates the completion of the basic score, irrespective of slight later retouchings.

afflicted with the revising mania: he had slightly revised no. 4 in 1886, and between 1888 and 1891 he entirely recomposed nos. 1 and 3 (the latter with the assistance of Franz Schalk).

Even worse, Bruckner's colleagues interpreted his malleability as giving them *carte blanche* to produce 'revisions' of their own. In 1890, no. 4 appeared in a first edition with the orchestration and the actual texture remodelled in Wagnerian style by Franz Schalk and Löwe, and with cuts probably stemming from Richter's performances. In 1896, no. 5 appeared in a first edition even more drastically cut, reorchestrated and recomposed by Franz Schalk alone. The original editions of all the other symphonies were also tampered with, by the Schalk brothers, Löwe, or others. They contain, at the very least, unstylish alterations to the phrasing and dynamics, and unwarranted indications of expression and of tempo changes; some of them have cuts, or suggestions for cuts, and changes in the orchestration and the music itself, as well as occasional rebarrings. The worst case is Löwe's first edition of no. 9 made in 1903, seven years after Bruckner's death.

Bruckner had made muted protests against such things. He refused to ratify the Schalk-Löwe score of no. 4 with his signature; he begged Weingartner not to allow his alterations to no. 8 to get into the printer's copy, whatever he might do in performance; and he preserved all his original scores 'for future times'. But it was to no avail. Instead of the ideal situation postulated by our imaginary simple list, a sadly complicated one materialized:

No. 1 completed 1866; recomposed by Bruckner, 1890–1; spurious 1st edn. 1893.

No. 2 completed 1872; revised (with Herbeck's assistance) 1876; spurious 1st end. 1892.

No. 3 completed 1877; spurious 1st edn. 1878; recomposed (with Franz Schalk's assistance) 1888–9; spurious 1st edn. (Schalk) 1890.

No. 4 completed 1880; revised 1886; spurious 1st edn. (Franz Schalk and Löwe) 1890.

No. 5 completed 1876; never revised; spurious 1st edn. (Franz Schalk) 1896.

No. 6 completed 1881; never revised; spurious 1st edn. (Cyril Hynais) 1899.

No. 7 completed 1883; orchestration revised (with the assistance of Josef Schalk and Löwe) 1883; spurious 1st edn. (Schalk and Löwe) 1885.

No. 8 completed 1887; revised (with Josef Schalk's assistance) 1888–90; spurious 1st edn. (Schalk) 1892.

No. 9 left unfinished 1896; spurious 1st edn. (Löwe) 1903.

Thus by 1903 there were in existence no less than twenty-five different scores of the nine symphonies; moreover, the ten published ones did not represent Bruckner's own intentions, whereas the fifteen unpublished ones were either authentic or at least nearly so. It was to rectify this wretched state of affairs that the International Bruckner Society was founded in Leipzig in 1927, with the aim of replacing the spurious first editions with Bruckner's own 'original versions'. Between 1934 and 1950, nine publications were issued— seven edited by Robert Haas, and one each by Alfred Orel and Fritz Oeser[2] —which represented Bruckner's own original definitive scores of his symphonies—with one exception. This was no. 8: Haas accepted the manifest compositional improvements of the 1888–90 revision, but incorporated material from the first definitive version of 1887 which he believed that Bruckner had excised only under the influence of Josef Schalk. The ethics of this proceeding will be discussed later; but one immediate result was that it raised the total of existing versions to twenty-six. On the other hand, apart from this, the muddle had been entirely cleared up. The ideal situation postulated by our imaginary simple list had been practically recreated: we now had a published score of each symphony as first definitively completed by Bruckner himself, except for no. 8, and we had what was arguably the best possible score of that.[3]

But this happy ending was promptly annulled by fresh confusion. In 1945, for non-musical (political) reasons, Haas was deposed, and replaced by Leopold Nowak, who between 1951 and 1973 has brought out a new set of Bruckner Society publications, edited entirely by himself. In the cases of nos. 2, 3, 4, 7, and 8, he published more or less authentic editions of the *revised* versions as drawn up by Bruckner himself, plus the hitherto unpublished

---

[2] The last of these—Oeser's edition of no. 3—was actually issued by the Brucknerverlag; but although not commissioned by the Bruckner Society, it belongs to the complete edition in spirit, and is accepted by the Society.

[3] Haas also published (in the Society's Critical Collected Edition, not for performance) the 1890-1 score of no. 1, as being a revision undertaken entirely by Bruckner himself.

original 1887 version of no. 8, thereby not adding to the total of existing scores. With nos. 1, 5, 6, and 9, on the other hand, he reissued Bruckner's original definitive versions as already published under the Haas regime, but with slight divergences which made his editions, from a strict point of view, different scores. And so the total was raised to thirty.

Meanwhile, Bruckner scholars had been insisting that a full list must take into account the fact that, in the cases of nos. 3 and 4, Bruckner's first definitive versions had been preceded by earlier scores (four in all) which remained unpublished; and so the list finally reached its present intolerable state of complexity:

No. 1 (1) 1866, ed. Haas; (2) 1866, ed. Nowak; (3) 1891, 1st edn. of 1893; (4) 1891, ed. Haas (Critical Collected Edition).

No. 2 (1) 1872, ed. Haas; (2) 1876, 1st edn. of 1892; (3) 1876, ed. Nowak.

No. 3 (1) 1873, unpubd.; (2) 1874, unpubd.; (3) 1877, 1st edn. of 1878; (4) 1877, ed. Oeser; (5) 1889, 1st edn. of 1890; (6) 1889, ed. Nowak.

No. 4 (1) 1874, unpubd.; (2) 1878, unpubd.; (3) 1880, ed. Haas; (4) 1886, ed. Nowak; (5) F. Schalk and Löwe version, 1st edn. of 1890.

No. 5 (1) 1876, ed. Haas; (2) 1876, ed. Nowak; (3) F. Schalk version, 1st edn. of 1896.

No. 6 (1) 1881, 1st edn. of 1899; (2) 1881, ed. Haas; (3) 1881, ed. Nowak.

No. 7 (1) 1883, 1st edn. of 1885; (2) 1883, ed. Haas; (3) 1883, ed. Nowak.

No. 8 (1) 1887, ed. Nowak; (2) 1890, 1st edn. of 1892; (3) 1890, ed. Haas, with material restored from 1887 version; (4) 1890, ed. Nowak.

No. 9 (1) 1896, ed. Orel; (2) 1896, ed. Nowak; (3) Löwe version, 1st edn. of 1903.

Thirty-four different scores in all, and most of them published, liable to be used at any time! The 'Bruckner problem' has become sheer purgatory for the non-specialist musician or music-lover who simply wants to enjoy his Bruckner symphonies. But it has only become so, really, because it is such a paradise for Bruckner scholars, who are delighted to have as many versions as possible to compare, contrast, and classify. In fact, the extreme complexity of the above list is entirely illusory. More than half of those thirty-four 'versions' are not versions at all in any real sense: the total can be reduced to a considerably smaller number if we only concentrate on those scores which are more or less authentic and at the same time significantly different from one another.

To begin with, we may ignore, for all practical purposes, the early unpublished scores of nos. 3 and 4. These are not alternative performing versions, but scores which Bruckner discarded on the way to his first definitive versions. They are never likely to be published outside a critical collected edition, and are of interest only to students of Bruckner's creative development. The same really applies to the first score of no. 8, though since this was actually Bruckner's first definitive score of the work, which he improved only on the advice of others, it is interesting to have a published score of it. However, setting it aside with the rest, we reduce the total to twenty-nine.

Next, the first editions should be simply repudiated. These are not 'versions' either—not versions by Bruckner, that is. The monstrous distortions of nos. 5 and 9, by Franz Schalk and Löwe respectively, seem mercifully to have been dropped by everybody; but one still occasionally hears the first edition of no. 4, in which both men collaborated in misrepresenting Bruckner's intentions, and some of the others are liable to turn up from time to time. The rejection of these ten original editions (including the two of no. 3) shrinks the total further to nineteen.

Finally, faced with the two different Bruckner Society scores of each symphony issued under the Haas and Nowak regimes, we need not talk about two different 'versions' where they show no structural divergencies at all but only a number of subsidiary differences in texture and/or orchestration and/or phrasing. With nos. 1, 5, 6, 7 and 9, the two Bruckner Society scores represent, not different 'versions', but one and the same Bruckner score in two slightly different editions. So the list finally shrinks to fourteen, and the 'Bruckner problem' at last assumes manageable proportions:

No. 1 (1) 1866, ed. Haas or Nowak
      (2) 1891, ed. Haas (Critical Collected Edition)
No. 2 (1) 1872, ed. Haas
      (2) 1876, ed. Nowak

No. 3 (1) 1877, ed. Oeser
       (2) 1889, ed. Nowak
No. 4 (1) 1880, ed. Haas
       (2) 1886, ed. Nowak
No. 5 (1) 1876, ed. Haas or Nowak
No. 6 (1) 1881, ed. Haas or Nowak
No. 7 (1) 1883, ed. Haas or Nowak
No. 8 (1) 1887/90, ed. Haas
       (2) 1890, ed. Nowak
No. 9 (1) 1896, ed. Orel or Nowak

These are the only scores that anyone need consider in clarifying his mind about the Bruckner problem. In what follows, I shall discuss the textual situation of each symphony in turn, after giving briefly the facts about the two uncanonical early symphonies. For the lists of publishers of the first editions, in all cases I am indebted to the comprehensive list issued by Arthur D. Walker.

SYMPHONY IN F MINOR

This first symphonic attempt is known as the 'Studiensymphonie'—best translated as 'Study Symphony', and not, as one sometimes finds, 'Student Symphony', since Bruckner was thirty-nine when he completed it in 1863. A mainly impersonal exercise by which he set no store, it was not performed in his lifetime, though occasional performances have been given since. The full score is available on hire from Universal Edition.

SYMPHONY NO. 0 IN D MINOR

By dubbing this more mature symphony 'Die Nullte' (The Noughth), Bruckner indicated that it was not to be included in the canon. It received no performance in his lifetime; the premiere took place in his centenary year, 1924. The fact that it clearly reveals Bruckner's musical personality is due to its not having reached it definitive form until 1869, three years after no. 1, though it was originally composed in 1864—that is, two years *before* no. 1. There is only the one (1869) version, which is available in two published editions. That of Joseph Wöss, issued in 1924 by Universal (also by Philharmonia), and that of Leopold Nowak, issued in

1969 by the Bruckner Society. The latter must be taken as replacing the Wöss edition, which, although entirely faithful to the MS from the structural point of view, contains a lot of editorial phrasing, dynamics and tempo and expressive markings, plus a few misreadings of notation. However, one thing is worrying in the Nowak edition—the addition of a flat against the B for the second violins in bar 4 of the trio of the scherzo: it sounds improbable, and does not correspond with the equivalent note in bar 40, which is B natural. Could it be a misprint?

SYMPHONY NO. 1 IN C MINOR

(a) versions

1. ORIGINAL VERSION, completed in 1866 in Linz, and usually known as the 'Linz version'. It was first performed in Linz in 1868, with Bruckner conducting; the score was not published in his lifetime.

2. REVISED VERSION completed in 1891 in Vienna; and usually known as the 'Vienna version'. This is Bruckner's own radical recomposition of the symphony: retaining the general layout, he recast the music in multifarious detail, altering bar-periods, melodic lines, harmony, texture and orchestration, and even rewriting the material completely in places; he also added extra indications of tempo-changes. This version was first performed in Vienna in 1891, under Hans Richter, and was published two years later: see (*b*) below.

(b) First Edition

REVISED VERSION, anonymous edition published in 1893 by Doblinger (later by Eulenburg, Peters, Philharmonia and Universal). This score, still the only available performing edition of the revised version, must be rejected as unauthentic, since it differs in many details from Haas's reproduction of Bruckner's own score in the Bruckner Society's Critical Collected Edition (see (*c*) 2 below). The differences are in orchestration, dynamics, phrasing, tempo-indications, and even time-signatures (in the first movement Bruckner's C is changed to ₵, with certain passages changing back to 4/4).

(c) Bruckner Society Editions

1*a*. ORIGINAL VERSION, ed. Haas: a reproduction of Bruckner's own score.

1*b*. ORIGINAL VERSION, ed. Nowak: a very slightly different reproduction of Bruckner's own score.

2. REVISED VERSION, ed. Haas: a reproduction of Bruckner's own score (in the Critical Collected Edition only, not available for performance). Nowak has not yet published an edition of this version.

With regard to Bruckner's own two different versions of the symphony, most Brucknerians favour the original; even Nowak, who in all other relevant cases preferred the revised versions, settled for the original version of this work.[4] The argument is that, in the revision, Bruckner largely obscured the bold originality of his first conception by squaring off bar-periods, rewriting some of the material in his more complex later style, and generally blurring the texture and orchestration.[5] However, since both versions are authentic Bruckner scores, conductors are at liberty to perform either, according to taste. But if choice falls on the revised version, the score and parts of the first edition should be brought into line with the edition of Haas (*c*) 2 above.

If choice falls on the original version, however, the question arises, as it so often will, 'Haas or Nowak?'. In this case the answer is that it hardly matters, since the two editions offer practically the same score. As with all the other symphonies (except no. 3, published by the Brucknerverlag) Nowak reprinted from the plates of the first Bruckner Society edition, making such alterations as his view of the MS necessitated: here they affect only 16 bars of the whole work.[6] Nowak gives no chapter and verse for these discrepancies, but they would seem to be different interpretations of difficult readings in the same MS that Haas used. They are as follows:

> I 68, fl; 89, ob, bn; 86–93, str.
> II 72, *Etwas zurückhaltend*, and 75, *A tempo*, both in Haas but not in Nowak; also 150, va.
> III Nil
> IV 2, vn 1; 4, vn 1 and 2, va; 5 va; 391, va.

---

[4] Hermann Levi actually advised Bruckner *against* revising this symphony—a unique reversal of the usual situation!

[5] The differences are too far-reaching to be listed here.

[6] I am leaving phrasing and dynamics out of account, since such differences as there are do not affect Bruckner's general style. In particular, I am not bothering with editorial emendations, such as where Haas has supplied a patently missing slur or accent, and Nowak has bracketed it to indicate that it is not in the MS.

Of these 10 discrepancies, the two affecting tempo are quite unimportant, since any sensitive conductor might well act spontaneously in the way the Haas edition indicates, even if using the Nowak edition. Another four (I, 89; II, 150; IV, 5 and 391) are tiny adjustments of inner parts which are completely unnoticeable in performance; and with one of them (IV, 391) it looks as if Haas may have corrected a slip on Bruckner's part, while Nowak preferred the faulty MS reading. A further difference (I, 86–93) is slightly more important: in this string unison, Haas has unrelieved quavers (minims or crotchets with strokes), whereas Nowak has straight minims or crotchets some of the time.

The other three differences are the most significant, since they affect thematic lines. In I, 68 Nowak gives the first two flute notes in dotted rhythm, whereas Haas has even quavers—but this is a mere fleeting moment. The different string readings in IV are as follows: bar 2 (vn 1), the last four notes are c'' -g' -e' flat-g' in Haas, c'' -g'' -e'' flat-d'' in Nowak; bar 4 (upper strings), the 2nd note is d''' in Haas, f''' in Nowak. The Nowak readings are certainly the stronger, but in any case the strings here are no more than a seething background to the powerful main wind and brass theme, so the differences are hardly noticeable.

Summing-up. The original version may be performed in either the Haas or the Nowak edition without making any real difference. The revised version, if desired, should be performed according to the Haas edition. But since the Haas and Nowak editions of the first version are so nearly identical, and since Haas's edition of the revised version simply reproduces Bruckner's own score, it seems pointless to bother with editors' names when designating which version of the symphony is to be performed. The only distinction to be made is between Bruckner's own two different versions, viz:

Symphony no. 1 in C minor (Linz version, 1866)
or
Symphony no. 1 in C minor (Vienna version, 1891)

SYMPHONY NO. 2 IN C MINOR
(a) Versions

1. ORIGINAL VERSION, completed in 1872 (in Vienna, as with all the remaining symphonies). It was first performed in 1873, with

Bruckner conducting (also in Vienna, as with all the remaining symphonies, except where stated otherwise). The score was not published in his lifetime.

2. REVISED VERSION (BRUCKNER AND HERBECK), completed in 1876 and performed that year, again with Bruckner conducting. At Herbeck's persuasion, Bruckner made cuts in the first, second and fourth movements, eliminated the repeats from both scherzo and trio, and altered bar-periods in all four movements; he also made an important change in the orchestration of the coda of the second movement. This version was published in 1892: see (*b*) below.

(b) First Edition

REVISED VERSION (BRUCKNER AND HERBECK), anonymous edition published in 1892 by Doblinger (later by Eulenburg, Peters, Philharmonia and Universal). This score must be considered unauthentic, since it differs in several respects from Nowak's Bruckner Society edition of Bruckner's own score: see (*c*) 2 below.

(c) Bruckner Society Editions

1. ORIGINAL VERSION, ed. Haas. Despite Nowak's statement in the preface to his own edition that 'Haas confused the two versions', it seems certain that Haas reproduced Bruckner's first score exactly. He did, however, indicate with 'Vi-de' signs the passages that Bruckner marked there for cutting in the revised version; thus he left it to the conductor to act according to his own inclination.

2. REVISED VERSION (BRUCKNER AND HERBECK), ed. Nowak. This is described on the title-page as '1877 version', which is merely different nomenclature (Bruckner made a few further alterations in 1877, after the performance of the version). Nowak again reprinted from Haas's plates, making the necessary alterations and indicating in his preface that the passages marked 'Vi-de' must be cut to represent the revised version. He also printed separately, after the slow movement, its original coda from Haas's edition, as an interesting but not-to-be-used alternative (pp. 73 *bis* and 74 *bis*). The complete list of differences between Haas and Nowak (and of the cuts in both editions) is as follows:

    I Tempo marking, *Ziemlich schnell* in Haas, *Moderato* in Nowak; 460, Haas has no marking, Nowak *Langsamer*; 488,

Haas no marking, Nowak *Tempo I*; Cut, 488–519, Vi-de, both scores; 566, in Nowak this is followed by an extra bar (timpani roll only), before Haas's 567.

II Title, *Adagio* in Haas, *Andante* in Nowak, but both have the same tempo marking, *Feierlich, etwas bewegt*; Cut, 49–69, Vi-de, both scores; 179 to end, slightly different bar-periods; 200 to end, solo instrument, horn in Haas, clarinet in Nowak.

III Tempo marking, *Schnell* in Haas, *Mässig schnell* in Nowak; Haas has repeat marks for both halves of scherzo and trio— none at all in Nowak; 123, this bar is repeated by Nowak, before Haas's 124; Coda, Nowak has two extra bars of general pause at the beginning.

IV Slight alterations in subsidiary voices, 95 cb, 349, 351, 361, trb 2; Cuts, 540–562 and 590–651 (the latter 590–655 in Nowak), Vi-de, both scores; 647 and 649 (Haas's numbering), in each case two bars of general pause follow in Nowak.

So here the choice between Haas and Nowak is simply the choice between the original version and the revised version; and only one decision seems possible. As the whole purpose of the founding of the Bruckner Society was to get back to Bruckner's own intentions, and to get rid of elements originating in the influence of his colleagues, it seems curious that Nowak should have counteracted Haas's fulfilment of that purpose by publishing for performance revisions in which the influence of Bruckner's colleagues is unmistakable. Here it is not even in dispute, as Nowak himself admits. To quote his preface:

> Johann Herbeck ... advised Bruckner to make alterations, and this was to be the first instance of the well-meaning persuasion that Bruckner was to be subjected to for the rest of his life ... we know that it was only with the greatest reluctance that Bruckner accepted these suggestions...

With that statement, Nowak condemns his own edition. The truth is that if Bruckner had refused to listen to Herbeck, and the symphony had come down to us in its original version only, nobody today would have imagined that any cuts were necessary (why did Haas indicate them, one wonders?), or that any repeats needed omitting, or that the coda of the slow movement needed rescoring. Indeed, anyone suggesting the cuts that Herbeck wished on to

Bruckner would surely have been regarded as a crank, since they upset the proportions of the structure, reducing the nicely judged codas of the first and last movements by half, and giving the second theme of the slow movement no time to establish itself properly before the return of the first. And anyone suggesting that the clarinet should replace the horn at the end of the slow movement would surely have been thought insensitive to a stroke of genuis. The latter change was probably made because the high horn solo gave trouble at the first performance, but it can be brought off today by a really good player, and it is exquisite, whereas the clarinet is comparatively colourless. Even Nowak, by printing the original passage separately, showed his reluctance to lose it altogether.

The change of title for the slow movement and the different tempo indications for the first and third movements hardly matter, nor do the slight alterations in subsidiary voices in the finale. On the other hand the rebarrings are mainly damaging, the one at the end of the first movement being particularly irritating. Whereas in the original version the last note comes at the very end of the final 16-bar period, in the revised version it comes at the beginning of an imaginary new period, in the orthodox traditional way. No doubt Bruckner's delightfully unrhetorical conclusion worried Herbeck, and he persuaded him to change it to the more banally emphatic procedure. The anonymous editor of the first edition of 1892, incidentally, demanded an entirely inflated emphasis. The three versions can be compared (Ex. 1):

Ex. 1

Summing-up. It seems incontrovertible that only Haas's edition of the original version should be performed; but some conductors will still no doubt prefer the revised version, in which case they should certainly use the Nowak edition, not the first edition of 1892. And so again, the two different versions can be designated simply, without editor's names—but definitely, I would say, with a mention of Herbeck, to exonerate Bruckner from total responsibility for the revised version:

Symphony no. 2 in C minor (original version, 1872)
or
Symphony no. 2 in C minor (Bruckner-Herbeck revision, 1876)

SYMPHONY NO. 3 IN D MINOR

Symphonies 1 and 2 represent Bruckner's first period, in which his full individuality had yet to flower; no. 3 marks the start of his maturity, which simply continued throughout his life without dividing into the usual second and third periods. And it was with this work, in which he first attempted the new monumental type of symphony he was to cultivate from then on, that his difficulties began—his *own* difficulties, that is, as distinct from those forced on him by his colleagues. Whereas each of the first two symphonies was soon built up into a single definitive score, it proved necessary to make three shots at no. 3: the dates are 1873, 1874, and 1876–7.

To call the first two of these 'Versions 1 and 2' and the 1877 score 'Version 3', as some Bruckner students insist on doing, is pure pedantry. The first two scores were mere discarded attempts, which have never been published or performed; they were superseded by the 1877 score, which can only be regarded as the first definitive version.[7]

(a) Versions

1. FIRST DEFINITIVE VERSION, completed in 1877, and first performed that year with Bruckner conducting. It was published in 1878: see (b) 1 below.

2. REVISED VERSION (BRUCKNER AND FRANZ SCHALK), completed in 1889, and first performed the following year under Hans

---

[7] Hans-Hubert Schönzeler (to whom I am grateful for many suggestions) has pointed out to me that Bruckner did at least consider the 1874 score definitive enough to show it to Wagner, who accepted its dedication; and in his book on Bruckner he designates this 1874 score the 'original version'—the *Urfassung*. However, as we are concerned here only with possible *performing* versions, we have to ignore it.

Richter. This is a partly cut and partly recomposed transformation of the 1877 score, carried out by Bruckner in collaboration with Franz Schalk; it was published in 1890: see (*b*) 2 below.

(b) First Editions　1. FIRST DEFINITIVE VERSION, anonymous edition published in 1878 by Rättig. I have not seen this score, but since it has never been reissued, and has been superseded by the Brucknerverlag edition of Oeser (see (*c*) 1 below), the question of its reliability is purely academic. According to Oeser, it differs in certain respects from Bruckner's own score, so it may be regarded as unauthentic.

2. REVISED VERSION (BRUCKNER AND FRANZ SCHALK), ed. Franz Schalk and published in 1890 by Rättig (later by Eulenburg, Peters and Philharmonia). This must also be considered unauthentic, since it differs in many small details from Nowak's edition of the same score (see (*c*) 2 below). These differences (in texture, orchestration, phrasing,dynamics, expression markings and tempo indications) are due to further editing by Schalk.

(c) Bruckner Society Editions

1. FIRST DEFINITIVE VERSION, ed. Oeser (Brucknerverlag): a reproduction of Bruckner's own score of 1877. It is described on the title-page as 'version of 1878', which is merely different nomenclature (Bruckner made a few more alterations that year).

2. REVISED VERSION (BRUCKNER AND FRANZ SCHALK), ed. Nowak: a reproduction of the Bruckner-Schalk score of 1889, without the alterations made by Schalk for the first edition of 1890.

So again we are faced with a straight choice between two alternatives—the first definitive version and the revised version; and here there are three separate reasons for choosing the former. In the first place, as with no. 1, Bruckner partly *recomposed* the work for the revision, rewriting certain passages in his more complex later style, which seems out of place in the comparatively simple world of the original.[8] Also, as with no. 2, he let a colleague persuade him to make cuts; and further, in this case, he allowed that colleague to do some of the cutting for him, *and by means of recomposition*. Here, for a second time, Nowak condemns his own edition by what he says in his preface:

---

[8] As with no. 1, the differences are too far-reaching to be listed here in full.

> The finale ... was copied by Franz Schalk in a shortened version of his own, approved by Bruckner and used by him as the basis for his revision. Two of Schalk's shortened passages were accepted by the master ... Bruckner approved those changes not made by himself ... Josef [Schalk] wrote to his brother [Franz]: 'Your cuts and transitions, by the way, were adhered to'.

Again, we can only wonder why, after Oeser's edition of the first version of 1877 had perfectly fulfilled the intentions behind the founding of the Bruckner Society, Nowak should have thought it necessary to issue for performance a revision so indisputably interfered with by one of Bruckner's colleagues. No. 3 is certainly the least perfect of Bruckner's nine symphonies (though not the least magnificent), but his attempt to improve it with the assistance of Schalk actually made it less perfect still. There may be two opinions about the passages completely recomposed by Bruckner himself, but there can surely be only one about the ruinous cuts which Schalk forced on the finale, and about such a clumsy piece of reworking as occurs in bars 155–60 in the first movement (Ex. 2).

Ex. 2

This passage gives an idea of what is meant by Bruckner's 'recomposing'. The raising of the pitch by a 3rd in bars 3 and 4 of this passage may seem an improvement, but the sudden augmentation of the characteristic three-plus-two figure at the fifth bar can only be called a minor calamity: it breaks up the lyrical flow of the second group, and at the same time introduces a most uncharacteristic note of bombast. No doubt Bruckner perpetrated this 'improvement' himself; but we have to remember that it was only due to the influence of Schalk that he ever started tinkering with the original work at all.

However, as with the other symphonies which Bruckner was persuaded to revise, some conductors will no doubt prefer the revision. In which case, it may be said that it scarcely matters whether they use Nowak's edition of the Bruckner-Schalk score of 1889 or Schalk's own edition of 1890, which was reissued by Eulenburg in 1961, in a new edition by Hans Redlich, freed from misprints. Since the 1889 score is itself unauthentic, in that it contains many elements stemming from the ideas of Schalk, why should a few more Schalkisms matter?

Incidentally, Arthur D. Walker has called Schalk's 1890 score a 'fifth version' (the Bruckner-Schalk 1889 one being the 'fourth'); and Redlich, in his preface, even made the total six (taking into account the Rättig publication of 1878). Moreover, Redlich looked forward to a possible 'seventh version, which will unite the achievements and characteristics of each of its predecessors'. If Bruckner himself could not make the symphony a perfect work of art, no-one else can now: merely to suggest such a possibility opens up the appalling prospect of an infinite number of different and equally useless 'versions' made by editors who think themselves free to pick and choose as they like.

Summing-up. Bruckner brought the symphony as near to perfection as he could in his first definitive version of 1877, and he never improved on it: this is surely the one that should be performed (in the Oeser edition, of course, which is anyway the only one now available). If the 1889 revision is preferred, the Nowak edition or Redlich's edition of Schalk's 1890 score can be used without making much difference. In designating the different versions, there is again no need of editors' names, but the three main scores should be clearly differentiated and a mention of Schalk seems essential:

Symphony no. 3 in D minor (first definitive version, 1877)
or
Symphony no. 3 in D minor (Bruckner-Schalk revision, 1889)
or
Symphony no. 3 in D minor (Bruckner-Schalk revision, ed. Schalk, 1890)

SYMPHONY NO. 4 IN E FLAT

With no. 4, Bruckner again found it necessary to make three shots before arriving at his definitive score. The first was in 1874, the second in 1877–8 (in this he composed a new scherzo—the present one—and a new finale): and the third was simply a recasting, in 1880, of the 1878 finale into its present form. As with no. 3, there is no need to talk of three different 'versions': the score arrived at in 1880 was Bruckner's *first definitive version* of the work.[9]

(a) Versions

1. FIRST DEFINITIVE VERSION, completed in 1880, and first performed the following year under Richter: Bruckner made slight modifications for a second performance that year under Felix Mottl in Karlsruhe. The score was not published in his lifetime.

2. REVISED VERSION, made in 1886, for a performance in New York under Anton Seidl; the revision is concerned entirely with minor modifications of the orchestration, except for one important formal modification, which is discussed below. This score was also not published in Bruckner's lifetime.

(b) First Edition

COMPLETELY SPURIOUS SCORE, drawn up during 1886–7 by Franz Schalk and Löwe, with cuts and with the texture and orchestration recast in Wagnerian style: it was first performed in 1888 under Richter, and published in 1890 by Gutmann (later by Eulenburg, Peters, Philharmonia and Universal).

(c) Bruckner Society Editions

1. FIRST DEFINITIVE VERSION, ed. Haas: a reproduction of Bruckner's score of 1880.

2. REVISED VERSION, ed. Nowak: a reproduction of the score which Bruckner prepared for Seidl in 1886 (reprinted from Haas's plates, with the necessary modifications).

The first edition of 1890 was prepared and published with Bruckner's permission, but he withheld his ultimate sanction by refusing to sign the copy sent to the printer. It was reissued by Eulenburg in 1954 in a new edition by Hans Redlich, freed from

---

[9] As with no. 3, Hans-Hubert Schönzeler prefers to regard the 1874 score as the 'original version'—the *Urfassung*—but again as we are concerned with possible *performing* versions, we must ignore it here.

misprints: in his preface, he calls it 'the fourth version', but he admits the spurious nature of some of the orchestration:

> It is difficult to believe that Bruckner could have sanctioned the blatant sonorities of piccolo-flute and cymbals, suddenly and erratically introduced for the first time in movement 4, bar 76 ... Both instruments introduce an element of theatrica-lity, totally alien to Bruckner's world of sonorities. Equally suspicious are the *pp* cymbals (à la *Lohengrin*) at bar 473 (movt. 4) and the effect of muted horns in the same movement's bar 147, to which significantly enough the 'aperto' sign is missing at bar 155.

Elsewhere Redlich finds 'felicitous touches'; but the truth is that the whole score is more than suspicious. Even worse than the Wag-nerian orchestration, which blurs Bruckner's stark outlines, is the recasting of the actual texture, which works more fatally to the same purpose. A typical example occurs in bars 87–92 of the first movement, where the firmly punching trombone rhythm, so characteristic of Bruckner's musical personality, is toned down, not only by removing the accents and changing the *f* marking to *mf*, but by actually altering the note-values (see Ex. 3, which gives the outline only).

Ex. 3

Things like this, not to mention the pointless cuts in the scherzo and finale, invalidate the Löwe-Schalk score. So when Redlich suggests that 'in a more distant future conductors will try to coalesce versions II/III and IV into an ultimate "practical version"', embodying the best solutions, taken from all existing versions of the symphony', it is surely as unrealistic as to hope for a 'seventh version' of no. 3. There are only two genuine versions of no. 4: Bruckner's own first definitive version of 1880, and his own revision of 1886.

But how genuine is the revision? It seems that the MS used by Haas for his edition of the first definitive version of 1880 was a copy of it made by Bruckner himself in 1890;[10] and the fact that Bruckner made a copy of it at this time could be considered not only (as Redlich admits) a 'silent protest' against the publication of the Löwe-Schalk score in 1890, but also an annulment of the revision made (in what circumstances we do not know) for Seidl's performance of 1886. It seems undeniable that Bruckner's final decision was to abide by his first definitive version of 1880.

In any case, there is really little difference between the two versions. The divergences in orchestral detail affect only 140 bars (about 7%), of the work, and they are quite unimportant, being almost entirely minor adjustments of the woodwind and brass parts which are scarcely noticeable in performance.They are too numerous to list here in full; the most interesting are as follows.

    I 19, ob; 459–62 ob
   II 21 db; 105–8, tpt; 193, brass; 201–3, hn; 217–8, tpt
  III (trio) 44–52, cl; 51–3, ob
  IV 19–22, ob; 51–5, ww; 187–92, hn; 249–52, ob; 449, hn

There are also several changes, in the finale, from ¢ to 4/4, which do not really matter, since these passages could only be conducted in four anyway. The really important difference, referred to in (*a*) 2 above, occurs in the last nine bars of the finale: in the 1886 revision, the trombone-and-tuba reiteration of the rhythm of the symphony's opening horn-motive is backed by repetitions of that motive itself on the third and fourth horns, whereas in the definitive version of 1880 these two instruments merely support the general tutti texture of the repeated tonic chord. It is not in fact very easy to hear the motive in most performances of the revised version, since conductors too often allow the two horns to be

[10] Pointed out by Redlich in the preface to his Eulenburg edition of the Löwe-Schalk score. In Robert Haas's book *Anton Bruckner* (Potsdam 1934), Plate 4 reproduces the first page of Bruckner's definitive score, and the date at the head of it is clearly 18 January 1890 (i.e. Bruckner made that year a fair copy of his first definitive score of 1880).

drowned by the *ff* brass and the other two horns; but in so far as it *can* be heard, it does represent a formal difference affecting the conception of the whole work.

Summing-up. The Löwe-Schalk score should be rejected altogether as a falsification of Bruckner's intentions. Ideally, the Haas edition should be used, as representing Bruckner's final adherence to his first definitive version,[11] though some conductors will no doubt opt for the Nowak edition of the revised version, with its return of the opening horn motive at the end of the work. Since both represent scores drawn up by Bruckner himself, they can be differentiated quite simply, without using editors' names:

> Symphony no. 4 in E flat (first definitive version, 1880)
> *or*
> Symphony no. 4 in E flat (revised version, 1886)

After nos. 3 and 4, the growing-pains of Bruckner's new monumental type of symphony were over, and he had no further difficulties, except with no. 8. So, with this one exception, there is no longer any need to tabulate versions and editions.

SYMPHONY NO. 5 IN B FLAT

Bruckner completed the work in 1876 and never revised it (though he slightly retouched it, up to 1878). This single definitive score was neither performed nor published in his lifetime; but in 1893 Franz Schalk made a version of his own, with cuts and with a comprehensive transformation of the texture and orchestration, for his first performance of the work in Graz the following year.[12] In this score, which was published as the first edition of 1896 by Doblinger (later by Eulenburg, Peters and Philharmonia), Bruckner had no part at all: he was too ill to attend the performance and was on his

---

[11] Hans-Hubert Schönzeler has drawn my attention to the curious fact that the two different printings of the Haas edition (1936 and 1944) show slight differences of orchestration in the trio of the scherzo: the most important is that the theme of the first eight bars, given to flute and clarinet in the 1936 printing, is given to *oboe* and clarinet in the 1944 one. The reason for this change is obscure; since Haas offered no explanation of it; however, it is so small a detail in the vast conception of the whole work that there is no need to differentiate between the two printings, even though conductors who favour the Haas edition will no doubt prefer one to the other, according to taste. (The 1944 Haas printing is the only published score of the work which has this feature; it can be heard on Klemperer's recording.)

[12] For an instance of how Schalk even recomposed passages of the work, see Redlich, *Bruckner and Mahler*, pp. 45–7, where the Bruckner and Schalk forms of bars 1–16 of the finale are quoted and compared.

deathbed when the score was published.

His own score was brought out by the Bruckner Society, edited by Haas: and Nowak's edition followed—a reprint from Haas's plates with scarcely any alterations. The significant differences are as follows.

    I   309 va; 314, tpt 2
   II   Nil
  III   71–4, bass trb, tuba
   IV   589, vn 1 and 2

Of these four differences, three seem to be mere corrections by Nowak of misreadings by Haas, and are practically unnoticeable in performance. The other (III, 71–4) is a case where both editors are patently wrong: the bass trombone should obviously have a staccato crotchet *A* on the first beat of each bar, and the tuba should be tacet (a good conductor would naturally sort this out at rehearsal). It may be added that in both editions a large cut is suggested (bars 270–374 in the finale are marked 'Vi-de'), and that this, as with all other cases in the symphonies, should be simply ignored. Since the cut would completely upset the proportions of the movement, it could hardly have been thought of by Bruckner himself.

Summing-up. The spurious Schalk score has been abandoned by everybody, and it does not matter whether the Haas or the Nowak edition of Bruckner's own score is used for performance. So there is no need to mention editors' names or 'versions' when designating the work, which stands simply as:

Symphony no. 5 in B flat (1876)

SYMPHONY NO. 6 IN A

Bruckner completed the work in 1881, and never revised it. Only two movements (the second and third) were performed in his lifetime—in 1883 under Wilhelm Jahn; the first performance of the work (heavily cut) took place in 1899 under Mahler. That same year the first edition, edited by Cyril Hynais, was published by Doblinger (later by Eulenburg, Peters, Universal and Philharmonia); this must be considered unauthentic, as it contains alterations to dynamics and phrasing, unwarranted extra tempo indications, and suggestions for cuts.

Bruckner's own score was brought out by the Bruckner Society, edited by Haas; and Nowak's edition followed—a reprint from Haas's plates with a number of small modifications. Most of the discrepancies are manifest corrections by Nowak of misprints in Haas; many of them would be picked up anyway in rehearsal, since they are cases where two instruments are doubling each other but do not have the same note or accidental. In any case there are places where Nowak has failed to correct Haas (e.g. I, 96, cl 2; 181, db; and IV, 301, vn 2; 351, vn 1). The actual differences in texture, covering six bars of the first movement, are as follows:

I 29, hn 3, 4; 32, trb 2; 121, vn 2; 138, ob; 212, vn 2; 279, db

All these discrepancies are entirely or practically unnoticeable in performance, except only Nowak's extra two double-bass notes in bar 279, and these look rather curious (one would have expected Bruckner to stop this *pizzicato* pedal a bar earlier, as in the Haas edition).

Summing-up. The first edition seems to have dropped out now, as it should have done, and it does not matter whether the Haas or the Nowak edition of Bruckner's own score is used for performance, provided that the misprints in both are corrected. Again the work needs no more than its title and date for its correct designation:

Symphony no. 6 in A (1881)

SYMPHONY NO. 7 IN E

Bruckner completed the work in 1883 and never revised it. That same year, however, he was persuaded (and helped) by Josef Schalk and Löwe to recast the orchestration of a few passages, for the first performance in Leipzig the following year under Nikisch. It was in this form—but with further editorial retouchings by Schalk and Löwe and with additional tempo indications stemming from Nikisch—that the symphony was first published in 1885 by Gutmann (later by Eulenburg, Kalmus, Peters, Philharmonia and Universal).

The Bruckner Society brought out Bruckner's own score, edited by Haas; and Nowak followed with his edition of the same score, reprinted from Haas's plates but modified to include the orchestral alterations. There is no need to make a great deal of these, since they cover no more than 29 bars of the whole work, as follows:

   I 103–4, hn; 123–30, ob, hn, tpt, trb, tuba; 148–9, cl, bn; 154, 156, vn 1; 319–22, ob

  II 177–81, timp, trgl, cym; 192, trb; 216, str (pizz. in Nowak, not till 217 in Haas)

 III Nil

 IV 337–9, tpt

These discrepancies affect the sound of the work very little. As regards the really striking one, the famous cymbal clash and triangle-roll at II, 177, I cannot say I am worried: even if it is a Schalk-and-Löweism, Bruckner's climax is so pure as to ennoble these dangerously flashy weapons in the romantic orchestral armoury. (But it is a pity we should have to make such personal decisions.) In any case, much worse than things like this, in Nowak's edition, is the reintroduction (in brackets) of the extra tempo indications of the first edition. They have no place in Bruckner's score, being simply Nikisch's 'conductor's markings': Bruckner is supposed to have sanctioned them, but surely only for Nikisch's own performances. The *Alla breve* and *Molto animato* markings at 1, 233, and the plentifully scattered *ritard* markings in the finale, are particularly harmful, since if observed carefully (*cf* Klemperer's recording) they destroy the natural flow of the music (who can say how much or how little Nikisch meant by them?).

Summing-up. The first edition and Nowak's edition differ very little, and in view of their unwarranted tempo indications should surely be rejected in favour of Haas's edition, which is a clean reproduction of Bruckner's own definitive score. Again, whichever score is used, the work can be designated by its title and date alone:

Symphony no. 7 in E (1883)

SYMPHONY NO. 8 IN C MINOR
(a) Versions

   1. ORIGINAL VERSION, completed in 1887.[13] The score has been issued by the Bruckner Society (1973), ed. Nowak.

---

[13] The statement in the lists issued by Arthur D. Walker, that there was a first version in 1885, and that the score of 1887 is a second version, is incorrect. The 1885 MS—as confirmed in the monumental Bruckner biography of Göllerich (completed by Auer), IV 2, 532–557—is a full-length *sketch*, partly in pencil, partly in ink, partly in short score, partly in full score; the 1887 MS is a full-score realization of this, and thus the first genuine version of the work.

2. REVISED VERSION (BRUCKNER AND JOSEF SCHALK), completed in 1890, and first performed two years later under Richter. This is a recomposed and partly cut transformation of the 1887 score, carried out by Bruckner in collaboration with Josef Schalk; it was published in 1892 as the first edition: see (*b*) below.

(b) First Edition

REVISED VERSION (BRUCKNER AND JOSEF SCHALK), edited by Josef Schalk and published in 1892 by Schlesinger (later by Eulenburg, Haslinger, Peters and Philharmonia). This must be considered unauthentic, since it differs in a number of respects from Nowak's edition of the Bruckner-Schalk score of 1890; see (*c*) 3 below.

(c) Bruckner Society Editions

1. ORIGINAL VERSION, ed. Nowak; a reproduction of Bruckner's score of 1887.

2. REVISED VERSION (WITH MATERIAL RESTORED FROM THE ORIGINAL VERSION), ed. Haas.

3. REVISED VERSION (BRUCKNER AND JOSEF SCHALK), ed. Nowak. This was largely reprinted from Haas's plates, but with considerable modifications to make the score a reproduction of the Bruckner-Schalk score of 1890 (without the alterations made by Schalk for the first edition of 1892).

Here we face the most awkward problem of all. It was Hermann Levi's negative reaction to the original version of 1887 that led Bruckner to revise the work; and in doing so, he went through it with a fine toothcomb: in particular, he composed a new ending to the first movement and a new trio for the scherzo, as well as redisposing the tonal perspective of the Adagio. These manifest compositional improvements[14] Haas felt obliged to accept as such; but Bruckner had also made cuts in the Adagio and finale, and Haas felt these to be damaging, and almost certainly due to the influence of Schalk. So he restored the missing material from the 1887 score. Nowak, in his preface, declared Haas's procedure to be impossible, since 'different sources, according to the principles for the working out of a critical complete edition, can never be intermingled'; and so, for his own edition, he simply reproduced the Bruckner-Schalk revision of 1890 in a clean score.

---

[14] But was it the originals of these passages that worried Levi? Most unlikely—it seems that he was puzzled by the whole work.

Nowak may have musicological rectitude on his side, but this is a unique case, in which human ethics play at least as large a part as the musicological variety. Josef Schalk's interference in the revision must itself be considered unethical; and so Haas's conjectural restoration of what Bruckner's own revision would probably have been, if he had been left to himself, could be regarded as the setting right of a wrong. We may consider a single example, a passage in the second group of the finale, as it appears in the exposition (leading up to letter F) and in the recapitulation (leading up to letter Oo). This passage, which contains a reference to the Seventh Symphony, is followed in both cases by a completely new section in a slower tempo; Ex. 4 shows how it appears in the exposition in both the original version of 1887 and the revised version of 1890 (the example breaks off at letter F). In the original version Bruckner restated this passage in full in the recapitulation, with a climactic extension of two bars (Ex. 5, which breaks off at letter Oo). But in the Bruckner-Schalk revision of 1890, this recapitulatory passage is drastically and crudely truncated (Ex. 6, which also breaks off at letter Oo). And in the Schalk first edition of 1892 alone, the passage in the exposition is truncated as well (Ex. 7).

Nowak, musicologically faithful to the Bruckner-Schalk revision of 1890, has Ex. 4 in the exposition and Ex. 6 in the recapitulation, and gives his reasons as follows: 'Josef Schalk wrote in his letter of 5 August 1891, to Max von Oberleithner [who saw the edition through the press] that he wanted this abbreviation [the cut in the exposition, as in Ex. 7], since the "reminiscence of the Seventh" seemed "quite unfounded to him". He was not quite wrong, because the abbreviation before letter Oo [the cut in the recapitulation as in Ex. 6], made by Bruckner himself, eliminated the same passage in the reprise. Thus the balance of motives in the second version is disturbed, nevertheless, following Bruckner's decisions nothing is to be changed . . .'

Ex. 4

Ex. 5

Ex. 6

Ex. 7

In fact, this is one more case of a Nowak preface condemning a
Nowak edition—or rather condemning a score that Nowak has
edited. Bruckner could not possibly have made 'decisions' which
'disturbed the balance of the motives', since he was always eager
for his full-length scores to be published, if possible. It can only
have been that he made the cut in the recapitulation (Ex. 6) to
satisfy Schalk (and made a botch of it as can be seen), but that he
overlooked the equivalent passage in the exposition (Ex. 4). And
in 1891, when the score was being prepared for printing, Schalk
must have realized—the old man had forgotten! Hence his letter to
Oberleithner, asking for the truncation in the exposition (Ex. 7). In
spite of Nowak, Schalk *was* 'quite wrong' in tampering with
Bruckner's score at all, either by influencing Bruckner or by
altering it himself. Nevertheless, in making the cut in the exposition he did show that he cared about the 'balance of the motives',
whereas Nowak, by leaving out what Bruckner and Schalk had cut
in the recapitulation and keeping in what Schalk had cut of his own
accord in the exposition, achieved only a piece of musicological
pedantry which makes no structural sense at all. How much wiser
was Haas, in restoring the situation of the original version (indicated by Exx. 4 and 5), and thus shaking off the influence of Schalk

altogether![15] The same may be said of his other restorations, in this movement and in the Adagio. The cuts in the revised version are as follows:

III 209–18.
IV 211–30, 253–6, 584–98, 609–15, 671–4.

Apart from these, there are many other discrepancies between the Haas and Nowak editions, concerning texture and orchestration, because Haas restored more than material—what he considered felicities, which had been spoiled in the revision. A dangerous undertaking, no doubt, and yet his score always seems the more Brucknerian. The differences are too many to list in full here; the following are the most significant.

I 101, hn; 164–72, vln 1 & 2, bsn, hn.
III 24–5 and 41–2, bsn, brass; 60, fl, cl; 66–7, cl; 141–2, 151–2, vln 2; 160, vln 1; 260–1, brass.

In any case, these differences matter very little compared with the cuts.

Summing-up. The Nowak edition of the original version of 1877 is of purely musicological interest. No doubt there will always be controversy over the merits of the Haas and Nowak scores of the revised version of 1890; although my own vote goes unreservedly to the Haas, since it makes the best of both versions, there are still musicians who stand by the Nowak. Actually, as with no. 3, the Nowak and the first edition are so near to each other that it makes little difference which is used; as said above, the first edition is more logical in one respect at least. Whichever score is used, it should be clearly designated, and this is a case where editors' names should certainly be mentioned:

Symphony no. 8 in C minor (1887/90, ed. Haas)
Symphony no. 8 in C minor (Bruckner-Schalk revision, 1890, ed. Nowak)
or
Symphony no. 8 in C minor (Bruckner-Schalk revision, ed. Schalk, 1892)

---

[15] Nowak offers a technical argument against Haas's restorations—that material cannot be incorporated from the original version because that is a score with two of each woodwind and the revised version is a score with three; but it is quite invalid, since there are still many passages in Bruckner's revised version where only two of each are used.

SYMPHONY NO. 9 IN D MINOR

Once more, there is no need to tabulate. Bruckner left the work unfinished (lacking the finale) when he died in 1896, and his score was not published for thirty-eight years. The first edition, issued in 1903 by Doblinger (later by Eulenburg,[16] Peters, Philharmonia and Universal) was of a 'version' made by Löwe, with cuts and alterations to the texture and orchestration, for his first performance of the work that year. This score is entirely unauthentic, and is never used today.

Bruckner's own score was brought out by the Bruckner Society, edited by Alfred Orel, and Nowak's edition followed—an identical reprint from Orel's plates, except for a correction of one or two misprints. So the symphony stands simply as:

Symphony no. 9 in D minor (unfinished, 1896)

To conclude this investigation of the 'Bruckner problem'. I should like to offer my own personal list of the versions which I believe should be used for performance, as being the purest. It is in complete agreement with the conclusions of Robert Simpson,[17] and practically with those of Hans-Hubert Schönzeler—and it takes us back to the imaginary simple list with which we began.

(1) Linz version, 1866 (Haas or Nowak)
(2) Original version, 1872 (Haas)
(3) First definitive version, 1877 (Oeser)
(4) First definitive version, 1880 (Haas)
(5) Definitive version, 1876 (Haas or Nowak)
(6) Definitive version, 1881 (Haas or Nowak)
(7) Definitive version, 1883 (Haas)
(8) Revised version, 1890, with material restored from original version of 1887 (Haas)
(9) Definitive version, 1896 (Orel, Nowak, or Schönzeler)

Scores and orchestral parts of all the Bruckner Society editions of the symphonies are available as follows:

Britain: Haas's editions of nos. 1–2 and 4–8, and Orel's of no. 9, from Breitkopf & Härtel; Oeser's edition of no. 3 and

---

[16] Not to be confused with Eulenburg's 1963 publication of Bruckner's own score, ed. Hans-Hubert Schönzeler.
[17] in *The Essence of Bruckner.*

Nowak's editions of nos. 0–9, (plus the 1887 score of no. 8), from Bärenreiter.

USA: Haas's editions of nos. 1–2 and 4–8, and Orel's of no. 9, from Associated Music Publishers; Oeser's edition of no. 3 and Nowak's editions of nos. 0–9, (plus the 1887 score of no. 8), from Schirmer.

[1969, revised 1975]

The Facts Concerning Mahler's Tenth Symphony*

In view of various misleading statements which have been made concerning Mahler's Tenth Symphony, and the confusion that has arisen from them, it may be of value to set forth clearly the facts of the matter.

It was Mahler's custom to sketch a symphony during the summer and elaborate it in full score during the following winter. He sketched the Tenth Symphony in the summer of 1910, but instead of working on it during the winter of 1910–11 he made a further revision of the Ninth Symphony; since he died in May 1911, the work was never completed. Thus the Tenth Symphony—in the sense of Mahler's final definitive score, which would probably have been ready for publication by 1912—is forever lost to us; all we possess is the sketch.

This much is known to all lovers of Mahler's music, and there are those for whom that is all there is to be said. They maintain that, since Mahler did not live to complete the symphony, it does not exist as a work of art in any sense; they regard the sketch as a tragic might-have-been and a mere musicological curiosity, and they wish it to remain so. Some make an exception in the case of the opening Adagio movement, believing that it was brought near enough to completion to be performed, with a very minimum of editing, as a genuine piece of Mahler; but any attempt to make a performing version of the whole sketch, they tell us, is at best a misguided folly,

* After the BBC radio performance of the bulk of the Tenth Symphony in Deryck Cooke's realization in 1960, all further performances were banned by Alma Mahler, the composer's widow. This article was written for *Chord and Discord*, the Journal of the Bruckner Society of America, before the ban was lifted, in order to demonstrate, among other things, the musical unity of the work in its unfinished state. Because of copyright problems no music examples could be used in the original article.

After Alma Mahler's death in 1964, a further 44 pages of sketches for the Tenth Symphony came to light: their absence from the 1924 facsimile does not materially affect the substance of this essay. [D.M.]

at worst a sacrilege.

This view must command respect, in so far as it is based on the crucial and indisputable fact that exactly what Mahler's final score of the work would have been like is beyond all conjecture. But unfortunately some of those who hold it have supported it by denying or obscuring other crucial and indisputable facts, which offer a sound basis for the opposite viewpoint—the viewpoint of those who advocate making a performing version of the sketch. It is these facts that I wish to establish here.

(1) Mahler did not, as is still too widely stated, express any final wish that the manuscript should be destroyed. The statement that he did so was made by Richard Specht in his official biography of the composer (1913); but in 1924, Mrs. Mahler allowed the manuscript to be published in facsimile, and the first and third of its five movements to be performed in edited form; and the following year, Specht, in the seventeenth edition of his book, wrote an appendix, with Mrs. Mahler's sanction, in which he categorically withdrew his statement, and firmly advocated the completion of the work by someone conversant with Mahler's method and style.

(2) Schoenberg's remarks about the 'unknowable' Tenth Symphony, reprinted in his book *Style and Idea*, cannot be invoked as arguments against making a performing version of the sketch, since they were not based on an intimate knowledge of the manuscript. Indeed, Schoenberg can never at any time have made an intensive study of the manuscript or, being the man of integrity that he was, he would have retracted the remarks about it in *Style and Idea*, since they are utterly misleading in the impression they give of an inscrutable enigma.

(3) The manuscript is in no sense an inscrutable enigma. It can only be regarded as such by those who have not made themselves absolutely familiar with it in every detail by copying it out for themselves. Despite the apparently chaotic calligraphy, its supposed indecipherability has been vastly exaggerated. It is true that, in the case of occasional isolated notes, which are either illegible or manifest slips by Mahler in his notation, one is forced back on a conjectural reading; but in the case of something like ninety-five per cent of the manuscript, there can be no argument as to what Mahler set down, and indeed most of it can be written out by a good copyist, familiar with Mahler's calligraphy, who is prepared to make the necessary effort of concentration.

(4) All suggestions that the manuscript is fragmentary are quite false. The word 'sketches,' so often used to describe it, is only justifiable in that there is a separate sketch for each of the five movements (two of the opening Adagio—short score and full score), and some isolated alternative sketch-pages of odd passages and sections.* But the word is utterly misleading when it is used to convey an impression of separate fragments, the assembling and ordering of which is a matter of conjecture. Each of the five main folders contains a comprehensive sketch of a movement, with the pages clearly numbered. The order of these movements is clear from Mahler's final blue-pencil marking on each folder—I, II, III, IV, and V; and this order is in any case self-evident from the internal tonal and structural progression of the whole.

(5) Even in the case of each separate movement, any use of the word 'sketch' to imply something improvisatory and inchoate is misleading. Each sketch is a full-length, bar-by-bar laying down of an entirely intelligible and significant form, in which there are no lacunae, except perhaps one tiny one near the end of the fourth movement. As Richard Specht said in the appendix to the seventeenth edition of his biography, Mahler himself described the manuscript as a work already fully-prepared *in the sketch*; and indeed it is a comprehensive full-length sketch (1949 bars) of a five-movement symphony in F sharp, with every main idea fully-formed in melody and entirely intelligible in harmony, and with bar-by-bar thematic continuity from beginning to end. The sketch makes perfect sense as a continuous symphonic structure; so accuracy demands that we should describe the manuscript, not as '*sketches* for the Tenth Symphony' but—with Mahler—as '*the sketch of* the Tenth Symphony.'

(6) The Tenth Symphony does actually exist, then, as a musical work, in the basic sense of a significant and integrated structure. That Mahler would have modified this structure in detail is certain; but that he would have recast it wholesale cannot be imagined. Whatever may be lacking in textural detail—especially in the second movement—the sketch as it stands can be analysed as a symphony quite as meaningfully as any of Mahler's completed works; and analysis reveals a form as rich and complex and closely

---

* The complete surviving sketch material, published in facsimile in 1967, comprises (in brief): 1. Adagio: draft full score; short score; sketch. 2. Scherzo: draft full score; sketch. 3. Purgatorio: fragment of full score; short score; sketch. 4: short score; sketch. 5. Finale: short score; sketches. [D.M.]

integrated as any Mahler conceived. The brochure which Richard Specht wrote as a companion to the publication of the facsimile in 1924 offers a broad descriptive analysis which, apart from numerous misreadings, due no doubt to insufficiently prolonged study of the manuscript, provides as comprehensive an account of the work as could be made of a complete symphony. I would also refer the reader to my own summary thematic analysis (in music-type) in *The Musical Times* of June 1961, which indicates the main strands of the phenomenally intricate web of thematic cross-references and cyclic development from movement to movement; again the analysis gives the impression of dealing with a completed work. Neither Specht's nor my own analysis would have been possible if the Tenth were not complete in its whole essential thematic-harmonic-formal structure.

(7) This structure presents an emotional and psychological statement as intelligible as those of Mahler's other symphonies. The 'message' of the symphony is clear, and is of the utmost significance in that this was Mahler's last work—complementing *Das Lied von der Erde* and the Ninth Symphony as the final panel of his great posthumous last-period trilogy, and throwing crucial light on everything that went before. The final resolution of Mahler's life-long spiritual conflict is not to be found in the Ninth Symphony, but in the quite different Tenth. The following description may give an idea of the work's crucial importance to our full understanding of Mahler as man and artist: it should be studied in conjunction with the facsimile.*

SYMPHONY NO. 10 IN F SHARP MAJOR

1. ADAGIO. Draft full score, 275 bars, almost all 4/4. F sharp major-minor-major. Like the opening *Andante comodo* of the Ninth Symphony, but less desperately, this movement presents a sombre introspective conflict between two opposed ideas. These are: (1) the introductory *andante* motto-theme for unaccompanied unison violas (bars 1–15)—a disconsolate, homeless, searching melody, of shifting tonality, moving from B minor to D minor (the latter noted enharmonically); and (2) the main *adagio* theme in F sharp major (bars 16–19)—a passionate, large-spanned violin melody over rich harmonies for lower strings and trombones, which forges onwards yearningly, repeated in inverted and normal

---

* Or with the full score of the Performing Version, published in 1976. [D.M.]

forms, through acute tonal disruptions. At bar 31, after a threefold statement of the *adagio* theme, the *andante* theme returns, transformed into a melancholy F sharp minor violin melody with sparse string texture, generating more anxious material (bar 34) and taking in a quicker, troubled version of the *adagio* theme itself (bar 36); but at bar 38 it returns in its original unaccompanied viola motto-theme form, even more unsettled in tonality, to lead back to a resumption of the *adagio* theme.

This is the whole main pattern of the movement: the Adagio keeps launching off in F sharp major, confidently, only to give way to the melancholy F sharp minor melody; and the original motto-theme keeps coming back like a dark unanswered question. In spite of the glorious F sharp major outburst of the *adagio* theme (from bar 58), and the ascendancy of the anxious elements, first in B flat minor (from bar 91) and then in A minor and other keys (from bar 112), no resolution is reached. But eventually the latent tension of the movement suddenly erupts in a dramatic and unexpected outburst—a great organ-like sequence of chords in A flat minor for brass, with sweeping arpeggiando for strings and harp (bars 194–99), followed by a sustained fortissimo nine-note dissonance for full orchestra, with a high trumpet A piercing through it (bars 203–8). As in the opening movement of the Ninth Symphony, but in a different way, the climax brings dissolution: at bar 213, the music moves into F sharp major, not to resume the *adagio* theme, but for an extended coda, woven of regretful reminiscences of it and its former opponent, which mingle together in bitter-sweet resignation.

This first movement, it should be noted, initiates the motto-rhythm of the symphony ♩♩|♩., which is present in both of its main themes, and permeates the movement.

II. SCHERZO. Fast crotchets. Draft full score, 523 bars,[1] with various time-signatures, F sharp minor-major. This big scherzo movement complements the big opening Adagio, being in the same key, proportionate in weight, and contradictory in mood. It

---

[1] The numbering may vary, to a few bars, according as one interprets the sketch. Notes for guidance: (1) I count bar 44 (which is 4/2) as two bars of 2/2—bars 44 and 45. (2) Note the extra insert-bar after bar 53. (3) I take bar 163 as nullified by the single-line correction above the violins in the next bar, and divide this corrected line into three bars of 3/4—bars 163, 164, 165. (4) Bar 271 is only one bar: Mahler has deleted the line indicating an extra bar. (5) The bar after bar 307—the last on the page—is deleted; bar 308 is the first on the next page. (6) Note bar 434, crushed in between bars 433 and 435.

consists of a main scherzo-section with two trio-sections, the material of all three sections gradually mingling together in free development.

A. Main scherzo section, F sharp minor (bars 1–59)—fierce bustling music, mainly for strings and brass, with a nervous tautness due to constantly changing time-signatures, but full of a bold extrovert strength of spirit. Its brief C sharp minor introduction for horns and oboes (bars 1–4) presents the symphony's motto-rhythm ♫ ♩ which will permeate the movement; the main theme (from bar 4) makes much use of a falling octave, which will also play a large part in the fourth movement (a second scherzo). Statement (bars 1–22) and more forcible restatement (23–42) are followed by a brief extension (from bar 43) rising to a crashing climax (bar 55) which dies down swiftly. In bars 60–75, a brief transition dispels this mood with lighter treatment of the same material, switching through B flat, E and G, to F.

B. First trio, F major (bars 76–130). At the same tempo, still with changing time-signatures, the original fierce material is transformed into gay pastoral music in F major, featuring oboe, woodwind and horns, which is still permeated with the motto-rhythm. After the statement (76–96) and modified restatement (97–110), there is a brief string version in A (111–16), before the last woodwind statement in F (117–30).

A. Varied restatement and development of scherzo material, F sharp minor (bars 131–65). Restatement of the fierce scherzo material (131–41) is interrupted by more genial development in A flat and D (142–51), but resumes in F sharp minor (from bar 152), reaching a new unison climax (bar 158), which subsides swiftly into E flat (163–5).

C. Second trio, E flat major (bars 166–246). The mood changes completely, as the restlessly changing time-signatures and short, clear-cut motives give way to an easily flowing 3/4—a rolling waltz-rhythm in the bass, supporting a warmly affectionate Ländler melody for violins. This melody is first cousin to the main *adagio* theme of the opening movement, and appears, like that theme, in normal and inverted forms. (Although Mahler indicated no change in tempo, he would doubtless have marked this section with some such word as 'gemächlicher': compare his 'Etwas ruhiger' at figure 6 in the scherzo of the Fifth Symphony.) The Ländler melody, mainly for strings (166–86) gives way to a secondary theme, a slightly melancholy 'hurdy-gurdy' type of tune for oboe and other woodwind (187–202); then the Ländler melody is restated in E flat and developed (from bar 203), the secondary idea breaking in a more grotesque form for a brief restatement in E flat minor (235–46).

AB. Varied restatement of scherzo material, F sharp minor, taking in development of the first trio, in other keys (bars 247–300). The fierce restatement of the scherzo material in F sharp minor (247–54) is interrupted by cheerful development of the first trio, in E flat and other keys (255–69), but resumes in F sharp minor (269–79), only to be interrupted again by the same material, now in D (280–94). At bar 295, the motive of the Ländler theme of the second trio enters repeatedly, broadly augmented, with normal and inverted forms in combination, generating a climax.

C. Varied restatement of second trio, D major (bars 301–66). The Ländler motive swells out in sonorous augmentation on the horns, in 3/4, beginning a richly glowing restatement in D major of the second trio, slightly modified and developed. The secondary theme does not recur in its original melancholy form, but cuts in towards the end, as before, for a brief restatement in D minor (348–59).

BC. Continuation of development of first trio, fused with elements of second trio, F major and C major (bars 367–416). With a return of the changing time-signatures, the cheerful material of the second trio is developed by brass and strings in F (367–76), taking in a quicker version of the Ländler motive in C (377–86) and in F again (387–408). From bar 408, the tonality begins to shift, as the second trio's material starts to change back into that of the fierce scherzo section, and there is a growth of tension towards a climax (408–16).

AC. Slower, more lyrical episode, developing materials of scherzo and second trio, F sharp major (bars 416–44). For the second time, the mood changes completely: as in the Rondo Burleske of the Ninth Symphony, the vociferous music abruptly gives way to a passage of deep yearning lyricism in the original key of the symphony. (Again, Mahler indicated no change of tempo, but he would doubtless have added some direction; compare the 'Etwas gehalten' in the passage of the Ninth Symphony just mentioned—third movement, after figure 36). It is at bar 416 that the agitation of the previous section is dispelled and broken off abruptly, when the trumpet breaks in with a transfigured, radiant version of one of the spiky scherzo motives, in F sharp major, over sustained trombone chords. This is in a calm 4/4; then (bar 424), in a smooth alternation of 4/4 with 3/4, moving more and more towards a pure 3/4, solo horn and strings muse tenderly on the Ländler theme, augmented, making its relationship to the opening movement's main *adagio* theme more apparent than ever, especially since the key is now the same. This section reaches a passionate climax and breaks off abruptly at bar 444.

ABC. Bringing together of main elements of scherzo and both trios, various keys, moving back towards F sharp major (bars 445–92). Abruptly, turning to B flat, resuming the original lively tempo (Mahler would no doubt have marked 'Tempo I' here) and going back to the changing time-signatures, the music continues with the gay development of the first trio material, taking in the augmented Ländler motive (445–58). It moves back to F sharp major (459–69), away to D major (470–78), and back to F sharp once more (at bar 479)—F sharp *minor* this time. In this key the cheerful second trio elements change back to the fierce scherzo material and work up to a tense climax, while the augmented Ländler motive is heard at the same time in a Neapolitan G major on horns (486–90).

BC. Coda, being an apotheosis of the two trio themes, F sharp major (bars 493–523). The movement, so robustly confident in essence, culminates logically in a blaze of vital energy. Minor switches abruptly to major, and over a dominant pedal, the augmented Ländler motive rises excitedly on horns and trumpets (493–503), leading to a triumphant march-like statement of the first trio material (504–11). This rises to a further climax—a brilliant outburst of the second trio's original main oboe theme on trumpets, wind and violins (from 511), which is joined by the horns, whooping out the augmented Ländler motive (515–21); and the movement ends with a sudden bang, in the same jubilantly affirmative mood as the scherzo of the Fifth Symphony.

The folder of this movement, incidentally, is marked '2. Scherzo-Finale'; and it seems most likely that Mahler originally intended a symphony in two movements.* Indeed, in view of the close re-

---

* The various crossed-out titles on the folders of the second and fourth movements are most confusing; but in fact '2. Scherzo-Finale' is best understood in conjunction with '1 Scherzo (I. Satz)' (1st Scherzo (1st movement)), which appears on the folder of the fourth movement, and would seem to imply that at one stage Mahler had thought of placing this movement first and the present second movement last. [D.M.]

lationship between the *adagio* and Ländler themes, and the fact that the yearning of the *adagio* theme finds release in the scherzo's final jubilant transformation of the augmented Ländler motive, the two movements form a unified whole, like the first and second movements of the Fifth Symphony. Wherefore it would seem that the Adagio and scherzo combine to form Part 1 of the Tenth Symphony, and that the other three movements, abandoning F sharp and only returning to it in the closing pages of the finale, form Part 2.

III. PURGATORIO, *Allegretto moderato.* Short score, 170 bars of 2/4[2] with full score of the first 28 bars, B flat minor. This short movement, a *moto perpetuo* mainly of great delicacy, is the motivic and emotional source of the two large-scale movements which follow: like 'Von der Jugend' in *Das Lied von der Erde*, it follows a simple A-B-A pattern.

A. Main section, B. flat minor and major (bars 1–63).

(1) Introduction, *Allegretto moderato,* setting up a semiquaver *moto perpetuo* (bars 1–6); and troubled B flat minor theme, *Nicht zu schnell*, for violins, looking back to the anxious material of the B flat minor section of the opening movement. Statement (6–14) and restatement (14–22), followed by the two opening phrases of the theme, striking in like a refrain (22–4), as they will do throughout the movement.

(2) Hopeful B flat major theme, *Etwas fliessend*, for oboe (24–32), rounded off with the refrain (32–4).

(3) Even brighter B flat major theme, for flute (34–40), rounded off with the refrain (40–41). Themes 1, 2, and 3, and the refrain, are permeated with the motto-rhythm ♫ | ♩.

(4) Second B flat minor theme, much darker than the first, for bassoons and basses. The statement (41–52) is joined by the refrain (48–50), and the restatement (52–63) is likewise (59–61).

B. Central section, development in D minor and major (bars 64–121), introducing a new theme. In contrast with the main section, the development is violent. After fierce treatment of theme 1 in D minor (64–9) and of theme 2 in D major (69–81), followed by the refrain (81–3), the new D minor theme enters—a

---

[2] Bar-numbering: (1) note the indication of three inserted bars after bar 76. (2) note the indication for expanding bar 99 into two bars—99 and 100. (3) note the *da capo* at bar 125—repeat bars 6–34 as bars 125–53, then return to page 3 (bars 154–70).

brooding six-note motive, extended (83–9). Refrain again (89–91), then the new theme recurs, more intensely (91–5). New development of theme 1 in bars 96–106 leads to a great tragic outburst of the new theme (106–9), followed by an even more tremendous one (112–14). Then the development of theme 1 dies away in D minor, spectrally (115–21).

A. Curtailed restatement of main section, B flat minor and major (bars 122–70). The music switches abruptly from D minor to B flat minor, and after a shortened restatement of the introduction (122–5), Mahler indicates a *da capo* of themes 1 (125–41) and 2 (143–51), with their refrains. Then theme 3 is written out in slightly modified form, *sempre diminuendo* (153–67). The movement is dying away radiantly in B flat major with the hopeful flute theme, when a momentary upheaval provides an eerie conclusion, with the refrain darkly in the bass (167–70).

It should be noted that theme 1 of this movement (Ex. 1) is made up of short agitated motives, of which three are important. There are two three-note ones, both to the motto-rhythm: B flat, D flat, B flat (bars 13–14), to be called w; and C, D flat, B flat (bars 23–4, short score*), to be called x. The other is a seven-note one (bars 10–11), to be called y. These, together with the tragic six-note theme of the central section (Ex. 2—to be called z), are used pervasively in the last two movements.

Ex. 1

Ex. 2   Ex. 3

* The Performing Version follows Mahler's full score fragment and opts for C, D flat, C here, though the short score has B flat. So too at bar 34 where Mahler's short score has both B flat and C with a question mark against the notes. Accordingly the three-note motive x does not in fact appear in the Performing Version until the very last bar (Ex. 3). [D.M.]

IV. MOVEMENT WITHOUT TITLE. Short score, 580 bars of 3/4,[3] E minor moving to D minor. Although this movement has neither title nor tempo marking, it is clearly a fierce *Allegro pesante* in the lamenting vein of the 'Trinklied' of *Das Lied von der Erde*, conflicting with seductive waltz material. Again there is a main scherzo section and two trios, and the materials of all three sections mingle in free development; and all these elements are pervaded with the motto-rhythm ♪♩ and the three-note motive *x*, which formed the refrain of the Purgatorio and ended that movement (Ex. 3).

A. Main scherzo section, E minor (bars 1–115)—wild tragic music in Mahler's demonic vein, permeated with the three-note Purgatorio motive *x* to the motto-rhythm and to another rhythm ♩. ♪ ♩ (both rhythms pervade the whole movement).

A brief introduction (1–5) presents a grim motto of three sustained chords, descending by octaves, for wind, horns, and trombones respectively. The first chord is subdominant (an A minor secondary seventh), the second dominant (the dominant seventh of B minor); the third establishes the movement's main tonality with a 6/3 of E minor. This already adumbrates the tonal conflict of the whole movement between a tendency to fall despairingly towards the subdominant side (A minor, and further to D minor), and a struggle to move positively into the dominant, B major—a conflict which is finally lost. Against the first chord is thrown the falling octave of the second movement, against the second the Purgatorio motive *x*, both of which form the basis of the main theme.

(1) Violent, high-soaring main theme, E minor (5–11), developed to a climax (11–25), and extending by a secondary idea in the subdominant, A minor (24–41), which brings back the motto-

---

[3] Bar-numbering: Page ī: after bar 14, a bar is deleted. Page II: after bar 106, I have ignored the possible insert marked by Mahler with a query, as I believe it indicates a contemplated alteration in the structure. Page III: I take the first two bars of the upper line, and the four bars of the lower—bars 115–22; the single up-beat beginning the next page belongs to bar 122. Page IV: bar 144, ringed for possible deletion by Mahler, is reinstated by the word 'bleibt', and remains; after bar 158, I take the next bar as deleted. Page V: after bar 235, two bars are deleted. Page VI: at bar 307, note the extra bar. Page VIII: after bar 379, the rest of the page is deleted. Page IX: after bar 398, eight bars are deleted. Page Xa: after bar 506, one bar is deleted; after bar 508, one bar is deleted; then follow bars 509, 510, 511, 512 (deleted but reinstated with the word 'bleibt'), and 513, the last bar of page Xa. Page Xb: after bar 515, a bar is deleted.

[In the full score of the Performing Version, bar 394 is deleted by analogy with the bar deleted (by Mahler) between bars 14 and 15. Consequently all references to bar numbers after bar 393 in this article should be reduced by one. D.M.]

chords with full force (41–5) and a new working up of the main theme, in E major, to the first big climax (45–57).

(2) Transitional theme, beginning stormily in E minor (56–64), but changing to graceful waltz-like material in E major (64–72); this leads to a melancholy waltz-tune of the 'hurdy-gurdy' type in G minor in bars 73–83 (cf. the secondary theme of the E flat Ländler trio of the second movement); but the stormy theme bursts in again in E minor with a new continuation (83–98), which works towards a climax.

(3) The approach to the climax is a new idea in its own right—a fiercely lamenting passage which will recur throughout as a refrain (99–107). This brings the whole continuous non-stop scherzo section to a tremendous climax (107–14), into which the motto-chords enter with overpowering force (111–15) to herald a new section.

The climax subsides on to a curiously laconic link-passage, based on the Purgatorio motive x, which will recur: it modulates to C major, the relative of the subdominant A minor (115–22).

B. First trio, C major (bars 123–66)—seductive waltz-music derived from augmented lyrical variants of the Purgatorio motive x.

(1) Quiet, sentimental main waltz-tune, C major (123–37), with varied restatement (138–44).

(2) Secondary idea, C major (145–52)—characteristic waltz-material of the gay, leaping, syncopated kind.

(3) A confident, dashing theme bursts in, C major, and leads back to E minor (152–66).

A. Varied restatement and development of scherzo material (in conjunction with that of the first trio), basically E minor (166–247). First the waltz-tune B1 is developed in the stern mood and key of the scherzo material, E minor (166–73), the motto-chords striking in powerfully (170–74) to initiate this whole new section; and A1 itself is developed passionately, in E minor (174–84). Then the waltz-tune B1 returns to be treated lamentingly in the subdominant, D minor (184–201); this passage, shot through with the Purgatorio motive x, is almost a direct quotation from the 'Trinklied' of *Das Lied von der Erde* (see that movement, bars 69–75). It merges into the lamenting refrain A3 in A minor (202–10), which now takes in the Purgatorio motive x and reaches an unexpected climax—a broadly joyful one in A minor's relative C major (210–

18), which will also recur. After this, the waltz-tune B1 reappears in its original form for a brief hushed reference (219–25), but is swept away by the return of E minor and ferocious development of the scherzo theme A1 (226–43). This eventually calms down, and the laconic linking passage returns (243–7), marking the entry to the next section by modulating to A major.

B. Varied restatement of the first trio, A major (bars 248–90). The waltz-tune B1 is now restated joyfully (248–60); but though the key is the bright A major, it is still on the subdominant side of E minor. It is followed by B2, adorned with a new lilting treatment of the Purgatorio motive x (261–8), which soon works up to the former broadly joyful climax (269–77). The restatement then picks up B2 again quietly (278–86), but this soon leads to the laconic link-passage (287–90), which marks the appearance of a new section, by modulating from A major to C major (still the subdominant side of E minor). This time, however, the link-passage is developed briefly into a completely new idea, a quiet wistful episode in C major, consisting of statement (291–300) and restatement (301–11); this whole passage acts as an independent interlude prefacing the new main section, which it introduces by modulating back to A major.

C. Second trio, A major (bars 311–80). This second trio is in fact based on a verion of the dashing theme of the first trio, B3: it is stated powerfully (311–35), then restated and developed with passionate intensity (336–80). The music is hectically joyful for the most part, and works up to a great jubilant climax; but the subdominant key of A major still holds the field, and the climax runs inevitably into the first A minor harmony at the three motto chords, which turn the music savagely back to E minor. This initiates the final restatement of scherzo and first trio, in which the two sections are split in two and spliced into one another, so to speak.

A. Beginning of restatement of scherzo, E minor (380–410)*
After the introductory motto chords (380–84), only the main scherzo theme A1 is recapitulated, in contracted form (384–99), before the laconic link-passage breaks in and modulates to B major (399–410).

B. Beginning of restatement of first trio, B major (411–44). At

---

* See footnote 3 on p. 82. [D.M.]

last the movement has counteracted its fatal subdominant tendency by placing the joyful first trio in the bright key of the dominant major. The main waltz-tune is restated—a slightly ˙modified repetition of its former A major restatement (411–24, cf. 248–60), followed by the lilting idea (425–32, cf. 261–8), which works up to the broadly joyful climax (433–44). But this time the climax is shot through with fierce dissonance, and it subsides into a shadowy and anxious transitional passage in B minor (445–52), based on the Purgatorio motive x.

A. Conclusion of restatement of scherzo, B minor (bars 452–87). The dominant key is still maintained, though it has darkened from major to minor. This section is an almost literal repetition, in B minor, of the original scherzo section from the beginning of the 'hurdy-gurdy' theme of A2 (cf. 73–107): the 'hurdy-gurdy' theme itself (452–63), the 'stormy' theme (463–78), and the 'lamenting' refrain (479–87). This time, however, the lamenting refrain reaches the broadly joyful climax in its original form, in the relative major, exactly as in the first restatement of the scherzo (487–95, cf. 202–18). But the relative major is now inevitably D major, a less bright key than either A major or B major, and doubly subdominant of E minor.

B. Conclusion of restatement of first trio, D major (496–506). The joyful climax initiates an overlapping repetition of the end of the first restatement of the trio (cf. bars 269–86): the climax itself, as mentioned (487–95) and the leaping waltz-material B2 (496–506).

Coda, D minor (bars 506–80). Following the repetition of bars 269–86, the joyful climax should now strike in—and it does, but in an awesomely distorted form, as a doom-like outburst in D minor (506–17), taking in Purgatorio motive x. With this abrupt switch from major to minor, the conflict is fatally decided: the movement has been pinned down irrevocably in the double subdominant minor of D. The fury dies down (518–21), as the final stage arrives. The movement retreats into the distance with an empty and shadowy transformation of the leaping waltz-material B2 in D minor, which becomes more and more ghostly, and gradually disintegrates completely. The coda consists of statement (522–9), restatement (530–7), third statement (538–50), and finally a mere phantom of the waltz rhythm, dying away on percussion alone (551–80). The last solitary note is the deathly thud of a *fortissimo* stroke on a completely muffled drum.

The tonal conflict of this movement is the main crux of the symphony. The actual outcome was a despairing fall from E minor to the double subdominant minor (D minor, via A minor)—and D minor was the key of the tragic central section of the Purgatorio. But the exact equivalent in the opposite, optimistic direction would have led through the dominant major of B (which the waltz theme B1 actually reached) to the double dominant major, F sharp—the true key of the symphony. This is the hard journey which the finale has to travel, and it has to start from the opposite pole—the double subdominant D minor to which the fourth movement has retreated.

V. FINALE. Short score, 401 bars, mainly 4/4 or 2/2,[4] D minor moving to F sharp major.

Slow Introduction, basically D minor (bars 1–84). There is no tempo marking, but the music is obviously slow.

A. First section, D minor (bars 1–29). The *fortissimo* stroke on muffled drum that ended the fourth movement is the first sound to be heard. Then, with constantly changing time-signatures (as in the second movement), and in D minor (the tragic key of the central section of the Purgatorio, to which the fourth movement retreated), three of the Purgatorio motives are given out slowly and lugubriously in the depths: the seven-note y (2–3 and 5–6), the three-note w (8 and 10), and the six-note z (11–14). This material is given a statement (1–15) and a restatement (16–27). The progress of the music is painful, and continually broken off by loud muffled drum strokes. But at bar 27, a rising seventh on the horn, repeated, initiates a more yearning form of the motive z, which introduces the next stage.

---

[4] Bar-numbering: Page 1: the fragmentary looking bar after bar 25 must be counted—bar 26; the bar after bar 44 must not be counted—Mahler ringed it for possible deletion, and did not reinstate it with the word 'bleibt'. Page 2: at bars 58–9, despite the one-bar indication of the lower staves, I count the two bars of the upper ones; and bar 78 I count as two bars—78 and 79 (see the inserted seven-note motive). Page 3: at bar 130, note that there are three bars to the end of the page—130, 131, 132. Page 4: at bar 144, there are two bars after the double bar to end the line—144, 145. Page 6: after bar 243, the page is deleted except for the last six bars—244–249. Page 7: the bar after bar 274 must be counted—bar 275; on the next line, there are 9 bars to the double bar—276–84; at bar 288, the extra bar line is deleted—only one bar; after bar 299, the rest of page 7 is deleted; continue on the page 8 which begins with a B flat major chord (this replaces the other page 8) and then take pages 9 and 10, ignoring the superseded page which is not numbered.

B. Central section, D major and B major, 4/4 (bars 29–72).

(1) The rising seventh is taken up by the flute, to begin a long sixteen-bar melody of hushed, unearthly serenity, over harmonies of utter stillness, opening in D minor but immediately switching to D major (29–45). This melody, which is partly a reshaping of the 'hurdy-gurdy' theme of section A2 in the fourth movement, also makes calm use of z, and ends with a melting modulation to B major.

(2) The violins enter, *ppp*, with a hopeful flowing melody in B major, which has an important counter-melody in the inner parts, with rising and falling intervals (44–58).

(3) During this melody, at the point where it rises up to switch momentarily into E flat major, a solemn chordal motive enters beneath it, consisting of two serene statements of the remaining Purgatorio motive x (53–4).

(1) The music is retracing the steps of the fourth movement, from D minor, through D major, back to B major; now it turns to D major again to repeat the last stage more clinchingly. The serene flute theme B1 returns for a modified restatement, growing in strength and sonority, and modulates in a more forceful way to B major (58–66).

(4) The rising seventh takes over, beginning a new soaring theme which rises immediately to a great paean-like climax (66–72).

A. Return of first section, B minor and D minor (72–84). The soaring theme is cut off brutally by a loud muffled drum-stroke and the menacing return of the Purgatorio motives of the first section; these, despite the theme's attempt to continue, turn the music back the opposite way, from B major, through B minor, to D minor. The move to regain the symphony's main key of F sharp major, via B major, has failed, and the introduction ends darkly, in the depths.

Allegro Moderato, 2/2, D minor (85–268). The struggle has to begin all over again, from D minor.

A. First section, D minor (85–185): this consists of persistent alternation between the main allegro theme and various versions of the six-note motive z.

(1) Main allegro theme, D minor (85–98)—a swift, agitated, darting idea, in a desperate, cynical mood akin to that of the Rondo Burleske of the Ninth Symphony, but continually marked *sempre*

piano. It is made up of short motives—all quick versions of the Purgatorio motives *w, y* and *z*, as used in the introduction's first section. The theme is stated (87–94) and restated (95–8).

(2) Contrasting theme, shifting tonality (98–104)—a sardonically jaunty version of the six-note motive *z*, still *piano*.

(1) Return of main theme, D minor, with new extension, working up to a climax (104–20).

(2) The contrasting theme this time is the transformation of *z* back to its original tragic Purgatorio form, presenting an exact quotation of the two great passionate *fortissimo* climax-statements of it in the Purgatorio's D minor central section (120–27, cf. Purgatorio, 106–14).

(1) Return of main theme, *piano* again, with another new extension, working up to a different climax (127–45).

(2) The contrasting theme now takes the form of a big jubilant *fortissimo* version of the jaunty transformation of *z*—a theme of great romantic warmth in D major (145–53), with a stormy extension moving back to D minor (153–61).

(1) Brief ferocious reference to main theme, D minor (161–3).

(2) The contrasting theme returns, beginning in its jaunty version and continuing in the romantic one, D major (163–71). It is developed in agitation, working up to a big climax (171–5).

(3) Climax of whole first section—an unexpected one, since it presents an almost exact quotation from the fourth movement of the lamenting refrain with motive *x* (176–80) going straight over into the broad joyful climax (180–6), *fortissimo*, in the relative major of F. (Cf. fourth movement, bars 202–16 and 479–93: the two four-bar phrases of the lamenting refrain as in the fourth movement are presented simultaneously in the finale version.) The aptness of the fourth movement's joyful climax here is that it reveals itself in this new context as a version of *z*.

B. Central section, mainly F major and B major (186–251). In F major (a semitone below the symphony's goal of F sharp major), the introduction's rising seventh is heard (187–9), and as before it initiates the yearning version of *z* (189–92), and the serene theme B1 from the introduction's central section. But in the swift 2/2 *allegro* tempo (which Mahler would only have moderated slightly, one feels, with something like '*Etwas gehalten*'), this theme has to strive hard to establish itself at all. Opposed and halted each time by the cynical main *allegro* theme, and forced into tonal disruptions, it can only present its first two phrases, and these are full of agitation; nevertheless it holds tenaciously to the key of F major. After a statement (191–9) and restatement (199–209), an agitated extension (209–13) brings a further restatement (213–25), which calms the music down, and dispels the hostile *allegro* theme by modulating to the much-desired key of B major. (Here Mahler might well have indicated a further slackening of the tempo, towards that of the introduction's central section.) A calm, hushed reference to motive *z* in its most positive form (226–9) brings a final restatement of the serene theme B1—still two phrases, but now as serene as at first, and with the added nobility of soft trumpet tone (230–36). The movement has once more reached B major on its way back to F sharp; but now a brief tranquil extension (236–9) switches to A flat, and the introduction's solemn chordal motive B3 enters, with its original fragment of B2 above it (240–43). And from this tonal no-man's-land the motive falls sadly by the Neapolitan modulation to G minor (244–5); and the Allegro breaks in again fiercely. It works up to a climax (246–9), and in spite of an attempt to hold to D major at least (250–51), the tonality is jerked back forcibly to D minor, for a return of the Allegro's first section. (Mahler might well have indicated a gradual increase of tempo here, back to Tempo I for the return of the Allegro.)

A. Restatement of first section, D minor (251–68)—much curtailed, owing to a shatteringly dramatic interruption.

(1) Main *allegro* theme, D minor, *piano*, presented as on its second appearance (251–61, cf. 104–20).

(2) Contrasting theme, jaunty version, as on its first appearance (261–7, cf. 98–104). With incredible suddenness it works up to a tremendous and unexpected climax.

Return of first movement motto-theme and climax, shifting tonality (268–99). The climax is a fortissimo dominant ninth on G, and while the trumpet holds on to its high A, the violins descend from an octave higher with the second segment of the viola motto-theme of the symphony's opening (268–75, cf. first movement, 188–93). As they die away, the trumpet still holds to its high A, and the sustained *fortissimo* nine-note dissonance of the first movement enters, the trumpet note piercing through it; this time, however, against the dissonance two of the Purgatorio motives are thrown, in their finale *allegro* version—the grotesque three-note *w*, and the ferocious seven-note *y*, which attempts to reimpose the key of D minor (bars 276–84), cf. first movement, 203–8). Then, with the trumpet still holding its high A *fortissimo*, the horns strike in powerfully with a practically literal quotation of the first movement's viola motto-theme as it opened the symphony (285–99, cf. first movement, 1–15). While this proceeds *diminuendo*, the trumpet descends from its high A in two-part counterpoint similar to that between first and second violin in bars 184–93 of the first movement.

The tonal direction of this last passage is, of course, that of the symphony's opening motto-theme—B minor to D minor; and this may be taken as some indication of the extent to which Mahler had worked out the overall form of the symphony. *The whole tonal crux of the work—the fourth movement's retreat through B minor to D minor, and the finale's difficulty in breaking out of D minor into B major on its way back to F sharp—is already contained in embryo in the motto-theme which opens the symphony and introduces the F sharp major adagio theme.* It is, in fact, the finale's inability to leave D minor that has brought back the first movement's eruptive climax and motto-theme: the symphony has regressed to its original unresolved tension and its dark unanswered question.

As trumpet and horn die away, *pianissimo*, the motto-theme has brought us to D minor as it did originally, but it has pointed a way to the solution of the finale's problem: here is now an implication of F sharp major, since that key generally followed the motto-theme in the first movement.

But the finale does not go immediately into F sharp major; that was the first movement's too-easy and precarious answer to the original question. The music switches calmly to a new key—B flat major, the hopeful key of the major themes in the Purgatorio. (The tempo has also returned to the 4/4 of the introduction's central section: Mahler wrote '4/4' just before the dissonant chord, and this whole section will naturally be in the tempo of the equivalent passage in the first movement.)

Restatement of Introduction, central section, modified, B flat major moving to F sharp (299–374). The first section of the introduction is not restated: the finale has now left the dark key of D minor, and the grim D minor versions of the Purgatorio motives, so intensively exploited in the Allegro, once and for all.

B2. The serene theme B1 does not enter immediately: it is to the hopeful violin melody B2 that the music turns first, to begin a long passage of great quietude and serenity. A brief gentle reference to this theme, in B flat (299–304), leads to a more solemn and noble treatment of it in the same key, which exploits the rising and falling intervals of its original counter-melody rather than the flowing theme itself (304–15). At the end of this, the music melts, through a breath-taking modulation, into F sharp major. At last, almost without realizing it, the symphony has found its way home to its true key: where passion and violent struggle have failed, calm meditation and hope have succeeded. It is fascinating to note in Mahler's first version, the symphony did not return to F sharp at all, but ended in the B flat of the hopeful Purgatorio themes (see his rejected page 8, and the single unnumbered page). After the horn and trumpet counterpoint, the present B flat major passage did not follow: the music switched to B flat, but began immediately in that key the present F sharp major conclusion to the symphony. There can be no doubt that the addition of the B flat transitional passage, the modulation to F sharp, and the transposition into that key of the whole last section, was a conclusive master-stroke.

With the return home, passion returns, more sure of itself. B2 (the counter-melody still) is taken up in F sharp in a new version with soaring and sweeping intervals (316–23), but the passion is as yet subdued, in a soft dynamic.

B1. Quietly, tenderly, the serene theme B1 now takes over, also in F sharp (324–31), and then a brief return to the counter-melody of B1 (331–5) makes another glorious modulation, up a semitone into G major: this assured semitonal elevation of the symphony's main key counterbalances the semitonal failure to rise to it in the Allegro's F major central section.

B4. In G major, the soaring theme of the introduction's climax returns (335–40), but now devoid of all struggle, as full of peace as the G major music of the *Poco Adagio* of the Fourth Symphony.

B2. Still in G major, still softly, the hopeful violin melody B2 now steals in in its original flowing form (340–47), and rises up as before, ready to introduce the solemn chordal motive.

B3. As B2 reaches the heights, it switches key, as it did at first, but quite differently, magically, back to F sharp major, for the solemn chordal motive to strike in with a new nobility and majesty (348–9). A passionate reference to the counter-melody of B2 flares up and dies down (350–52), and the final stage is at hand.

B1. The serene theme B1 has been the real protagonist of the finale, being the first to raise the movement out of its dark D minor despair, and the temporary dispeller of the cynical *allegro* material; and now it comes fully into its own to bring the symphony to its ultimate climax. It is given out in F sharp major by 'all the violins, *fortissimo,* big tone' (Mahler's marking), in two tremendously passionate affirmations, corresponding to the two statements in the introduction: statement (353–61, cf. introduction 29–36), and, after a surging reference to B2 (361–5), restatement (365–74, cf. introduction 58–66). At the end of the latter, the passion ebbs, and the music returns to the rising passage of B2, in a dissolving A major/F sharp major *diminuendo*.

Coda, F sharp major (374–401). The symphony ends in a mood of transfigured serenity quite different from the bitter-sweet resignation of the endings of *Das Lied von der Erde* and the Ninth Symphony. As B2 continues in the upper part, there are ethereal references to the rising seventh and the solemn chordal motive, the latter continuing after B2 has died away (374–93). Then the rising seventh is heard low down, dying away (393–5); but it suddenly, unexpectedly, leaps up as a great rising twelfth, swelling out to *fortissimo*; the upper note is held tenaciously with full power, then in a long diminuendo, and finally the phrase descends stepwise, completing the six-note motive *z* to form a final benedictory cadence. The effect is of a great sigh of contentment at finding peace at last.

This description, despite its length, is only an outline, from which a thousand significant cross-relationships have had to be omitted. Those interested may pursue for themselves the myriad transformations of the four main Purgatorio motives during the last two movements, hardly a bar of which is free from one or other of them; and also the implications of such features as the fact that the opening motto theme of the symphony begins with the thematic pattern of the Purgatorio motive *x*, and the scherzo's opening germ-motive with that of its opposite number *y*.

Nevertheless, the above should be sufficient proof that the Tenth Symphony does exist, in the sketch, as a musical work of art, in the sense of a continuous, integrated symphonic structure, fully intelligible in its whole essential thematic, harmonic, tonal and formal argument. It is this crucial and indisputable fact that impels those who advocate, with Richard Specht, that a performing version of the sketch should be made.

But let us be absolutely clear that what we advocate is in fact simply this—*a performing version of the sketch*—and not a 'completion' of the Tenth Symphony. No one in his right senses can imagine that the work can be completed for Mahler, as Mahler himself would have completed it, for the following reasons.

(1) Here and there, owing to Mahler's hasty calligraphy, it is difficult, if not impossible, to establish exactly what Mahler wrote, or intended to write.

(2) Even allowing that these dubious features represent only a small proportion of the whole, a conjectural reading of which cannot affect the general purpose of the work, the manuscript is still only a comprehensive sketch, the bar-to-bar layout of which still awaited final revision.

(3) Even allowing that this revision of detail would not have changed the overall form of the work in any crucial way, there are sections in the second, fourth and fifth movements where continuity is preserved by only a single thematic line, without accompanying texture.

(4) Even allowing that most of these sections represent either exact or almost exact recapitulations of material exposed earlier, and can therefore be filled out with material already provided by Mahler himself, there are still a few short passages in the second movement where the texture has to be completed conjecturally, if the music is to make any genuine impact.

(5) Even allowing that these short passages again represent a small proportion of the whole, a conjectural filling-out of which cannot affect the general purport of the work, the texture of the second, fourth and fifth movements lacks in many places the wealth and perfection of detail characteristic of Mahler's completed scores.

(6) Even allowing that this is still, after all, a matter of detail rather than of essence, it is still necessary to complete the orchestration of the second movement, and to provide the whole orchestration of the last two, from the few significant hints scattered here and there by Mahler.

For these reasons, it is undeniable that a 'completion' of the Tenth Symphony is impossible. But on the other hand, it is not at all impossible to produce a performing version of the sketch, which shall allow Mahler's whole tremendous (if unperfected) conception to speak out clearly. Admittedly, to make the sketch as it stands performable, it is necessary to provide a certain amount of conjectural addition to the texture, and a large amount of conjectural orchestration; but these elements, in comparison with Mahler's own 'fully-prepared' thematic, harmonic, tonal and formal argument, sink to the level of the subsidiary, and in performance would be so dwarfed by it as to be barely perceptible.

It can be argued, of course, that the result would be artistically unacceptable, since it would not be a definitive, perfected, fully-achieved work of art. The answer to this is that we are dealing here with a unique case: rather than lament the loss of Mahler's own final definitive score of the Tenth Symphony, we should rather rejoice in what fate has so incredibly spared us—the full-length, continuous, entirely intelligible sketch of the whole five-movement structure. And we should do all in our power to make this structure capable of being experienced as living sound.

All true lovers of Mahler's music should ask themselves, with the utmost seriousness, the following question. Is Mahler's final symphonic masterpiece, so essential to our understanding of his life's work, to be lost to us simply because, lacking his own perfect end-product, we refuse to accept it in the form of its whole main essence, made audible through some subsidiary assistance by another hand?

[1962]

Mahler's Melodic Thinking

No one will deny, I think, that the great majority of those who identify themselves with the music of Mahler—professional musicians as well as musical laymen—are drawn to it by its intensely expressive character. What matters to them is not so much the music in itself—considered as thematic invention, thematic development, symphonic structure, and so on—as what that music has to communicate in the way of human feeling. I think it is also true to say that by far the larger proportion of the writing about Mahler's music—including most of my own—has been concerned with its content rather than its form. Mahler has been discussed very largely as an expressive artist, a visionary, and an important figure in the evolution of the modern view of the world: one with an early awareness of the void caused by the breakdown of traditional values, and of the need to find something to fill that void.

I know, of course, that in distinguishing between form and content, I am making a distinction that doesn't really exist: the two things are indivisible. 'Form' is simply a word we use to denote the technical note-by-note organization of a piece of music, and 'content' is simply a word we use to denote the potentiality of that organization to communicate life-experience to the listener. Content is not something separate from form: it *is* the form, as the form functions in communicating life-experience. If the form is changed, the content will change accordingly.

Nevertheless, the distinction is a useful one, since the two words enable us to approach a piece of music from two different viewpoints—as technical organization, and as life-experience communicated by that organization. What I am trying to say, in the case of Mahler, is that we have largely considered his music from the point of view of the life-experience it communicates, without paying much attention to the technical organization whereby that experience is communicated. We have tended to accept Mahler as a visionary, without making a close examination of his credentials as a composer.

This is only natural. If one finds that the music of a certain composer communicates an extremely significant life-experience, one is apt to talk about that, and take the technical means for granted; or else—and very rightly so, in my opinion—one assumes that the technical means must be of the highest order, otherwise the experience would not be so successfully communicated.

But is the experience as valuable as it seems to be? Those who do not love the music of Mahler, but rather detest it—and there are still plenty of such people around—maintain that the life-experience it communicates is of no real significance; and in explaining their opinion they indicate an equivalent emptiness in the musical organization. Mahler, they say, is a bad composer; and in the first place they talk of poverty of thematic invention, and describe Mahler's themes as sentimental, vulgar, or banal.

It would seem impossible to answer such a criticism, except by a mere denial: 'Mahler's thematic invention is *not* poor; his themes are neither sentimental, vulgar, nor banal; they only seem so to you because you misunderstand them in some way.' It is generally accepted that the artistic quality of a given theme is a pure matter of opinion, something that cannot be demonstrated, one way or the other, because we have no technical means of doing so. But I believe we do have the technical means, if we are prepared to apply normal methods of musical analysis in a much more microscopic way than usual—to analyse the construction of a theme in as detailed a way as we have analysed the structure of a whole movement, or a whole symphony, in the past. So I want to try to demonstrate the high quality of three of Mahler's themes by analysing them in such a way. This will, I hope, show his compositional mastery at work on a small scale.

I have chosen the three themes deliberately, because each is a type of Mahler theme which repels those who are unsympathetic to his music, and evokes one of the familiar adjectives 'sentimental', 'vulgar', or 'banal'. And the first theme is of the supposed 'sentimental' type—the long one which acts as the whole opening section of the second movement of the 'Resurrection' Symphony (Exx. 3–6). The first movement of the symphony is a huge sonata-structure, mainly in the rhythm of a funeral march; and this second movement is the equivalent of the minuet-and-trio of the classical symphony.

Mahler wrote a programme for the work; according to this, the first movement was intended as a vision of death—a Funeral Ceremony, as he called it—while this short and delicate second movement was intended as a nostalgic dream of past happiness, at the graveside. Now this idea in itself is enough to alienate certain minds, because they regard nostalgia as a disreputable emotion. It can be argued, however, that nostalgia is an entirely natural and normal human emotion, so long as it doesn't occupy too much of a person's life. It certainly doesn't occupy too much of Mahler's 'Resurrection' Symphony, but it is included, legitimately, as part of the area of human experience communicated by a work concerned with the ultimate meaning of life and death.

Even granted that nostalgia is a legitimate emotion for expression in music, the style in which Mahler expresses it here will still alienate a lot of people: it is the style of the Austrian rustic waltz known as the Ländler—which of course belongs to the world of popular music. But if one is alienated by the style, one is likely to miss Mahler's creative mastery in handling the style—the way he used it not to produce just one more piece of sentimental entertainment music, but to achieve a very moving expression of one aspect of human feeling—that 'nostalgic dream of past happiness' that I mentioned earlier. How did Mahler manage this? The nostalgia for happiness is pretty self-evident, being anyway part and parcel of popular Austrian dance-music of the slower kind; but what about the peculiar dream-like character of the music, that strangely suspended quality, as though it were moving in an unreal world?

The way Mahler achieved this was by the unique construction of the theme: he made it one continuous, seamless melody, which never retraces its tracks. Nothing ever happens twice in dreams and nothing happens twice in this melody—whereas in all other symphonic dance-movements of the tonal period, a lot of things happen twice.

To show what I mean by claiming that this Ländler-theme is a unique feat of melodic construction, it is necessary to take it to pieces. The whole theme is thirty-two bars long, and that, in a symphonic dance-movement, normally means four times eight: either we have an eight-bar strain repeated, followed by a different eight-bar strain repeated; or we have an eight-bar strain repeated, then a

different eight-bar strain, and the first eight-bar strain repeated
again.

Take the Ländler-like trio of the minuet of Mozart's Symphony
no. 39—which will remind us, incidentally, that Mozart wasn't
above drawing on the popular style when he wanted to. First there
is an eight-bar strain (Ex. 1), which is repeated. Then there is a different eight-bar strain (Ex. 2) and finally, the first eight-bar strain
is repeated once more. Four times eight equals thirty-two—and we
have heard one of the eight-bar strains three times, as we are liable
to do in popular dance-music itself.

Ex. 1

Ex. 2

Now Mahler's Ländler-theme certainly begins as if it were going
to behave in something like that way. It starts with the traditional
eight-bar strain (Ex. 3), which we might well expect to be repeated

Ex. 3

in the conventional way. And indeed, Mahler makes as if to repeat
it; but he uses this pretence at a repeat as the beginning of a different eight-bar strain (Ex. 4). Here another possibility opens up:

Ex. 4

perhaps this is the end of a rather long sixteen-bar strain—as sometimes happens—and he is going to repeat the opening at this point. But again, this doesn't happen: the music flows on, over any suggestion of a repeat, with yet another strain (Ex. 5). And here is a

Ex. 5

very curious thing: there are only four bars this time, and even more curious, we feel that these four bars are the last four bars of an eight-bar strain which must have begun further back, across the eight-bar grouping: a very subtle case of overlapping.

These four bars complete the sixteen, but at the same time they start a new eight, overlapping, and this is why the music flows right over the possibility of a repeat at the sixteenth bar. As we approach the sixteenth bar, it seems as if it is going to be the last bar of the second eight-bar strain, but it actually materializes as the fourth bar of an eight-bar strain which overlapped at the thirteenth bar. So we have now had twenty bars so far—three eights, but two of them overlapping four of their bars, to create an asymmetrical effect of eight bars, four bars, and eight bars.

By now, there is no question of any kind of repeat; but how long can this freely-developing melody hold out? It gathers itself together for one final strain—not of eight bars this time, but of twelve (Ex. 6)—and then some little echo-phrases form a short codetta of six bars (bars 33–8)—and so into the trio-section.

Ex. 6

This is not making too much out of what may seem to be just a pretty little tune: it's a case of art concealing art. This Ländler-theme exemplifies three important elements of Mahler's compositional practice. In the first place it shows the originality and unorthodoxy of a composer who is so often accused of plagiarism and banality. The section of thirty-two bars is not eight-eight-eight-eight, with some of the eights being mere repetitions—it is a seamless, non-repeating melody, with irregular phrase-lengths of eight-four-eight-twelve.

Secondly, it shows the economy and compression of a composer who is often said to take too long over what he has to say. By writing a melody which never turns back to repeat itself, Mahler crammed into those thirty-two bars enough material to serve other composers—even composers like Mozart, Beethoven and Schubert—for sixty-four bars or more.

And finally, this flowing, freely-developing melody shows the symphonic sweep of a composer who has been so often dismissed as a miniaturist who tried vainly to compose on a large scale. This may perhaps seem a strange remark to make: it may appear that the melody considered here is in fact a typical bit of miniaturist work. But after all, it is the equivalent of the classical minuet, and in such a context a long melody of thirty-two bars, without any repetitions, is anything but miniature: in fact it is just about the most broadly symphonic minuet-theme ever composed.

My second example—the opening of the third movement (the scherzo) of the Fifth Symphony—has been chosen to try to demonstrate Mahler's equally original and unorthodox methods of rhythmic construction. This movement is another Ländler, but of the quicker type, more like the quick sections of a Viennese waltz. And if the music we have just been considering belongs to the Mahler type that strikes the unsympathetic listener as sentimental, this music belongs to the Mahler type that gets criticized for being vulgar. The form of the whole movement is rather complex; but we are only concerned here with the opening section, or rather with the beginning of that, which consists of a short waltz-tune (Ex. 7), with two variations.

I am sure that the kind of people who, when they hear this music, consider it vulgar, get a false impression of what they have heard. Because its style is something like that of the Viennese waltz, they

Ex. 7

take it for granted that it is written in the normal rhythmic structure
of the Viennese waltz—the continuous series of eight-bar strains—
and they find it practically indistinguishable from a Viennese waltz.
And so they think that Mahler is merely spinning out music of the
popular type, under the impression that he's composing a
symphony—in other words, that he's writing vulgar music instead
of true art-music. And what they imagine they have heard, I think,
is something like this—a conventional melody consisting of two
eight-bar strains (Ex. 8), (and so on, for the two variations).

Ex. 8

If Mahler had written that, I think he could be fairly accused of
vulgarity. What he actually wrote was something slightly similar
but crucially different. In the first place, the movement begins with
a striking symphonic motive (*a* in Ex. 7) which is quite separate
from the waltz-theme, and which plays an important part later in
the symphonic development of the movement. Immediately after
it, the waltz-tune begins, with a slight delay on its first main note,
which makes a satirical nod at the habits of popular waltz
orchestras. However, leaving out the delay, we do have the first
four bars of a conventional eight-bar waltz-strain (*b* in Ex. 7), and
we get bars 5 and 6, in the expected way (*c* in Ex. 7). So we can't
help expecting bars 7 and 8 of the waltz-tune to be something like *x*
in Ex. 8.

In fact we don't get anything of the sort—we are left to tread on a stair which isn't there. The seventh and eighth bars that we are about to take for granted are just left out altogether; and the tune turns straight to its second strain (the first four bars of which are marked *d* in Ex. 7). This time we expect bars 5, 6, 7 and 8 of the second strain to be something like *y* in Ex. 8; but instead, bars 5 and 6 are left out, and we have only 7 and 8, the two ending bars, with the rhythm shifted slightly (*e* in Ex. 7)

This is a very strange way of composing a waltz-tune. And when the variations begin, it gets stranger and stranger. To take only the first variation, its first strain is more or less the same—six bars, leaving out 7 and 8, but the second strain now shrinks to five bars, by leaving out 4, 5 and 6 (Ex. 9). And in the second variation, the numbers for the two strains are six bars and seven bars. And so it goes on throughout the movement, each time this section comes round. The music keeps on playing havoc with one's rhythmic expectations: nobody could possibly waltz to it.

Ex. 9

This quite extraordinary kind of compositional technique is the reason why Mahler's waltz-movements are anything but vulgar pieces of popular waltz-music. Together with the leaping counterpoints that clash with the tune, and the vividly clear orchestration, these rhythmic contractions account for the pungent Mahlerian personality of the music, which gets across to those who feel the strangeness of it; but fails to make any impression on those who take the style for the real thing—the popular waltz-style for an actual popular waltz. This is because Mahler treats the style half affectionately, half satirically: the music is waltz-music, but the waltz is a tipsy, staggering one. The movement is full of joyous vitality; but owing to the continual truncations of the conventional rhythmic structure, it is also full of the characteristic Mahlerian tenseness and impatience—it just can't wait to get on with it.

So again we find this supposedly long-winded composer compressing and contracting his material all the time. The waltz-tune and the first two variations, if they were written in the normal rhythmic structure, would take up sixteen bars each—forty-eight bars in all; as Mahler writes them, they are twelve, eleven, and thirteen bars respectively—thirty-six bars instead of forty-eight.

My last example is one that demonstrates Mahler's highly original methods of harmonic construction: the first theme of the Adagio-finale of the Ninth Symphony, a theme which has been much condemned by those who are unsympathetic to Mahler, as being utterly banal (Ex. 10). By 'banal', they mean something commonplace, something that has been done over and over before, something stale, with nothing new to offer. The style here is that of the popular Victorian hymn-tune: some people have said that this theme lives in the world of Moody and Sankey; others have gleefully pointed out that it begins like the famous hymn 'Abide with me' by W. H. Monk:

Ex. 10

The only way a composer can get away with using a theme in the popular hymn-tune style, as the basis of a symphonic Adagio, is to make it something startlingly original—either rhythmically, mel-

odically, or harmonically. Rhythmically, Mahler does nothing
original here at all: he follows the normal hymn-tune pattern of
four symmetrical strains, each consisting of four bars. Melodically,
one has to say that he is original, since the tune is quite different
from any known hymn-tune, despite the chance resemblance of the
first brief phrase to the opening of 'Abide with me'. But I shall
consider the tune's melodic originality later, since it is bound up
with the harmonic originality, which is quite extraordinary.

Let us begin with that much-maligned first phrase of four notes.
It may coincide by accident with the first four notes of W.H.
Monk's tune, but the whole point of the phrase is its *harmonic* progression, which is made what it is by its last chord (marked *a* in Ex.
10). Monk's harmonic progression (Ex. 11) is conventional, but

Ex. 11

Mahler's is absolutely unconventional: it immediately disrupts the
tonality by lowering the root of the final chord a semitone. This is a
strange progression, but not an unprecedented one: a century
earlier, Beethoven had used the very same effect in the slow introduction to his E flat major piano sonata known as 'Les Adieux'
(Ex. 12b). But Beethoven did this when the phrase came round the
second time. He began the sonata with a conventional progression
(Ex. 12a), and only on repeating it, some bars later, did he use the
unconventional progression which disrupts the tonality. Mahler,

Ex. 12

however, used the unconventional progression to begin his theme, on its first appearance; and of course this is a familiar way composers have of extending the boundaries of musical language—taking over a procedure, already used by a previous composer as a special effect, and making it a starting-point. (For as we shall see, this progression is the basis of the whole character of Mahler's theme.) And immediately, there are good grounds for believing that Mahler was deliberately *quoting* Beethoven's phrase—as opposed to that of W.H. Monk: Beethoven wrote over it the word 'Le-be-wohl' (Farewell), and when Mahler was composing his Ninth Symphony, he regarded the work as his symphonic valediction.

To continue examining Mahler's harmony. The disruptive chord is for the moment treated as a passing inflection. Its suggestion that the music should change key before it has really got going is ignored: the theme switches straight back to the main key, and ends its first strain in that key (*b* in Ex. 10)—though the recovery of the main key is only achieved by a painful dissonance quite alien from traditional hymn-tunes (the fourth chord in bar 1). Thus a feeling of uneasiness is left, at a 'hymn-tune' which so early shows signs of tonal instability.

The second strain of the melody tries to dispel this uneasiness, by sticking firmly to the main key; but the troubled mood of the music is still there, in some unexpected dissonances in the fourth bar. This second strain ends the first half of this hymn-tune. For the third strain, beginning the second half, Mahler follows orthodox symmetry by turning back to the first strain, but he varies it in the most unorthodox way. In the first place, he raises it in pitch by a third. If he had done this with straightforward harmony the result would have been as in Ex. 13. But what Mahler actually does is to

Ex. 13

give an expressive melodic inflexion to the first four-note phrase, and to lower its final chord by a semitone. This is, of course, the same unconventional progression as in the first strain, but this time it drags the melody down with it (*c* in Ex. 10), and the music doesn't immediately recover the main key, as in the first strain. On the contrary, it stays out of the main key; and what is more, it immediately repeats the unconventional harmonic progression, from this outlying key, to move even farther away from the main key. We can best appreciate this extraordinary unorthodoxy by comparing Ex. 13, the 'conventional' version of the third strain, with bars 5 and 6 of Ex. 10.

We have now reached the fourth and final strain, which must re-establish the main key, and end in it. How does Mahler manage this? There is one obvious device that he could have used to switch back immediately, for the whole of the final strain, and that is the ambiguous chord known as the German sixth. If Mahler had used this stale trick, and then written his final strain entirely in the home key, the result would have been quite banal. Beginning at the end of the third strain, we might have had this:

Ex. 14

But Mahler's way back is a gradual, surprising, and painful one, which firmly re-establishes the main key in the end, though in a tense and unexpected way (bars 7 and 8 of Ex. 10). The hollow resolution on to the melodic key-note alone, instead of on to the key-chord, is of course a highly original fingerprint of Mahler's.

To all of which the response might be: 'What's so wonderful about that?—Mahler wrote a sentimental melody of the most banal kind, and then tacked on to it some fancy harmonic progressions to disguise its banality'. But that would be totally wrong—for the simple reason that the harmonic progressions, as we have seen, are not just tacked on to a melody: they are part and parcel of the melody, and they carry it far from the main key, making it anything but banal. The melody only, without the harmony, is a very unorthodox one, because of the way the harmony has affected it, almost removing the sense of key towards the end. The point of this kind of harmonic technique is that it communicates that special sense of spiritual torment which is so characteristic of Mahler. The constant key-switches—and they get more extreme as the movement continues—disrupt the tonality of the melody so severely that it seems as if it will never find its way back to the main key; yet it always does, with a most painful effort. The melody itself, by its very nature as a hymn-tune, stands as an affirmation of faith, and the disruptive harmonic progressions represent the doubts and disbeliefs that continually assail it. As long as we are not so repelled by the hymn-tune style that we cannot hear how different this music is from any conventional hymn-tune. Mahler's peculiar vision of spiritual torment comes straight out of the music to us, owing to his masterly command of subtle and original harmony.

[1972?]

The Word and the Deed:
Mahler and his Eighth Symphony

Every century is the heir of its predecessor, and it is the tragedy of the twentieth century that it has tried to disown its great progenitor, the nineteenth. In western Europe much of the vast spiritual capital inherited, through the nineteenth century, from the eighteenth, and ultimately from the Renaissance—the philosophy of humanism—has been allowed to moulder away in the bouts of discouragement which have followed first one world holocaust and then another. Yet we of the twentieth century, discouraged though we may be, are still committed to the heavy responsibility handed on to us by the nineteenth—that of trying to better the conditions and the quality of human life throughout the world; and we have no other spiritual capital to draw on than the philosophy of humanism. To turn back to outgrown religious dogmas, or to fall back on a cynical nihilism and hedonism—two attitudes which are indeed all too widespread—is a declaration of spiritual bankruptcy.

What this has to do with music—and particularly with Mahler's music—may not seem altogether clear at first. Yet composers have insisted on having their say, in their music, about what we human beings are, and what we are doing, and where we are going; and Mahler was concerned more than most composers with saying things of this kind. But the twentieth century's attempt to disown the nineteenth has also had its effect in the musical sphere; the definitive musical statements of the humanistic position by certain great nineteenth-century composers are dismissed, according to the modern dogma of 'pure music', as illegitimate flirtations with philosophy and metaphysics.

Mahler especially comes under fire from this angle, which is a disturbing sign that the present popularity of his music may be largely a craze for its fantastic sound, which has brought no understanding of its real and profound significance. For instance, in a recent broadcast talk it was approached from a characteristic twentieth-century point of view—the psycho-analytic; and while the first and last works—the immature cantata *Das klagende Lied* and the incomplete Tenth Symphony—were singled out as psychological documents of some validity, the whole definitive canon of Mahler's life's work—the nine symphonies and *Das Lied von der Erde*—was waved aside as 'music built around abstract concepts projected from his inner self'. Similarly, in a recent article in *The Listener,* Mahler was reproved for his supposed 'escape into a world of vague religious, mystical, and metaphysical ideas, a world out of which the majority of his symphonic works were born'.[1]

Statements like these show how curiously confused is the present-day attitude to the problem of musical meaning; musical criticism is certainly years behind literary criticism, which has long since recognized that a work of art—however apparently metaphysical its intention—is not an abstract statement of an intellectual proposition; it is an expression, through the manipulation and development of certain appropriate symbols, of an attitude to life, and an evaluation of man's various potential states of being. Mahler, as I have said, was concerned with expressing certain humanistic positions, and the Eighth Symphony is particularly important in this respect. In bringing together a great religious text, the old Catholic Latin hymn *Veni Creator Spiritus*, and a great humanistic text, the final scene of Goethe's *Faust*, and in assembling some hundreds of performers to present the work in a large hall to thousands of listeners, Mahler clearly intended to make an artistic statement concerning the contemporary situation, which should have importance for common humanity. What we have to do is to try to understand just what this statement amounts to.

Mahler's music, like Wagner's and Beethoven's, arose out of the great crisis in civilized history which occurred in the nineteenth century. If I were asked to choose a motto for the nineteenth century, I should pick that famous slogan of Karl Marx: 'The philosophers have only interpreted the world in various ways; the point is to *change* it'. Humanism had been a projected plan of campaign for a long time, but only in the nineteenth century, with the French Revolution already a *fait accompli,* were men in a position to put the plan into action.

[1] Mosco Carner in *The Listener* of 21 May 1964.

For a time, of course, this new dynamic, humanistic conception of progress existed alongside the old static religious conception of man as a humble, fallen creature; and so it is that we find, in Schiller's *Ode to Joy,* which Beethoven set as the choral finale of his Ninth Symphony, the religious exhortation 'Seek your Creator above the starry spheres', even though Schiller's and Beethoven's attitudes were undoubtedly centred on the humanistic declaration 'All men shall be brothers'. But there was always a strong tendency for the emphasis to shift over entirely from the religious viewpoint to the humanistic one; and this eventual transformation found classic expression in a passage in Goethe's *Faust.*

In scene three of part one, Faust, that incarnation of restless humanistic man, seeking a new knowledge beyond the accepted knowledge of mankind, suddenly feels an urge to translate the New Testament from Latin into German. He opens it at the beginning of St John's Gospel, and begins construing: 'In the beginning was the Word'. But this literal translation fails to satisfy him: the expression 'the Word' must surely stand for something more dynamic. He tries again: 'In the beginning was the meaning ... no.... In the beginning was the power ... better...'. And then he finds what he has been looking for: 'In the beginning was the Deed'.

This was the new discovery of the nineteenth century. Life is not a static condition but a dynamic process. Man was to find less and less and less satisfaction in communing with the Word—the immaterial and intangible Spirit—and more and more satisfaction in doing the Deed—in trying to put into action the humanistic ideals of the brotherhood of man, freedom, and human self-realization. And, finally, most thinkers and artists who wished to change the world abandoned the religious conception of man altogether, in favour of a completely atheistic humanism. There was no longer any need of 'the hypothesis of God', as Laplace had put it. Voltaire's witticism that Man had created God in his own image was expounded seriously by Feuerbach, who declared that God was Man—meaning man's projection of his ideal self; and, inevitably, this was soon taken to mean that Man was God. It is a scarcely recognized fact that hardly a single nineteenth-century composer of the first rank believed in the God of the Christian religion.

An even less understood fact—and unless we understand it we shall never begin to comprehend the so-called 'late-romantic' period from 1880 to 1914—is that this crucial change in human thought, summed up by Nietzsche in the startling phrase 'God is dead', had an unexpectedly demoralizing effect on the later nine-teenth century. Once the first flush of enthusiasm was over, and it became evident that it was beyond man to *be* his ideal self, the absence of any supernatural being on which to project this ideal self was felt as an acute and irreparable loss. Take only three character-istic types of late-romantic musical emotion—Delius's transience-haunted regret, Puccini's despairing eroticism, and Richard Strauss's aching sense of hollowness—these are so many musical manifestations of the traumatic spiritual experience undergone by man as a consequence of abandoning his belief in God and then finding himself incapable of being his own God and of building a heaven on earth in which to achieve fullness of being. As the poet Rilke lamented: 'The world has fallen into the hands of men'.

Nor should it be assumed that this sense of being forsaken by God vanished with the late-romantic period; we still find it acutely alive today, in a more bitter form, in the literary work of Ionesco and Beckett, even if we may have difficulty in finding equivalents in the pure abstractions of present-day music. Beckett curses God for not existing—which is exactly what Hilaire Belloc accused Thomas Hardy of doing. We are faced here, in fact, with the central problem of our age—what faith we can possibly have as a basis for our actions—and the roots of this problem are to be found in the later nineteenth century. Mahler is the composer who holds the central position in this three-cornered struggle between religious faith, humanism, and nihilism; and that is his fundamental significance for us today.

Mahler was a Jew who was brought up in a free-thinking world without any belief in the religion of his own race, but whose deep spiritual need impelled him to turn to the Christian faith, in the Catholic form of his native Austria. He became a converted Catholic; and although there was a certain coincidental expediency in this move, in that it was necessary for his musical career in anti-semitic Vienna, the genuineness of his fundamental motive was never in doubt. If any words can be said to ring with sincerity, they are those of Mahler's wife in her book: 'He was a believer in Christ-ianity, a Christian Jew, and he paid the penalty; I was a Christian pagan, and got off scot-free'. But Mahler was also, by virtue of his cultural tradition, a humanist. If he gave few outward signs of his humanism, it was probably because he took it for granted; it was certainly there, as one particular anecdote makes clear. One May Day in Vienna, both he and a fellow-composer, Hans Pfitzner, ran into one of the socialist processions of workers, marching along to band music. According to Mahler's wife again, Pfitzner was furious at the sight of so many proletarian faces, and escaped down a side-street, whereas Mahler accompanied the workers for some distance, and said afterwards that they looked at him in such a brotherly way—they *were* his brothers, he said, and they were also the future.

This brings us to the subject of Mahler's musical expression of his beliefs, since his works are permeated with the sound of the brass-band march. It is always assumed that this came simply from his having lived during his early childhood near a military barracks, but it seems obvious that a composer will only reproduce musical elements heard in his formative years if they have any inherent meaning for him. We can hardly imagine that if Ravel, for instance, had spent *his* childhood near a barracks, his music would have shown any signs of it. The brass-band march was, of course, the central symbol of the humanistic attitude, owing to its evocation of man on the road towards some positive human goal, and its element of vulgarity embracing all mankind including the common man. The first great humanistic march was naturally the *Marseillaise,* which accompanied the tramping feet of the French Revolution. March-music entered the classical symphony—bringing with it its unavoidable touch of vulgarity—when Beethoven used the march style for his three great humanistic statements: the ultimate march-like transformation of the graceful theme of the Eroica finale, the battering main theme of the finale of the Fifth Symphony, and, most significant of all, the unequivocal brass-band march, complete with drum and cymbals, and surmounted by a male-voice chorus, which hymns the brotherhood of man in the choral finale of the Ninth. The funeral march also played its part, honouring the burial of humanistic heroes, in the *Marcia Funebre* of the Eroica Symphony, and in Wagner's mighty Funeral March for the death of his humanistic hero Siegfried, which the fastidious Romain Rolland significantly found so repellent for what he considered its tasteless vulgarity. It was Mahler who brought this tradition to its head, by including in nearly all his symphonies either triumphal marches to celebrate humanistic aspirations, or funeral marches to lament the burial of humanistic hopes, or both.

But being a product of the later, disillusioned humanistic period, Mahler was acutely conscious of the insufficiency of humanism, in its pure, godless aspect, owing to the insufficiency of man himself. In consequence he revived, from a new standpoint, the earlier attitude of Beethoven's Choral Symphony, attempting a new fusion of humanism with religious belief; and for the expression of this belief he turned to the central musical symbol for the Christian faith which had been handed on to him by the devout Bruckner—the chorale. In several of Mahler's symphonies, march and chorale appear side by side, or are transformed one into the other, or are even fused into a single thematic idea. And so much of his music, far from being concerned with abstractions, or with vague metaphysical ideas, is simply an existential meeting-place for humanism and faith in God—for the Deed and the Word. It is a place where a bold attempt is made to erect a spiritual bridge over the abyss of nihilism, of a kind which may be the way forward for disillusioned modern man, who can hardly hope to return to the unreflecting childlike faith that made possible the music of a composer like Bruckner. This is particularly true of the Eighth Symphony of 1907, which may be regarded as the Choral Symphony of the twentieth century, as Beethoven's Ninth was that of the nineteenth century.

In the Eighth Symphony, the Word and the Deed are set side by side, both in the text and in the music. The old Catholic hymn *Veni Creator Spiritus,* which Mahler used for the first part of the symphony, is actually an invocation to the Word—to the Holy Ghost of Christianity, as Creator Spirit. And the text of the symphony's second part—the final scene of Goethe's *Faust*—may be described as the free rendering of the Catholic Latin of the Word into the humanistic German of the Deed. The salvation of Faust's soul symbolizes the indemnification of his humanistic quest, in spite of its failure; and this is granted because, as the angels sing, 'He who ever striving drives himself onwards, that man we can redeem'. And likewise, in the music, the two great symbols are the Brucknerian chorale, standing for the Word, and the nineteenth-century brass-band march, standing for the Deed.

But there is a strange thing here, which reveals Mahler's profound artistic and human originality. We should expect the musical and verbal symbols to go simply in harness together—as they actually do in Beethoven's Choral Symphony, where the lines concerning the brotherhood of man become the basis of the march-music, while the words 'Seek your Creator above the starry firmament' are set to a kind of self-abasing religious hymn. But in Mahler's Eighth, the verbal and musical symbols are crossed with one another, to amazing effect. It is the setting of the *Veni Creator Spiritus*—the Word—that is the great striding triumphal march in the humanistic tradition; and it is the final scene of Goethe's *Faust*—the Deed—which is based on a religious chorale, and reaches its climax with that chorale. This extraordinary artistic cross-fertilization can mean only one thing: that the symphony offers a multiple symbol of the humanizing of religion and the spiritualizing of humanism—and the fusion of both into one faith. The Word *becomes* the Deed: in other words, the God the symphony addresses is not the static God 'out there', but the dynamic God 'in here'—in man's inner being: but it addresses this God, not as man's projection of his own ideal self—the purely human God of Feuerbach—but as the immaterial and intangible Creator Spirit which inspires and impels man's questing aspiration.

The truth is that the texts themselves provide a sound basis for this musical act of unification. The hymn *Veni Creator Spiritus* is more than a humble Christian prayer for personal salvation in another world. It is concerned with Pentecost—the great moment of inspiration, when the Holy Ghost descended and spoke in many tongues through the mouths of the Apostles, and was interpreted by Peter in the words of the prophet Joel: 'Your sons and your daughters shall prophesy, your old men shall dream dreams, your young men shall see visions'. In other words, it is concerned with the time when the Christian faith itself was at its most dynamic, and it suggests the march of men towards higher things: it addresses the Creator Spirit as *DUX*—leader—and contains the lines 'Scatter the foe; with Thee as our leader going before us, may we shun all that is evil'. And conversely, in the final scene of Goethe's *Faust,* the indemnification of Faust's humanistic quest is granted, not only because of his restless striving and driving himself onwards, but also through the Christian virtues of repentance, compassion, and forgiveness, symbolized by the intercession of 'a penitent, once named Gretchen'—the woman he had betrayed. Indeed Goethe, by his recourse to Christian symbolism at the end of his great drama, was clearly intent on stressing the truth that man has need of God for the achievement of his aims; and Mahler's chorale backs him in this.

But Mahler lived during the later period of humanistic self-doubt; and by bringing back on the orchestra alone the theme of his triumphal march to end his great symphony, in a new form which reaches up imperiously to the heights, he was evidently concerned with reminding us of the converse and complementary truth: that God—whoever or whatever God may be—has need of man for the fulfilment of the dynamic creative purpose of things.

[1964]

Delius: A Centenary Evaluation

Although Frederick Delius lived most of his life on the Continent, his music has never gained the slightest footing in any continental country, except for a short-lived popularity in Germany before and just after the first world war, which has long since died out. Only in this country has it won any kind of lasting recognition; and it is a truism to say that this has been almost entirely due to the advocacy of Sir Thomas Beecham, who for half a century, from 1909 until his death in 1961, pursued a consistent policy of thrusting Delius's music on the attention of the British public.

But I am convinced that Delius's popularity in this country has been a factitious, ephemeral affair. It only really began with the 1929 Delius Festival, when it was given a great send-off by the presence of the heroic figure of the blind and paralysed composer himself, who had emerged from comparative obscurity; and afterwards it was sustained by the magnetic personality of Beecham. At other concerts, I have never noticed any tumultuous applause after a Delius work, though the performances were often good enough to elicit enthusiasm from an audience of genuine Delius-lovers. The wave of popularity began to dwindle after the Festival of 1946, with the progressive decrease in Beecham's performances of the music, and it has reached a very low ebb in the last few years. It seems certain to me that only a minority of the English musical public has ever really loved Delius.

The same is true of the musical profession, whose attitude tends to create the general climate of opinion; I have met far more English musicians who disliked Delius's music than who admired it. It is significant that there has been no thorough and comprehensive study of his music. Consider the main literature on this composer—only four books in all, and only one of them is a critical study of the complex style and form of the music. Eric Fenby's moving account of how he worked as amenuensis to the stricken composer threw invaluable light on Delius's personality and his method of working, but it naturally was not concerned with a critical examination of his output.

Compare with this the extensive list of books on Elgar, several of which are detailed critical studies, and one of which is a volume in the 'Master Musicians' series—an honour significantly denied to Delius.*

My own explanation of this general unpopularity is that Delius is a peculiarly individual, isolated composer—a composer *sui generis*—whose style is incomprehensible to most people, because they expect it to conform to certain traditional standards which are outside its terms of reference. And the cause of this isolation was the anomalous social position of Delius himself. Alone among composers of any standing, except perhaps Busoni, he had no roots in any single national culture. His Dutch-German ancestry; the English environment of his childhood and youth; his years of wandering in Scandinavia, the United States, and Germany; his final settling in France for the main part of his life—all this made him into a stateless artist. He was technically an Englishman; he was born in Bradford and spent the formative years of his life, until the age of nineteen, entirely in England; he spoke with a Yorkshire accent, and was even a cricket enthusiast; but he was never at home in this country. And despite his German blood, and the fact that he called himself Fritz Delius till he was forty, he was not at home in Germany either; he preferred to make his home in France. Yet he never became the slightest bit gallicized, for after a few years in Paris, spent mainly with an international artistic group, he retired to the country, and lived more and more as a recluse at Grez-sur-Loing, cut off from French life.

Not unnaturally, this isolated, cosmopolitan existence produced an isolated, cosmopolitan musical style. The normal composer is a national composer, in the most fundamental sense: whether he uses the folk-music of his race as Janáček did, or only its traditional classical style, as did Brahms, he expresses the spirit of his people; and so he bases himself primarily on an appeal to his compatriots—his reputation begins at home. Then, by a seeming paradox, this national quality enables him to appeal to groups in

---

* No longer true: Alan Jefferson's 'Master Musicians' study of Delius was published in 1972. [D.M.]

other countries, as a recognizable representative of his own race.

But Delius's style is a non-national amalgam of influences from the various countries with which he had connexions. It blends together Scandinavian elements from Grieg, features of the Negro music of Florida, aspects of the German style of Wagner, procedures from French impressionism, and has at times a strong English pastoral idiom which Delius may possibly have originated. None of these predominates as a main national stream, on to which the others have been grafted; and in consequence Delius has fallen between all the national stools, particularly those of Germany, France and England. His rich Wagnerian harmonic texture appealed for a time in Germany, when his music was still 'modern' and 'difficult'; but when it lost its newness, the presence of strong elements of French impressionism became apparent, and the Germans, who have never appreciated Debussy, judged it vague and amorphous. In France, Delius's impressionistic elusiveness might have appealed if it had not been weighted down with a particularly rich German texture; the French found his music Teutonically heavy and woolly, on the few occasions when they had a chance to hear it. In England, the English pastoral element was the main reason for the temporary response to Beecham's advocacy; real Delius-lovers in this country have been chiefly attracted by the music's power to evoke the open air and the English countryside; but the equally strong German and French elements always made him an exotic for the majority. This is one reason why the English have never taken Delius to their hearts, as they have the truly English Elgar and Vaughan Williams.

Three other points are worth mentioning in connexion with England. In the first place, sensuous and emotional chromaticism, which plays such a large part in Delius's music, has been regarded by the majority of English musicians as something unmanly, morbid, almost sinful—surprising though that may be in a people which produced Purcell. Then there was Delius's entirely un-English attitude to life—his hedonistic, Nietzschean, anti-Christian self-centredness—which can be felt in his music; this even upset some of his warmest admirers, such as Fenby and Hutchings. Lastly, in regard to the present, there is the unfortunate legacy of the false identification of Delius with the English pastoral school in the nineteen-thirties and forties. The young musicians of today, who hardly know Delius's music, see him as belonging to the orbit of Vaughan Williams, Bax, and Ireland, which, with the unkindness always shown by the English to their leading composers, they are busy debunking as hard as they can.

Like other composers, Delius wrote a number of inferior works, and some of the out-and-out Delius worshippers have not made a clear distinction between good and bad. Beecham, for example, sang the praises of the early Piano Concerto, which Delius himself regarded as a poor work; he also dug out the quite immature opera *Irmelin*, and in his biography of Delius he advocated more performances of the early works in general.

If we want to take the best of Delius, we have to agree with Eric Fenby, and reject all the music he wrote up to 1899, before the age of thirty-seven, and I would say most of the music he composed after 1916, from the age of fifty-four onwards. His main claim to an abiding place in musical history lies in some fifteen works, almost all written between these two dates. These are the large-scale *Mass of Life*; two shorter choral works, the *Songs of Sunset* and the *Songs of Farewell*; the opera *A Village Romeo and Juliet*; three tone-poems involving voices—*Appalachia, Sea-Drift,* and *The Song of the High Hills*; four purely orchestral tone-poems—*Brigg Fair, In a Summer Garden, Eventyr,* and *Song of Summer*; the suite *North Country Sketches*; two orchestral miniatures—*On Hearing the First Cuckoo in Spring* and *Summer Night on the River*; and a single one of his four concertos—the one for violin.

Taking these works as a basis, the first positive quality of Delius's music is surely the intense individuality of his style; and this is in itself a token of genius—for I agree with what Mosco Carner has said of Puccini: 'It is a sign of genius if an artist has been able to create a world which, by the force of his imagination and gifts, he compels us to recognize as peculiarly his own'. Second, and hand in hand with this originality, goes an ecstatic sensuous beauty. Such a remark may seem naïve in an age which has explained beauty away in terms of 'significance'; but in music, sensuous beauty is an irreducible quality—a great quality, which some composers have pursued more avidly than others; Mozart, for example, more than Haydn, as we realize if we think of the Clarinet Concerto and Quintet.

It was by absorbing the influence of Wagner that Delius first found himself. We can hear this clearly in one of the few places in his first really mature work where the influence has not been quite fully absorbed: in *A Village Romeo and Juliet*, of 1901, the 'dawn' music is unmistakably Delius, but it betrays a debt to the 'dawn' music in *The Twilight of the Gods*. The second main influence was the impressionism of Debussy. This is rather more elusive and difficult to pin down; but the opening of *Brigg Fair*, for example, with its flute arabesques, its impressionistic string, harp and horn texture, and its free progressions of dominant sevenths and ninths, is obviously unthinkable without the example of *L'après-midi d'un faune*.

Wagner's romantic melodic and chromatic harmony, and Debussy's arabesques and sensuous progressions of dominant sevenths and ninths—absorbing those of Grieg—might seem to account for Delius's mature style, allowing that he made something very individual out of his sources. But there was another, equally strong influence—the Negro plantation songs which he heard in Florida in the eighteen-eighties; he was fascinated, not only by their melodic style but by the original type of harmony which the Negro workers used to improvise when they sang them. His tone-poem *Appalachia* is based on an old Negro slave melody, and the final slow choral statement of the tune is a stylization of the Negro harmony which Delius heard. In places, it strikingly anticipates the use of such harmony by jazz composers like Gershwin, many years later, showing that Negro jazz originated its own harmonic style, and did not derive its dominant ninths from Debussy, as is generally assumed.

Delius's style is a peculiarly limited one: he confined himself largely to a very personal harmonic basis, and to a slow or slowish tempo, to express a particular aspect of human feeling, concerned with the beauty of nature and the transience of human life. This means that he lacked the wide expressive range characteristic of the very great composer; but we need not criticize him for that. The wise composer confines himself to expressing only what he is fitted to express, and if he does this with mastery, he can claim his own place in musical history. In any case, Delius's expressive range is often declared to be much narrower than it really is. The aspect of human feeling which he dealt with has itself many aspects; and the third positive quality of his music is his amazing variety within his limited range.

It is often said that there is a lack of rhythmic interest in Delius's music, and a lack of formal grasp, which place him on the level of a mere amateur, who is only successful on a miniature scale. It cannot be denied that there is some truth in this accusation, when applied to all but his best music; but when it is directed against that, it is carried to such lengths as to be a particularly flagrant example of the general incomprehension of Delius.

Delius's rhythm and form, like his melody and harmony, are isolated, cosmopolitan products, which have no national home. He followed the same iconoclastic path as Debussy, rejecting traditional rhythmic and formal methods, and evolving new procedures of his own; but he mainly retained the slow, fluid rhythmic style of Wagner's *Tristan*, which was unacceptable for new music in France after Debussy. On the other hand, he largely rejected in Wagner the traditional method of rigorous thematic development, in favour of Debussy's mosaic-like type of construction; and this made him unacceptable to the symphonically-minded Germans— and to the English, too, since most English musicians regarded the symphonic tradition as the ultimate yardstick for measuring everything.

In evolving his own rhythmic style and formal method, Delius presented further difficulties to his hearers by limiting himself far more than Debussy. Intent on expressing his own inner world, he largely rejected the more extrovert, incisive aspects of rhythm and form as useless for his purpose. This means that there are none of those clear-cut rhythmic shapes, exciting thematic-rhythmic developments, and sharp contrasts of conflicting themes and keys which we find in the work of almost every other tonal composer. Delius softened the edges of rhythm and form, within the general orbit of a slow tempo, until his music took on all the aspects of a stream of pure rhapsody. And it is this illusion of rhapsody that has given rise to the general misunderstanding.

For the sense of rhapsody *is* an illusion. Pure rhapsody—in the sense of a continuous stream of ideas which have no thematic, rhythmic or formal connexion—is a myth. The truth is that Delius pursued as close a thematic, rhythmic and formal logic as Debussy. I believe that if any of Delius's propagandists had taken the trouble to make and publish meticulous analyses of his best works, it would have been realized that he had, as Eric Fenby has said, 'a well-nigh perfect sense of form for what he wanted to say'.

The further positive quality of Delius's music—a most unexpected one—is the fascination of his original thematic, rhythmic, and formal methods, within his limited range. Again, there is a remarkable variety, for these methods are used in a different way in each work. I have spent a good deal of time analysing his finest works, and I have been amazed at his endless resource within such a restricted orbit. But this very fluidity makes it out of fashion amid the mechanized rhythms and forms of the new music.

Delius was the creator of a highly individual and beautiful art, which is limited to exploring a single area of the human spirit, but does so with comprehensiveness and mastery. It may be a narrow art, but it goes very deep; it says many things that no one else has said; and there is no case for neglecting it, except that of passing fashion. A just treatment of Delius's music, after the centenary year, would be to go on performing the best of it, but not whole concerts and festivals of good and bad alike, as in the nineteen-thirties and forties. To hear too much of any composer can deaden his impact, but Delius, with his confined expressive range, cloys the appetite sooner than most. Only two of his outstanding works occupy a whole evening—*A Mass of Life* and *A Village Romeo and Juliet*—and these do possess sufficient variety to prevent any sense of satiation. The others are normal-size concert-works; and the best way to feature them would be to set them between works by other composers of the most extravert character, from the classical and modern periods. In this way, their special quality would be set in high relief as one of the finest manifestations of late-romantic music.

[1962]

Delius and Form:
A Vindication

I

> In fact ... the intellectual content of Delius's music is peril-
> ously thin.—Peter Heyworth, *The Observer*, 4 February
> 1962.

> For Delius, admittedly, form was unimportant.—Rollo
> Myers, letter to *The Listener*, 15 February 1962.

'In fact' ... 'admittedly' ... these statements sound very authoritative; they seem to be offered as no less than the simple truth. But
if we really *are* after the truth in musical criticism we can reach it
only by establishing real facts, which do really have to be admitted.
In fact, the pretended facts quoted above are mere expressions of
groundless opinion. I intend to prove this, and to establish the
actual facts of the matter, which are actually undeniable.

This may sound arrogant. But after all, we must all be tired by
now of the never-ending stream of uninformed opinion, mas-
querading as authoritative judgement, which constitutes so much
musical criticism (and even more musical journalism). If we are
ever to put musical criticism on a basis of truth, we shall have to
work from the startling, but once-for-all definition of 'certainty'
given by the great American philosopher Charles Sanders Pierce:
'In sciences in which men come to agreement, when a theory is
broached, it is considered to be on probation until agreement is
reached; after it is reached, the question of certainty becomes an
idle one, *since there is no one left who doubts it*' (my italics).

So I want to stress, firmly, that I offer these two essays, not as a
personal point of view, to be commended, condemned or waved
aside in vague journalistic phrases, but as a reasoned aim at the

truth, which must either be *proven wrong* by hard factual reasoning, based on firm technical grounds, or else accepted as conclusive. In short, it is intended as a first attempt towards a scientific musical criticism; and it concerns Delius because of all composers he stands in need of rescuing from the confusion of fashionable dogma and loose journalistic opinion.

Fact No. 1. The classical method of analysis, while able to demonstrate the existence of a definite form in professional works using classical methods of construction, is so imprecise that it cannot establish *incontrovertibly* whether that form is adequate or inadequate. *Proof:* Musicians with professional analytical equipment disagree amongst themselves about the formal adequacy of even certain highly-regarded works, a notorious example being Schubert's Ninth Symphony.

Fact No. 2. The classical method of analysis has so far proved incapable of demonstrating even the *existence* of a form in works which do not use classical methods of construction, such as those of Debussy and Delius, let alone of establishing whether it is adequate or not. *Proof:* There are no writings in which the classical method of analysis has succeeded in throwing any light on the forms of works of this kind. *Consequence of Facts 1 and 2.* In the existing state of analytical knowledge—*i.e.* that based on the classical method of analysis—the statement that 'the intellectual content of Delius's music is perilously thin' is not a fact, but an opinion.

Fact No. 3. The application of the term 'intellectual content' to Delius's music begs the question how large a part the intellectual or rational faculty plays in different types of composition. In the forms of works written to a *strict* pre-formulated scheme, such as canon, the intellectual faculty plays a large part; in the forms of works written to a *flexible* pre-formulated scheme, such as fugue or sonata, the intellectual faculty plays a fair part; but in the forms of works written to no pre-formulated scheme of any kind, the intellectual faculty plays no part at all. *Proof*: Debussy and Delius—the chief composers of works of this kind—both disavowed the use of the intellectual faculty ('ingenuity') in composing their music.

Fact No. 4. The faculty which builds up the form in works not written to a pre-formulated scheme is the imagination, controlled by an intuitive sense of satisfactory shape. *Proof:* No formal proof is possible, but in the absence of the intellectual faculty, no other explanation exists. The utterances of Debussy and Delius give support to this explanation. *Consequence of Facts 3 and 4.* The term 'intellectual content' is inapplicable to the music of Delius, as to that of Debussy.

Fact No. 5. The proportion between (1) concern with the form as such, and (2) concern with the form as extra-musical expression, varies from composer to composer. *Proof:* Wagner's writings about his own works are almost entirely concerned with extra-musical expression, Stravinsky's almost entirely with form as such.

Fact No. 6. Even composers who are most concerned with extra-musical expression are also preoccupied with form. *Proof:* Wagner, although so concerned with extra-musical expression, evolved new formal methods of his own.

Fact No. 7. No composer of any standing is not concerned with form. *Proof:* Delius, of all composers the most purely concerned with extra-musical expression, was aware of the need for a technical command of basic structural devices, as the following of his remarks indicate: 'Towards the end of my course with Ward—and he made me work like a nigger—he showed great insight in helping me to find out just how much in the way of traditional technique would be useful to me. . . . A sense of flow is the main thing, and it doesn't matter how you do it, so long as you master it.' *Consequence of Facts 5, 6 and 7:* The statement 'For Delius, form was unimportant' is false, as it would be of any reputable composer.

Fact No. 8. From about 1850 onwards, the formal methods of all reputable composers differ so fundamentally—whether they use classical methods or not—as to be personal to themselves; and the methods of one are no standard for understanding those of another. *Proof:* It is impossible to understand the form of Wagner's music according to the methods of Brahms, or of Debussy's according to the methods of Richard Strauss.

Fact No. 9. It has been necessary for critics to make a new act of understanding for each of these composers, in the matter of their formal methods; and general critical understanding has only arrived after a specialist has studied the composer concerned and publicly explained his formal methods. *Proof:* There was general critical bewilderment over the formal methods of Wagner, Debussy, Strauss, Stravinsky, Bartók, Schoenberg, etc., until a growing body of literature appeared in each case which elucidated the formal methods of the composer concerned.

Fact No. 10. No one has publicly explained the formal methods of Delius. *Proof:* The extant writings on Delius either ignore the question or apply the classical method with inevitably fruitless results.

Fact No. 11. It is only possible for a critic to offer a helpful judgement of a composer's formal methods when he has become familiar with that composer's works and analysed them carefully. *Proof:* The only helpful judgements we possess of any composer's formal methods, by a critic, are those by one who has made a special study of the composer concerned, such as Ernest Newman in the case of Wagner—in which event the critic no longer functions as such but becomes a specialist; critical judgements made without a study of the composer's music—such as those of Hanslick on Tchaikovsky—invariably contain demonstrable errors of analytical fact. *Consequence of Facts 8, 9, 10 and 11:* Since the critics quoted at the head of this article neither know Delius's music intimately nor have studied and analysed his works, their pretended judgements concerning his form are mere groundless opinion.

Fact No. 12. A new method of analysis has come into being of recent years—two different examples of it being Rudolf Réti's 'Thematic Process' and Hans Keller's 'Functional Analysis' —which, by examining meticulously the bar-to-bar organization of music, can demonstrate the presence of a form in works not written to any pre-formulated scheme. *Proof:* Réti succeeded in demonstrating in Debussy's apparently amorphous 'La cathédrale engloutie', a clear monothematic structure. *Consequence:* This type of analysis should be applied to Delius's music, to see whether it can explain his formal methods; and until this has been done, and the results carefully examined and assessed by those professionally equipped to do so, journalistic opinion should be suspended on what is still a matter of idle conjecture.

II

One can't define form in so many words, but if I was asked, I should say it was nothing more than imparting spiritual unity to one's thought. It is contained in the thought itself, not applied as something that already exists.—Delius.

> It has always been my opinion that Delius had a well-nigh perfect sense of form for what he had to say—Eric Fenby.

> Delius lapsed into rhapsody—Peter Heyworth, *The Observer*, 25 March 1962.

In the previous essay I tried to prove conclusively that Delius's formal methods are *terra incognita*, and that all wholesale journalistic condemnation of his music on structural grounds is so much idle opinion, based on ignorance of the true facts. I also suggested that, since the classical method of analysis has proved powerless to judge the formal adequacy of a given professional work, and especially of works by composers with such personal formal methods as Debussy and Delius, the only possible solution of the problem is to apply to one of Delius's works the new analytical methods, stemming from the writings of Schoenberg, which have come into being recently; and I indicated that there is hope of success, since Rudolf Réti, by means of his 'Thematic Process', succeeded in demonstrating a taut formal coherence in Debussy's apparently amorphous 'La cathédrale engloutie.'

Some people have been amused at the idea of applying to the 'rhapsodic' Delius methods we know mainly from Hans Keller's use of them in his 'Functional Analysis'. 'You can't really be serious?' I have been asked. Indeed, I am: in this article, I want to make a main onslaught on the hitherto unbroached question of Delius's handling of the formal element of composition, by applying the new method, in my own way, to his Violin Concerto.

> Seeing that the principles of classical structure are utterly foreign to Delius's nature, we may admit that the finest music in his concertos is the most purely rhapsodic; therefore the violin concerto is better than the others. Even in this work, Delius cannot write one coherent rhapsodic flight of lyricism from start to finish. Who could? He is forced to find substitutes for the variety and contrast of classical ritornello, though he did not know the fact in such terms. Denied advancement by metabolism, germination, or apotheosis of themes, he uses sudden adventitious changes of time and texture . . .—Arthur Hutchings, *Delius*.

It is small wonder that present-day musical journalists, finding Delius's music somehow distasteful owing to its fluidity, and being unable to discern any form in it, should fall back on the word 'rhapsody' as a blanket term of disparagement (it has been much bandied about as such in this centenary year)—since Delius's admirers who find the music much to their taste, seem equally unable to discern any form in it and have fallen back on the word 'rhapsody' as a blanket term of approbation. In his book on Delius, Professor Hutchings, himself an adept at the classical method of analysis, seems to have been so hypnotized by Delius's singularly fluid outpouring of beauty as to have lost his analytical faculty altogether: after the introduction to the Violin Concerto quoted above, he devotes only one page and two music examples to what is one of Delius's most concentrated structures, and does not even attempt to describe its overall shape (as Harold Rutland does succinctly in a few lines in his sleeve-note for the Pougnet-Beecham recording), let alone its subtle interior organization.

In any case, what on earth does 'rhapsody' mean? If it means anything concrete at all, it must mean an undisciplined outpouring of ideas with no inherent connection, which are not organized into a coherent form. But the idea that such a thing can exist, except in music of such feebly amateur quality as to be beneath consideration, is a chimera. It is certainly inapplicable to Delius's finest works, except as a mere metaphor to evoke that wonderful spontaneous poetic flow of his, that miraculous freedom (akin to Debussy's) from all the clanking machinery of traditional formal methods. The truth is that where Delius does indulge in rhapsody is in his very worst works, which are indeed so amateurish as to be beneath consideration. The Violin Concerto, on the other hand, is a superb example of germination and rigorous thematic development, but of a uniquely plastic kind, far removed from the traditional hammer-and-chisel type.

Let us see how far the classical method of analysis will take us in understanding the work. It will certainly make clear the main outline of the form. The work is continuous, but falls into five sections:

(1) With moderate tempo (sonata exposition)   93 bars
(2) Slowly ('slow movement' = 'development')   73 bars
(3) Ad libitum (accompanied slow cadenza)   30 bars

(4) Tempo I (sonata recapitulation)	61 bars
(5) Allegretto (scherzo/finale, referring back to 1)	83 bars

Judged simply as an overall plan, this is a highly original solution of the problem of compressing the four movements of a normal sonata work into a single movement, which develops the initial material throughout. It can be schematically expressed as follows:

(1) *Sonata-form first movement,* the exposition and recapitulation being separated by (a) a development section which is the:

(2) *Slow movement,* and (b) a cadenza, bringing the recapitulation (see 1) which leads to the:

(3) *Scherzo*-theme, which turns out to be the main material of the:

(4) *Finale,* the second theme and coda of which refer back to (2) and (1).

But of course, a plan is one thing, carrying it out another. However, still using the classical method of analysis, we find, surprisingly enough, that it can demonstrate the existence of a very complex form, in detail, stage by stage:

I EXPOSITION (93 bars):

Introduction (orch) (2 bars)	2 bars 4/4
First Group (38 bars):	
A (vln)	6 bars 4/4
B (vln and wind)	5 bars 12/8
C (vln and wind)	3 bars 12/8 (1 of 6/8)
dev. of B and C (vln and orch)	5 bars 12/8 (1 of 4/4)
A1 (orch ritornello)	2 bars 4/4
dev. of A (vln)	4 bars 4/4
D (vln)	2 bars 12/8
dev. of A (vln)	10 bars 4/4
reference to B (orch)	1 bar 12/8
Transition (37 bars):	
New version of D (vln)	6 bars 12/8 = 4/4
D (vln)	2 bars 12/8
dev. of A (vln)	7 bars 4/4
reference to D (orch)	1 bar 12/8
dev. of B (vln)	3 bars 12/8
A1 (orch ritornello)	2 bars 4/4

dev. of D (vln and orch)	14 bars 12/8
A1 (orch ritornello)	2 bars 4/4
Second Subject (16 bars):	
E (brass)	5 bars 4/4
dev. of B (orch and vln)	3 bars 12/8 (1 of 6/8)
E (orch)	3 bars 4/4
reference to A (vln and wind)	5 bars 4/4

2 DEVELOPMENT—SLOW MOVEMENT (73 bars):
    Statement (38 bars)

(*i*) F (A and B fused) (vln)		14 bars 6/4
(*ii*) G (vln)	24 bars	4 bars 4/4
dev. of F in 4/4 (vln)		16 bars 4/4
G (oboe and vln)		4 bars 4/4

    Restatement (35 bars):

(*i*) F (vln)	13 bars 6/4
(*ii*) G only (vln and orch)	22 bars 4/4

3 ACCOMPANIED SLOW CADENZA (30 bars)

                                30 bars 4/4 (1 free; 1 of 6/4; 1 of 7/4)

4 RECAPITULATION (61 bars):
    Introduction omitted
    First Group (39 bars):

same as exposition until 28th bar, with slight rescoring, harmonic tonal changes:	27 bars 4/4 and 12/8
then contracted—	
dev. of A (vln and orch)	9 bars 4/4
D (wind)	2 bars 12/8
reference to B (orch)	1 bar 12/8

    Transition (11 bars):

New version of D (vln)	6 bars 12/8 = 4/4
D (vln)	2 bars 12/8
dev. of A (vln)	3 bars 4/4

    Second Subject (11 bars):

| E (brass—wind—tutti) | 11 bars 4/4 |

5   SCHERZO-FINALE (83 bars):
   Statement (30 bars):

(*i*) Scherzo-Theme H (orch)		8 bars 12/8
(*ii*) Second theme J (vln)		7 bars 4/4
(new form of G)	22	
dev. of J in 12/8 (vln)	bars	6 bars 12/8 (1 of 6/8)
J (vln)		9 bars 4/4

   Link (vln) (1 bar)   1 bar 12/8
   Restatement (52 bars):

(*i*) H extended (orch)	24 bars 12/8 (1 of 6/8)
(*ii*) Coda, based on A (vln)	28 bars 4/4

What does this broad analysis tell us? Four things, which are of crucial importance. First, that Delius, far from indulging in rhapsody, was concerned with evolving a very original and intricate, but entirely clear form, involving nine main ideas, with thematic cross-references. Second, that the work was written with a strong feeling for rightness in the proportions, since the balance of the various movements and sections, in the matter of numbers of bars, cannot be faulted. Third, that Delius was aware of the need for reshaping and compression on restatement (compare exposition—93 bars—and recapitulation—61 bars). Fourth, that the rhythmic organization is most original, alternating 4/4 with 12/8 or 6/4 throughout.

But the classical method of analysis can take us no farther. If it is powerless to demonstrate the adequacy of the form in works constructed on classical patterns, it is even more helpless here: in the sonata movement, as can be seen, Delius does not keep his themes neatly distinct from one another, but while he is developing one he introduces another in the middle of that development, and so on; moreover, it is useless to attempt to work out the tonal scheme on classical principles, since Delius, like Debussy, does not use tonality to oppose themes against one another in a dynamic perspective, but to create an 'impressionistic' flow of changing atmospheres. The only way of trying to demonstrate any true coherence in the form of the Violin Concerto is to use the new methods of analysis, which can at least demonstrate a logical connection in the sequence of A, B, C, etc., and their various developments, by scrutinizing closely the bar-to-bar evolution of the thematic argument.

In applying the new methods (in my own way), I shall ignore Delius's wonderful harmony, and confine myself to the thematic and rhythmic elements. This will not only save much-needed space in the matter of music type, but will also give the lie to the following recent statement by a musical journalist: 'Delius is not a particularly interesting melodist ... his most natural rhythmic state is inertia ... the one field in which he claims our attention is his use of lush, chromatically-sliding harmony to evoke a haze of dreamy, motionless musing.'

1 EXPOSITION. The orchestral introduction is a motto of two 4/4 bars, out of which the whole work grows. In this (and only one other case), I shall give the harmony, since it indicates the weight given to the motto, and contains an element which eventually becomes thematic. The motto is given in Ex. 1, together with its abstracted thematic shape (shape I) and its abstracted rhythm (P). The essence of this rhythm is the characteristically Delian syncopated accent on the second beat.

Idea A of the first group (Ex. 2) enters immediately, also in 4/4: in its second bar it swings into the rhythm P, with the falling second which opens the motto. The falling second is the basis of the descending scale-pattern of A. In the fifth bar of Ex. 2, the violin takes up figure x from shape I to rhythm P, in a new form; in bar 6, it appears to go off into rhapsody if one does not notice that the orchestra supports it with a repetition of x in its new form (Ex. 3, which underpins bar 6 of Ex. 2). In any case, the violin's bar of 'rhapsody' is a free variant of A.

A, in using the rhythm P in its second bar, superimposes on it a new rhythm Q to a thematic figure y (Ex. 2, bar 2, and Ex. 4): this figure will be pervasive, and its rhythm (a Delius 'fingerprint') even more so.

At the end of Ex. 2, the two-bar development of x implies two further bars to complete the period of two four-bar phrases, but Delius contracts here by weaving in immediately a second idea in 12/8 (B)—see Ex. 5. As Professor Hutchings says, Delius 'knew the need for such duality'—but on the other hand the change of time is not 'adventitious': it begins the opposition between 4/4 and 12/8 (later 6/4) which is the individual rhythmic basis of the work. Also the new theme B grows out of what has gone before: it is at once a new fluid form of shape I and a new fluid form of rhythm P (Ex. 6).

In rhythm P, the second note is emphasized by both syncopation and length; in its new form in B by syncopation only, marked by an accent in Ex. 6.

After the threefold statement of B in Ex. 5 (a contraction of an implied fourfold one), the melodic line proceeds immediately by developing B in a different form, B1, which gives a new thematic shape in three different versions—shape II (i), (ii), and (iii)—see Ex. 7.

After this two-bar development of B in Ex. 7, the melodic line continues immediately by weaving in a third idea, C—which is a quicker form of shape II (i); as with B, its implied fourfold statement is contracted into a threefold one, its half-bar length necessitating the single bar of 6/8 (see Ex. 8). The one bar of apparent rhapsody which follows, concluding Ex. 8, can be seen to be thematic, since it continues C's version of II (i).

After this single bar of 'rhapsody', the melodic line continues immediately with one statement of B, a one-bar contraction of C in 4/4 and resumed development of B in 12/8 in another new form (Ex. 9). This shows the extraordinarily subtle organic coherence of Delius's apparently wayward flow.

So far I have illustrated my analysis from the beginning, bar by bar, to show how closely Delius pursues his thematic argument, but from now on I shall take this for granted, since, for the sake of space, I shall have to confine myself to illustrating only the turning-points of the form. A score would help the reader at this point.

The development of B continues for three bars, culminating in a new forceful form of A—a two-bar contraction of it over a dominant seventh on B flat, which acts as an orchestral ritornello A1—see Ex. 10 (Professor Hutchings regrets that the opening 'eschew[s] the chance of germination, by cross-reference and interplay, possible only when introductory material is ritornellic': the introductory material is certainly not—it is germinal—but the first theme, A, is clearly used as a ritornello in the forceful form A1 over its dominant seventh on B flat.) The violin responds by developing A1 (see Ex. 10 again).

This development continues for four bars; then a fourth idea, D, is woven in (Ex. 11). This is a new brooding version of x as developed in Ex. 2—see Ex. 12. D is set out as a new thematic shape (shape III) in Ex. 13. After this, the development of A is resumed (see bar 3 of Ex. 11) and continues for ten bars; then a quiet reference to B brings the first group to an end.

The transition opens with an apparently new idea which, being in fact a flowing transformation of D, may be called D1 (Ex. 14); after six bars of this, D itself is reaffirmed. Then eleven bars of development of A, D and B bring back the orchestral ritornello A1, with its dominant seventh on B flat, more forcibly. Finally, another fourteen bars of intensive development of D bring the third and climactic statement of the orchestral ritornello A1, still with its dominant seventh on B flat; this time it goes straight into the powerful second subject, E (Ex. 15). But E is a highly contrasted and contracted refashioning of D, or shape III (see Ex. 16—the F natural which opens A1 in Ex. 15 is retained by the harmony throughout the two bars before E enters). Also E's rhythmic shape is a new dynamic version of the basic rhythm P (see Ex. 16 again).

Modified repetitions of E are interrupted by lively references to B, and followed by quiet references to A, which end the exposition by glancing back to its beginning.

Obviously sonata-form is merely a way of explaining what happens in this work: the music can in no way be said to be in sonata-form (in the normal sense)—it is an example of Delius's free yet thematically coherent formal method of evolving a form out of an initial idea. The concentration of his formal organization should be clear at this point; from now on, for reasons of space, I shall merely indicate the derivations of the new main ideas.

2 DEVELOPMENT=SLOW MOVEMENT.   Since the exposition has itself contained so much thematic development, the development section takes the form of a slow movement devoted to lyrical (but closely organised) treatment of new transformations of the exposition's main material. The main idea of the slow movement, F, takes up shape II (ii) and continues with shape I to a fusion of rhythms P and Q (see Exs 17, 18 and 19). In its second bar, the strings accompany the violin's version of shape II (ii) by a version of shape I, with its second group of three notes inverted; this interpretation is confirmed when in the fourth bar the violin itself has I in its original shape (see Ex. 18).

At the end of the fourteen-bar statement of F, notes three, four and five of shape I are treated as a separate thematic figure, z, which generates the second idea of the movement, G (see Ex. 20). The rhythm of G is yet another, drawn-out form of the basic rhythm P (see Ex. 21). The whole slow movement is made up of alternation and interweaving of F and G (see general analysis above) and nothing else.

3 ACCOMPANIED SLOW CADENZA. The slow movement ends with dying references to G, and the cadenza begins with a characteristic piece of violinistics (Ex. 22). If anywhere, a composer might be forgiven for 'lapsing into rhapsody' in a cadenza; strange, then, to find Delius meticulously picking up thematic shape II (i) from the end of the slow movement as a starting-point for his 'free' passage-work (see Ex. 22 again). The cadenza itself, however, is not built out of shape II (i). The ascending arpeggios of Ex. 22 are followed by falling ones, and the cadenza takes this pattern as its basis, in the form of a 'new' figure, consisting of one bar of ascending and one bar of descending arpeggio (Ex. 23). Delius used to improvise *harmonically* on the violin, in *arpeggios outlining chords,* and this cadenza is no doubt a formalized example of the fantastic and wonderful harmonic arabesques he used to draw from the instrument. For formalized it is: its arpeggio pattern is a taut fusion of idea A (with the rhythm P) and shape II (iii)—see Ex. 24.

The cadenza is built entirely out of fourteen beautiful variations on this basic idea, to sustained wind or string chords. Three times it is expanded into a three-bar pattern, by extending either the ascending or the descending arpeggio to two bars; but more interesting, in the case of this 'rhapsodic' composer, is that it is twice contracted into a single bar (as in Ex. 25). The final descending arpeggio takes the form of excited woodwind figures, which waken the music from its musing for a powerful orchestral statement of A, which opens the recapitulation.

4 RECAPITULATION. There is no need to analyse the recapitulation in detail. As indicated in the general analysis above, for twenty-seven of its sixty-one bars it restates the process of the exposition exactly, with modifications in the scoring, the harmony, and the tonal disposition, after which it drastically compresses the remainder. The second subject, E, uninterrupted this time, works up to an *fff* climax, heralding the final stage of the work.

5 SCHERZO-FINALE. The main scherzo material, H, begins by taking up, in more lively form, shape II (i) as at the end of the slow movement and the beginning of the cadenza (Ex. 26—compare Ex. 22). This is a subtle stroke: the recapitulation is 'ignored', as it

were, since in the implied *four-movement* form, the scherzo-finale *continues after the slow movement and cadenza*, not after the end of the first movement. This interpretation is confirmed by the fact that the whole shape of H is implicit in certain phrases of the cadenza (see Ex. 27).

In this scherzo-theme, Delius uses for the first time regular sequences of four-bar periods, and each bar has the four-square rhythm of H. This may be regarded, perhaps, as the one weak spot of the work. Even so, not for the reason given by one musical journalist—that this section shows how 'deadly' Delius is when he 'tries to be animated', that the attempt to dance here is 'depressingly languid'. On the Pougnet-Beecham recording, the music has the delicately lilting movement of an English country dance, and we do not ask more from Delius, since we do not expect him to burst suddenly into the electrifying rhythms of Stravinsky or Bartók. Even the four-bar periods can be defended, as characteristic of many dance-movements of great composers. Nevertheless, it has to be admitted that when this theme is extended, on its second appearance, to twenty-four bars, the effect of the continuous repetition of the rhythm of H, together with the persistent pattering of the soloist's *moto perpetuo* semiquaver accompaniment, does become a little wearisome; and that Delius's one attempt to stave off monotony—a 'fading-out' of the rhythm in bars 11–13 together with a contraction to a 'half-bar' of 6/8 in bar 12—does not really achieve its purpose. However, this is a single and comparatively slight flaw which should not unduly worry those who can respond to the strange charm of the music itself.

The second idea of this movement, J, introduces the finale element, and also brings the threads of the work together: it is a refashioning of shapes II and I and of the rhythm Q, as an urgent version of the main idea of the slow movement, F, which itself goes back to the thematic origins of the whole work (see Ex. 28—compare Ex. 17). After the recurrence of the scherzo material H (the twenty-four-bar extension mentioned above), J does not return, but instead there is an extended coda of just over the same length, which is a concentrated summing-up, in Delius's most exquisite elegiac vein, in the form of an intensely chromatic treatment of the first two bars of A; it dissolves, at the end, into an unclouded F major, with added sixth. Since J was concerned with elements of A, the coda, recalling A itself, is a perfect equivalent for the expected restatement of J, and a perfect ending for the work, looking back to its beginning.

In the closing bars, woodwind references to the pervasive rhythm Q make a final unifying comment. In Ex. 29b, the first clarinet figure is a version of shape I, ignoring the shape's third note (the repeated D) and taking A as the fifth note instead of C. This is confirmed by the clarinet's second figure in Ex. 29b, which uses for its fifth note not A but A flat—the crucial harmonic inflexion of the fifth note of the original motto (see Ex. 29a and Ex. 1). But the flute's imitation of the clarinet figure in Ex. 29b is a version of the second bar of the concerto's first theme—A. So A itself is ultimately derived from shape I, not only by transforming the motto's initial falling second into a descending scale, and incorporating into its second bar the rhythm P, but also by refashioning the motto itself as the pervasive little melisma *y* to the rhythm Q (Ex. 29c).

In other words, the whole material of the work, thematic and rhythmic, is evolved out of its initial two-bar motto—with what *entirely unrhapsodic, rigorously organic* mastery I believe to have demonstrated conclusively.

[1962]

Ex. 1

Ex. 2

Ex. 3

Ex. 4

Ex. 5

Ex. 6

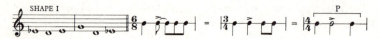

Ex. 7

Ex. 8

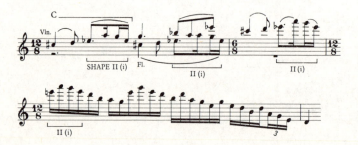

Ex. 9

Ex. 10

Ex. 11

Ex. 12   Ex. 13

Ex. 14

Ex. 15

Ex. 16

Ex. 17

Ex. 18

Ex. 19

Ex. 20

Ex. 21

Ex. 22

Ex. 23

Ex. 24

Ex. 25

Ex. 26

Ex. 27

Ex. 28

Ex. 29

The Unity of Beethoven's Late Quartets

This article is based on an illustrated talk I gave for the BBC's Third Programme on 31 March 1962. Since it involves the application of the new method of analysis—and not only to a single work, but to a group of five—I should like to make four points clear at the start in order to avoid the more elementary kinds of misunderstanding.

(i) Certain simple pitch-patterns have been used constantly by all composers throughout the whole tonal period. Thus, in the present context, the two pitch-patterns which I claim to be the thematic basis of Beethoven's last five quartets are not necessarily confined to Beethoven's musical language; for example, the one which consists of a simple sequence of fourths, ascending or descending, has been used as a principal thematic idea by Britten in *The Turn of the Screw* and Wagner in *The Ring*. What this means is that tonal melody is a language common to the whole period, and that in consequence the whole *corpus* of the music of this period can be discussed as a homogeneous whole, a continuous tradition, just as a complete literature can. This is what I have done in my book, *The Language of Music*.

(2) Within this period, each composer, in drawing on this common fund of melody, has tended to adopt certain of the basic pitch-patterns more exclusively than others, and to use them throughout his whole output. Again, in the present context, the sequence of fourths, ascending or descending, is not confined to Beethoven's last quartets, but was used by him as a principal thematic idea in some of his other works, for example the Piano Sonata in A flat, op. 110. What this means is that each composer's personal remoulding of pitch-patterns drawn from the common fund is part of his enduring musical language; and his complete output can be discussed as a homogeneous whole, a continuous expression of a single personality, just as the whole output of a literary artist can. I have done this in my article 'The Musical

Symbolism of Wagner's Music-Dramas' [see p. 25] in which I have demonstrated how Wagner used one particular pitch-pattern— best known in its form as the 'Day' motive in *Tristan*—in every one of his music-dramas except *The Mastersingers*, and always with the same basic psychological connotation.

(3) As the foundation of a given work, a composer will often use one of the basic pitch-patterns that form part of his personal language (sometimes he will use an entirely original pattern, apparently created *ex nihilo*). In such a case, he will usually remould the pattern afresh, giving it new tonal inflections and/or a new rhythmic articulation; and this accounts for the individual character of the theme itself—its difference from themes in his other works which use the same basic pattern. In any case, within a given work, he will create an overall structure from his basic, initial theme, in an entirely new way; and this accounts for the individual character of the work—its difference from any of his other works which may be based on a similar type of theme. This means that each of his works must be analysed as an entity in itself—as a continuous working out of a single idea—to show the particular way in which the basic theme is metamorphosed into the other themes of the work. This is what I do in applying the new method of analysis to a single work, as in the analysis of Beethoven's Seventh Symphony in my article 'In Defence of Functional Analysis' in *The Musical Times* for September 1959.[1]

(4) Sometimes, however, a composer will use the same basic pitch-pattern as the foundation of a whole group of closely-related works. In this case, each work still has, of course, its own completely individual character as a self-contained piece of music, in the sense of (3) above; and it can only be properly analysed as an entity in itself. Nevertheless, the new method can be usefully applied, in a broad way, to the group of works as a whole, to demonstrate that, in spite of the individual character of each separate work, the whole group has a wider unity, owing to its source in a single basic pitch-pattern. This is what I am doing in the present article, in connection with Beethoven's late quartets; except that I treat the single, initial basic pattern as soon bifurcating—giving rise to

[1] To avoid another misunderstanding, I must stress that the conception of the later themes of a work being *evolved from* the initial one is my own; the orthodox view of Hans Keller, the creator of the special technique of Functional Analysis, and his disciples, is that the later themes are *related to* the initial one, which is thus not given precedence over the others.

another basic pattern which assumes equal importance with its progenitor, and acts in conflict with it.

The *reason* why I am applying the new method in this broad way to Beethoven's late quartets is that it may help to open up a path towards elucidating what is generally felt to be the enigmatic character of these works. The *justification* of treating them as a group is, in the first place, that they are widely agreed to belong together, as a more or less self-enclosed area of Beethoven's output. I am naturally aware that Beethoven did not from the outset conceive the quartets as a single work of art: he wrote them as five separate works, in response to various commissions, and he obviously regarded them as separate in that he allowed them to be published in a different order from that in which they were composed. Nor is the set necessarily fixed and definitive in every detail, since we are faced with the perplexing riddle of the two alternative finales to the Quartet in B flat, op. 130. Again, the number of five was not necessarily intended: other 'late quartets' might have followed, if Beethoven's life had been extended.

Nevertheless, on a deeper level, the set may be treated as a single phenomenon. These were not only Beethoven's last five quartets, but his last five compositions of any consequence; and in the sense that every great artist's lifework is a continuous expression of the deeper layers of his personality, Beethoven was using instinctively the chance provided by the commissions as an opportunity to write a kind of musical diary, in which he set down the inner experiences of his last years. And from this point of view, we have to accept the set exactly as Beethoven wrote it, ignoring all ambiguities arising from practical considerations as a side-issue. So first, I shall ignore the possibility that the set might have been extended by one or more quartets, and take the number five as self-sufficient; indeed, many people have felt that the last of the set—the Quartet in F, op. 135—has an air of finality which makes it a curiously fitting conclusion, by a stroke of fate, not only to the last quartets, but to Beethoven's life-work as a whole. Also, I shall accept the *Grosse Fuge* as the genuine finale of op. 130, since it was Beethoven's first thought, and it seems unlikely that he would have had a second thought if his publisher had not pressed him.

Finally—and this is most important—I shall ignore the numbering, and the opus numbers, of the published edition, since these give us a totally false idea of the genuine sequence of the works as musical events in Beethoven's life. I shall number the quartets 1 to 5, in the order in which Beethoven actually composed them:

no. 1 in E flat	(op. 127)
no. 2 in A minor	(op. 132)
no. 3 in B flat	(op. 130)
no. 4 in C sharp minor	(op. 131)
no. 5 in F	(op. 135)

What I hope to show is that the set of five constitutes a self-contained unity, a single continuous act of creation, in which Beethoven persistently developed certain implications of two basic pitch-patterns.

The first thing we notice, if we look at the set as a single entity, is that the overall shape of the whole is a kind of arch. The two outer quartets—no. 1 in E flat and no. 5 in F—are both normal size works in the usual four movements, in major keys, and basically[2] concerned with pleasurable emotions, despite certain darker components. Then, moving inwards from both sides, we have no. 2 in A minor and no. 4 in C sharp minor, which are both on a larger scale, with more than the usual four movements (five in fact—see below), in minor keys, and basically tragic in character, despite certain brighter components. Finally, in the centre, we have no. 3 in B flat, the largest-scale of all, not only with more than the usual four movements (six in fact), but with the enormous *Grosse Fuge* as its finale; this work is again in a major key, matching the two outer quartets, but the emotional character of the work can hardly be contained within the term 'pleasurable', being rather compounded of a tremendous positive depth and power which it is difficult to give a name to. All this makes no. 3 in B flat the natural apex of the arch.

In general, most attention has been paid to the central three quartets, no doubt because they are the most unorthodox, complex, and adventurous—the most profound in a sense. And within this inner group of three, some light has been thrown on the question of the unity of the set. The following discoveries, well known by now, have been made.

[2] I use the word 'basically' to mean that the outer pillars of the structure—the first and last movements—set the basic character of any work, within which other highly contrasting elements will usually be contained, much as *Hamlet* is 'basically' a tragedy, in spite of its considerable comic element.

(1) Nottebohm showed that Beethoven had used the same pitch-pattern, as a principal thematic idea, in the first movement of no. 2 in A minor (as a kind of opening motto-theme) and in the finale of no. 3 in B flat (as a kind of opening motto-theme, and as subject of the *Grosse Fuge*): see Exx. 17 and 37.

(2) Marion Scott showed that this pitch-pattern is also present as a principal thematic idea in the first movement of no. 3 in B flat (as a kind of opening motto-theme): see Ex. 29.

(3) Bekker showed that the pitch-pattern is also present as a principal thematic idea in the first movement of no. 4 in C sharp minor (as the subject of the fugue): see Ex. 40.

(4) Someone—who, I cannot trace—showed that the pitch-pattern is also present in the finale of no. 2 in A minor (in the complex of opening theme and accompanying figure): see Ex. 25.

Like any other musicians, I became acquainted with these discoveries years ago, long before the new method of analysis had made itself felt in this country; and at that time I also noticed, and wondered why Bekker had failed to realize, that the pitch-pattern is also present in the finale of no. 4 in C sharp minor (in the two opening phrases, and in the second theme): see Exx. 48, 49 and 50.

This meant that, for me, all six main pillars of the three central quartets—their opening and closing movements—were built around the same basic pitch-pattern; and thus the three works obviously belonged closely together as a unified, homogeneous group.

Now it seemed curious to me that, since the whole set of five quartets clearly belonged together in spirit and technique, this unity of the inner three should not extend over the outer two as well. But a glance at the opening of no. 1 in E flat told me that this was apparently not the case (see Ex. 1). This opening too is a kind of motto-theme—a brief slow introductory idea—but any connection between it and the unifying pitch-pattern of the central three quartets seems remote indeed: it is a bright, upward-thrusting, major pattern involving a triadic shape and an ascending sequence of ascending fourths; whereas the other pitch-pattern is a dark, sinuous, minor shape, involving the top four notes of the harmonic minor scale.

There was only one other possibility, if the five quartets did in fact possess an overall thematic unity. Since the shape of the set was an arch, and the two outer quartets had so much in common, could it be that the bright major pitch-pattern that opened no. 1 was another contrasting motto-theme, running right through the whole set—being predominant in no. 1, subsidiary to the dark minor motto-theme in nos. 2, 3 and 4, and predominant again in no. 5? If this were so then perhaps the dark minor motto-theme was present subsidiarily in no. 1 predominant in nos. 2, 3 and 4, and subsidiary again in no. 5? A good argument against this being true was that no one had ever noticed any such thing. However, I decided to treat it as a hypothesis, and to try and verify it. I believe that I have in fact verified it; and my findings are set out below in the form of a skeleton analysis. Incidentally it goes without saying that this skeleton should not be taken as my idea of a genuine analysis of Beethoven's late quartets: it is not intended as such, but only as a schematic representation of what I believe to be the thematic unity of the group.

Before going on to this representation, however, I should briefly stress that much of it depends on the principles assumed by those who employ the new method of analysis: inversion, retrograde motion, retrograde inversion, octave transposition, and interversion (the switching around of the notes of a phrase). I shall not attempt to argue these principles here, owing to lack of space, but I must point out two things. In the first place, Nottebohm, Marion Scott and Bekker, in their analytic findings, were already taking these principles for granted (or at least two of the thorniest, octave transposition and interversion), long before the new method emerged. Secondly, and more conclusively, Beethoven himself obviously took all the principles for granted, and worked on them persistently in the late quartets, in the conscious process of thematic development (in the old sense). Inversion can be seen in Ex. 17; retrograde motion in Exx. 11 and 13; retrograde inversion in Ex. 61; interversion in Ex. 49. I believe that all these were conscious uses of the procedures concerned, except possibly Ex. 13—but in any case an undeniably conscious use of exact retrograde motion is to be found in the fugue of the Piano Sonata in B flat, op. 106 (Hammerklavier). As for octave transposition, it occurs in many passages; see the first movement of no. 2 in A minor (violas and cellos, bars 92–6).

QUARTET NO. 1 IN E FLAT (OP. 127)

I. The six introductory bars provide the thematic source of the set of five quartets—what I have called the bright major motto-theme:

Ex. 1

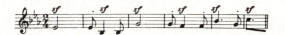

This may be set forth as a basic pitch-pattern A, divisible into two overlapping segments *x* and *y*:

Ex. 2

Throughout the set, A is represented either by itself, or as *x* or *y*. The derivation of the main *allegro* theme is from *y:*

Ex. 3

This subtle relationship becomes clearer in the development of the main *allegro* theme in bars 85f.:

Ex. 4

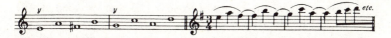

The 'second subject' is also derived from *y*—the first phrase by inflected inversion, the second (making all clear) by an ornamentation of the direct form:

Ex. 5

In the middle of the development (bars 116–134), the gentle character of the music is suddenly disrupted by an unexpected outbreak of violence (Ex. 6). This is an ornamented minor version of *x,* as shown in Ex. 7:

Ex. 6

Ex. 7

And this abrupt and scarcely explicable outburst is the moment of bifurcation mentioned above; for from this transformation of *x* (part of A) springs B, which is what I have called the dark minor motto-theme—the protagonist of the central three quartets. Here it is only in embryo form, which I represent by calling it (B)—with brackets:

Ex. 8

The close relationship between A and (B) can be seen in the notation of *x* in Ex. 7.

II. The relationship between the theme of the variations and A is a latent one, which becomes explicit in Var 2:

Ex. 9

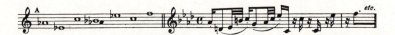

In Variation 3, the compression of the theme gives rise to a new form of *y* (to be called *yy*), in which the two ascending fourths are set a third apart, not a second:

Ex. 10

III. The scherzo theme is built from a version of A, which is formed as a sequence of the pattern *yy*. This makes clear how *yy* can be taken as a legitimate version of *y:*

Ex. 11

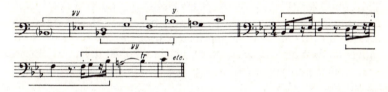

The theme is immediately answered by its inversion (bars 6–10), and this inversion forms the basis of the trio theme:

Ex. 12

This relationship is further clarified by the fact that one part of the trio theme is a practically exact retrograde form of the scherzo theme (Ex. 13, cf Ex. 11):

Ex. 13

IV. The finale opens with a brief introduction (bars 1–4), clearly modelled on Ex. 13, and out of this the main theme materializes, as a repeated little figure which is a remoulding of the first five notes of the main theme of the first movement. Only one note is different (Ex. 14a); and with the last two notes of the introduction, as they sweep into the theme, the identity is a complete, if ornamented one (Ex. 14b):

Ex. 14

This subtle relationship is eventually clarified at the point of recapitulation (bars 187f.), where the finale's main theme is answered by a version of itself which is the identical pitch-pattern of the first movement's main theme, even to the actual pitch itself (Ex. 15a). The finale's main theme is also a version of *x,* and as such rounds off the quartet (Ex. 15b):

Ex. 15

The finale's 'second subject' springs from *yy:*

Ex. 16

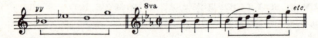

Thus the largely pleasurable and positive mood of no. 1 in E flat arises from the predominance of the pitch-pattern A, and particularly its second segment—the ascending sequence of ascending fourths, either in the original form *y* or the derivation *yy.*

QUARTET NO. 2 IN A MINOR (OP. 132)

I. In the slow eight-bar introduction, the pitch-pattern (B), adumbrated in the first movement of no. 1 in E flat, now emerges in its definitive form as 'the dark minor motto-theme' of the three central quartets; and thus, in the present thematic analysis, (B) sheds its brackets and becomes simply B. Note that Beethoven uses this theme in both its direct and inverted forms:

Ex. 17

This motto theme permeates the basic material of the main Allegro, acting as a counterpoint to the first subject, which seems to grow out of it, being much concerned with the notes A, G sharp, F and E. The transitional theme, however, presents a new, combative minor form of *y*, arising from contrapuntal imitation:

Ex. 18

The second subject—like the first subject of the main Allegro in the first movement of no. 1 in E flat—begins with a three-note segment of *y* (Ex. 19a); but whereas we might expect to find this segment repeated, either in descending sequence (cf Ex. 1), or in ascending sequence, thereby materializing the full direct form of *y* (Ex. 19b), the segment is in fact repeated in retrograde form (Ex. 19c):

Ex. 19

We can now look back at the first subject again, and see that it has already provided the basis for the second (a similar state of affairs to that in the first movement of no. 1 in E flat): the second subject is made up of retrograde and direct forms of the first (Ex. 20a). This means that the first subject also consists of a three-note segment of *y* (*y* inverted, that is—Ex. 20b):

Ex. 20

If this analysis by means of three-note segments of *y* be thought suspect, it will seem less so, in retrospect, when we reach the end. The reader may be reassured by a glance at Exx. 59 and 60—the phrases 'Must it be?' and 'It must be' in no. 5 in F. These are in effect three-note segments which, in sequential repetition, build up the full form of *y* direct and inverted; as can be seen in Exx. 19c and 20b, both the first and second subjects of the present movement are concerned with the phrase which is to become 'It must be'. Moreover, it should be realized that the pathetic effect of the second subject is due entirely to its refusing to fulfil the obvious expectations of ascending sequence indicated in Ex. 19b, and thereby both to materialize the full form of the optimistic *y*, or to rise up from B flat as far as C.

II. The direct form of *y* is the source of the main material of this 'would-be-happy' dance-movement; the inverted form that of the salient idea of the Ländler-like trio:

Ex. 21

III. In the *Heiliger Dankgesang*, the chorale theme itself remains a kind of supra-formal visitant from outside; but the radiant main idea which forms the contrapuntal background and

linking material is a version of *x* (Ex.22a). Moreover, the strong
modulation to D major for the vital second theme brings the notes
A and D, and thus practically the whole form A is present, the last
two notes fulfilling a structural function (Ex. 22b):

Ex. 22

The vital second theme itself ('feeling new strength') is also a
version of *x*:

Ex. 23

IV. This forceful march-movement's single theme is a free
version of A:

Ex. 24

V. The return of the tragic element, in the brief recitative, leads
back to A minor for the finale; and at the opening of this, as in
countless places in the first movement, the dark B is the main basis
of the texture:

Ex. 25

The main *allegro* theme itself, however, is a version of *x*—not in the bright major form which has brought so much alleviation in this quartet, but in a wild, agitated minor form:

Ex. 26

The finale's second main idea is a fierce transformation of *y*, in inverted form:

Ex. 27

At the end of the quartet, darkness is magically turned to light, as the first theme goes into the major to become a version of the original bright form of A:

Ex. 28

The ending itself is not simply joyful, however, but equivocal, being shot through with sombre elements (the minor sixth of the scale, chiefly).

QUARTET NO. 3 IN B FLAT (OP. 130)

I. The *adagio* introduction presents as motto what Marion Scott has called in 'incarnation' of the dark pattern B. It has lost its absolute darkness, however, being in brooding chromatic major form:

Ex. 29

The main *allegro* theme is a version of *y* in its direct form:

Ex. 30

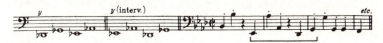

II: This enigmatic scherzo movement is basically harmonic in character, not melodic; its bass is composed of fourths in descending sequence which constitute a form of *y*:

Ex. 31

The theme of the dancing trio section is a free version of *x*:

Ex. 32

III. This movement, after beginning with another 'incarnation' of B (bars 1–2), has a serene main theme built from *yy*:

Ex. 33

IV. The relationship of the haunting *Alla tedesca* melody to the inverted form of *y* is a latent one, and only comes out in the ornamental form of the theme in bars 89f.:

Ex. 34

The second strain, however, is a straightforward version of *yy* in inverted form:

Ex. 35

V. The deeply-moving Cavatina theme uses the three-note segment of *y* which has already appeared in the first movement of no. 1 in A minor, and is eventually to become the phrase 'It must be' in no. 5 in F (Ex. 36a). Again we expect the natural sequence that would give the full form of *y* inverted (Ex.36b); and again the theme's expressive character—its soaring serenity—springs from its refusal to follow the simple sequence:

Ex. 36

VI. As Nottebohm pointed out, the dark minor motto-theme B, used as the basis of no. 2 in A minor, returns in the finale of no. 3 in B flat. As in the first movement, it is given out as a motto in brooding, chromatic major form—but loudly, not quietly. Note that the direct and inverted forms are used, overlapping, with inflection and interversion:

Ex. 37

This becomes the subject of the *Grosse Fuge,* the counter-subject of which is based on the inverted form of *y:*

Ex. 38

The end of the quartet, like that of no. 2 in A minor, is a bright major version of A—not complete, but as its first segment *x:*

Ex. 39

QUARTET NO. 4 IN C SHARP MINOR (OP. 131)

I. As Bekker pointed out, the fugue subject is a version of the dark motto-theme B:

Ex. 40

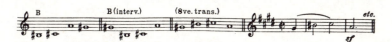

But the fugue subject may be looked at in another way as well. Its second phrase is an inversion of its first (Ex. 41a); and it is thus formed of a three-note segment of *y,* in direct and inverted forms (Ex. 41b):

Ex. 41

As the fugue progresses, it begins to support the method of taking three-note segments of B for the purpose of analysis, for the second phrase of the subject begins to move in sequence as a counter-subject and materializes the full form of *y*, inverted:

Ex. 42

II. The main theme of this movement centres on the inverted form of *y*; this is shown most clearly on its second appearance:

Ex. 43

III. What is called 'no. 3' in the score is in fact no more than a link: the true third movement is the set of variations which follows. As with the variations in no. 1 in E flat, the relationship of the theme to A is latent; it becomes manifest when Variation 5 establishes a clear connection with the direct form of *y* (Ex.44a). The accents in bars 3 and 4 indicate a simultaneous relationship with *yy* (Ex. 44b):

Ex. 44

IV. The E major *presto* movement centres on the interval of the rising fourth; the various appearances of it, in ascending sequence, make up versions of *y*:

Ex. 45

The inverted form of *y* is also present in various forms.

V. I take the so-called 'no. 6' (the G sharp minor movement) as a slow introduction to the so-called 'no. 7' (the finale), and group the two together as 'no. 5'. The theme of the introduction is a minor variant of *x,* which achieves its expressive character of extreme melancholy by failing to rise to the upper dominant, D sharp, and falling back to the tonic G sharp:

Ex. 46

The contrasting strain is based on the inverted form of *y:*

Ex. 47

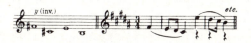

As in no. 2 in A minor and no. 3 in B flat, the opening of the finale proper brings back B as a motto. It can be looked at in two separate ways, which overlap:

Ex. 48

Ex. 49

The relationship of the finale's main theme to A is a latent one, which becomes manifest at the end of the movement (see Ex. 51). The second main theme (Ex. 50) is rhythmically identical with the first movement's fugue subject (cf Ex. 40), and is in fact an interversion of it; thus it is also a version of B:

Ex. 50

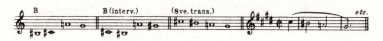

As in no. 2 in A minor and no. 3 in B flat, the ending makes manifest the direct form of A. Here, as in no. 3 in B flat, it takes the form of *x,* but it is back in its dark minor version—a feature which helps to make this ending the most tragic in all Beethoven's music:

Ex. 51

QUARTET NO. 5 IN F (OP. 135)

I. This enigmatic movement opens with the three-note segment of *y* which is to become 'It must be' (Ex. 52a): at bar 170, it actually takes on the descending sequential form it will adopt in the finale (Ex. 52b—cf Ex. 60):

Ex. 52

The second idea centres on the direct form of *y* (Ex. 53a); but in the recapitulation, by means of ornamentation, it takes on the form of the dark motto-theme B (Ex. 53b):

Ex. 53

The 'second subject', however, gives to B a gay, carefree major form (Ex. 54) for the first time in the whole group of quartets; and this eventually dispels the dark version (Ex. 53b) in the coda:

Ex. 54

II. The scherzo is based on the opening four notes of *x* in its
original bright major form; again the expressive character of the
theme—in this case its peculiarly inhibited animation—is due to its
failure to rise to the upper dominant, C, and its return to the tonic
F. The relationship with A is clearest at the first restatement of the
theme (bars 25f.):

Ex. 55

The trio section is built on a rising figure of five notes, spanning a
fourth, which eventually occurs in rising sequence, presenting the
full direct form of *y* (Ex. 56). The direct major form of *y* also acts
structurally, as the statements of the trio theme are each a tone
higher:

Ex. 56

III. The main theme of the slow movement is a serenely
flowing version of *x* in its original major form:

Ex. 57

B here makes its last appearance in the closing bars: its dark spell is
finally exorcised as it takes on a calm major form (bars 43f.):

Ex. 58

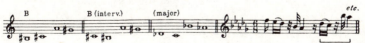

IV.   In the finale, the idea of the three-note segment of *y* comes right into its own. In the introduction, 'Must it be?' is a three-note segment, which in ascending sequence presents the full direct form of *y*:

Ex. 59

(Must it be?)

The main *allegro* theme—'It must be'—is a major inversion of 'Must it be?', and thus is a three-note segment which in descending sequence presents the full inverted form of *y*:

Ex. 60

(It must be)

The continuation of the *allegro* theme, as Schoenberg pointed out, is the retrograde inversion of 'It must be', otherwise the simple retrograde form of 'Must it be?' Again, sequential treatment (descending) results in the full inverted form of *y* (Ex. 61). Compare, incidentally, Ex. 42: the later stages of the whole group of quartets show a growing tendency towards sequential treatment of three-note segments of *y*.

Ex. 61

(It must be) (Ret.) (Ret. inv.)

The 'second subject' is a final, disembodied, dancing version of A, as is made clear on its last appearance (bars 216f.):

Ex. 62

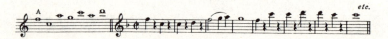

One final word about this quartet. Beethoven's obviously conscious use of retrograde inversion in the finale may perhaps justify the employment of this principle as an analytical tool in general.

The question now arises, what does one hope to prove by all this? As far as I am concerned, I have been interested in the problem only for the following reason. Once we have established that Beethoven, in his last quartets, was exploring continuously the implications of two basic elements of musical language, we are in a position to establish what it was that he has said in these enigmatic works, by applying the principles set forth in *The Language of Music*.

Or perhaps I should say '*I* am in a position'. I must confess that I have been disappointed at the refusal of all and sundry to try and attempt to apply these principles, in spite of the fairly general praise which the book received. For example, 'Our Music Critic' of *The Times* began a recent article with the question 'What is Beethoven's last string quartet about?' Now, this question was once believed to be insoluble; but one might have thought that it had been brought at least a little nearer to being answered by the fairly comprehensive analysis of musical vocabulary contained in my book. But 'Our Music Critic' continues as if the book had never been written, falling back on the empty Hindemith/Stravinsky dogma of 'pure music'. He says: 'One does not usually ask the question about a piece of music [!], particularly in the Viennese classical period [shades of my detailed expressive analysis of Mozart's Fortieth Symphony!]; if one did, the answer would come in terms of themes or phrases, relationships of key, or perhaps the sonorous implications of certain instrumental combinations and their logical consequences...'. What sterile intellectualism is displayed in this mechanistic approach! Are we to go on persistently burying our heads, ostrichwise, in the arid sands of formalism, and steadfastly refuse even to try and understand the emotional and spiritual significance of the music of the great humanistic period?

'Our Music Critic' scorns the idea, put forward in the romantic period, that the 'difficult decision' of the finale is about death and how to meet it; first, because the 'decision', in the music, is 'a high-spirited dervish dance in which the violins tumble over one another in their glee'; and secondly, because the verbal phrase 'It must be' was taken by Beethoven, humorously, from a remark made by an amateur musician who was reluctant to fork out for the hire of some parts ('Oh well, if it must be . . .'). To which one might reply that, in works of art concerned with spiritual realities, as we suppose Beethoven's last quartets to be, the idea of facing death with a high-spirited dance is not at all unfamiliar (cf 'Tomorrow shall be my dancing day', etc.); and the use of a phrase with an originally humorous connection as a text for a highly serious disquisition touching lightly on fundamentals is not at all uncommon (cf almost anything by G. K. Chesterton). If the quartet were about the problem of facing death, one would hardly expect Beethoven to be necessarily portentous—the man had a sense of humour; and a sense of humour need not imply flippancy—it can often cut deeper than earnestness, in that it is born of a cheerful acceptance of the discouraging limitations of the human condition.

But 'Our Music Critic' will not have it that the last quartet has anything to do with Beethoven's character and life: he says 'a more satisfactory solution may be found if we consider [the quartet] as a musical composition and not as some sort of codicil to the Heiligenstadt Testament . . .'. He regards the work as one in which 'Beethoven contrasts the new manner with the old [more matter, and less manner!], and attempts, not without difficulty, to reconcile them'. And he says that 'because this is an argument about music, the *Entschluss* [decision] is not a moral or philosophical, but a musical decision'.

A *musical* composition . . . a *musical* decision . . . what *is* a piece of *music*, after all? The whole argument of *The Language of Music*—that music is an indissoluble whole of form-and-content—is ignored in favour of the fashionable use of the word 'musical' to mean 'purely formal'. 'Our Music Critic' should have said, more precisely, not 'a musical composition', but 'a piece of pure musical form'; not 'a musical decision', but 'a purely formal decision'. Everybody is not agreed that 'music' means 'note-patterns without any connotations of any kind'; at least, not yet, though the time may well come, at the rate things are going.

If I seem to be pressing the claims of *The Language of Music* unduly, it is simply because the book is a serious attempt to grapple with such undeniable realities as the fact that Beethoven wrote on one of the sketches for the Adagio of this particular quartet the words 'Sweet song of rest or song of peace'—a fact which 'Our Music Critic' mentions, but the ultimate implications of which he refuses to face. And yet, in passing, and quite self-contradictorily, he does admit that this quartet is concerned with—oh, not moral or philosophical arguments, I do agree—but with the character and life of the man who actually wrote it. What he insists on calling, at the end of his article, 'an argument about music' (*sc.* 'about form') he has previously described as 'an argument between the young Beethoven and his older self, *between extraversion and introversion*' (my italics). Despite the abstract way of putting it, there is something concrete here. If music is pure form—pure patterns—it cannot be about things like extraversion and introversion, since these are hard psychological realities of the artist's inner being. In my opinion, our misguided music critic has here, in spite of himself (or rather in spite of his adherence to fashionable dogma) caught a glimpse of the inner meaning of Beethoven's last quartet—and in consequence of the whole set of five.

Obviously, to attempt to elucidate their whole inner meaning in detail would require a large book, not a mere essay like this; but I offer the following brief indication of what I believe to be their central significance. I hasten to add that what follows, like the first part of this essay, is in no way meant to be an exhaustive solution of the problem concerned.

In the above schematic examination of the quartets' thematic unity, I said that the largely pleasurable and positive mood of no. 1 in E flat arises from the predominance of the pitch-pattern A. And I described A as 'a bright, upward-thrusting, major pattern, involving a triadic shape and an ascending sequence of ascending fourths'. If there is anything at all in the theories of *The Language of Music*, this pitch-pattern must express an unbounded humanistic confidence and joy—the main characteristic of the youthful (and mature) Beethoven; and indeed, I believe that most people 'feel' the theme this way.

Now the basis of this mood was the central nineteenth-century belief in the progress and perfectibility of man, and the new ultra-humanistic creed (opposing the orthodox religious one) that Man was his own god. It is this mood which gives Beethoven's 'middle-period' compositions—especially works like the Eroica, the fifth, the seventh, and the 'Emperor' Concerto—their blatantly optimistic character, which the nineteenth century so adored, and which the twentieth century finds so hard to swallow. But when Beethoven composed the E flat Quartet, he was already in middle age (fifty-three, to be precise)—a time when the ebullient confidence of early maturity gives way to a broader wisdom (and when, as 'Our Music Critic' points out, extraversion gives way to introversion); and for the humanistic artist of Beethoven's time, the change was characterized by the growing realization that if Man was his own god, the artist himself, as an individual man, was after all mortal. (Compare Hazlitt's famous essay which begins 'No young man ever thinks that he shall die'.) And this consciousness of the approach of waning powers and ultimate extinction must have been all the more appalling to a great creator like Beethoven. Indeed, for some years earlier, certain 'last-period' works such as the late piano sonatas, had shown a growing tendency to give up storming the heavens and to accept the limitations of man's position in the universe as a mortal being.

And so, despite the bold humanistic confidence of the bright motto-theme A of the E flat Quartet, the general mood of the quartet itself is more mellow. In particular, the downward motion of the first theme of the main Allegro (Ex. 3) is essentially an expression of acceptance; and the attempt of this theme to follow an optimistic upward course in the development (Ex. 4) provokes that totally unexpected outburst of violence (Ex. 6) which gives rise to the dark motto-theme B. The mood of this passage is one of agitated anguish—note the insistent minor sixth of the scale—G flat. However, this is an isolated moment; and despite troubled moments elsewhere, the main mood is a happy one, and the culmination is a finale largely full of joy (though of the 'last-period' accepting kind, manifest in the tendency of the main themes to centre around a few notes without sky-rocketing upwards).

But it was after composing this quartet that Beethoven was afflicted by the serious illness referred to in the Quartet in A minor—in the 'Sacred Song of Thanksgiving from a Convalescent to the Deity'. This illness would undoubtedly have brought home more forcibly to Beethoven the fact that the days of his creative activity were numbered—which would explain the emergence, as the main basis for the quartet, of the dark motto-theme B, with its searching ascent to the anguished minor sixth, and its sorrowful sigh of the minor sixth falling to the fifth. And this theme remains the protagonist throughout the central three quartets. Admittedly, their inner movements cover all kinds of moods, from grave to gay, with the peculiarly detached wisdom of the 'last period'; but these are subsidiary sections enclosed within the more powerful opening and closing movements, based on the dark motto-theme B, which even dominates the bright motto-theme A by forcing elements from it into wistful, sorrowful and despairing versions (Exx. 19, 20, 21b, 25, 26, etc.).

In the A minor Quartet, the main mood is tragic, though there is a hopeful reference to the original major form of the bright motto-theme A at the very end (Ex. 28). This hope is realized in the B flat Quartet: the motto-theme B is fought against (A actually returns in its original form, as its segment *y*—Ex. 30); it is modified into less gloomy forms (Exx. 29 and 37); and it is forced to serve the purposes of a last tremendous affirmation of vital energy—the *Grosse Fuge,* which at the end brings back the original form of A triumphantly (Ex. 39). But the C sharp minor Quartet immediately turns back both B and A to despondent forms (Exx. 40 and 41—how sadly the opening fugue-subject falls on to the anguished minor sixth!); and the end of the quartet is the most tragic in all Beethoven's music, with its illusory brightening to the major which only has the effect of turning the music wearily to the subdominant.

Hence, it would seem, the dark opening of the last quartet: the 'It must be' version of the inverted form of A (in its segment *y*)—which has been pervading the music ever since the first *allegro* subject of the A minor Quartet—is brought right into the foreground as an abrupt, crucial question (Ex. 52). It is as though, with the utmost detachment, a final attack is to be made on the whole problem that has made the central three quartets so oppressive: granted the fact of eventual decay and extinction, how to accept it and retain one's belief in the purpose and significance of existence? The mood of the first movement is altogether equivocal, presenting bright and dark versions of both A and B in alternation (Exx. 52, 53a, 53b, 54), and coming to no settled conclusion. But after the peculiarly inhibited gaiety of the scherzo with its frenzied outburst of unquenched vitality in the trio, and then the sublime serenity of the Adagio, in which the proud confidence of A is put to sleep in a 'sweet song of rest or song of peace', the finale brings the resolution. The salient carrier of A's confidence—its final portion *y*—appears in the minor, ascending, in the form of three-note segments, as the fiercely protesting question 'Must it be?' (Ex. 59). And the answer is the ultimate acceptance of the inevitable—'It must be'—but a glad, vital acceptance worthy of the indomitable

Beethoven. The phrase *y*, in its original major form, is presented
again in three-note segments, *inverted;* and not sighingly, as in Ex.
19c, nor gloomily, as in Ex. 20, nor wistfully, as in Ex. 21b, nor
even with noble resignation, as in Ex. 36; but swiftly, and with a
new bubbling gaiety.

It is fascinating to place the two bases of the great arch, made by
the five quartets, side by side, to show how Beethoven's quite
different end is in his beginning:

Ex. 63

At the opening of the first quartet, the joyous main theme rises up
with all the massive power of humanistic optimism; at the end of
the last quartet, it trips downwards with an almost humorous non-
chalance born of the deeper wisdom of accepting Man's ultimate
limitation. The closing lines of a great final group of poetic
masterpieces—the *Duino Elegies* of Rilke—offer a curiously
similar resolution. The first Elegy begins by storming the heavens
in search of happiness; the last ends as follows:

> Und wir, die an *steigendes* Glück
> denken, empfänden die Rührung
> die uns beinahe bestürzt
> wenn ein Glückliches *fällt.*   (Rilke's italics)

> (And we, who think of happiness *climbing,*
> would feel an emotion
> that would almost startle us,
> if a moment of happiness were to *fall.*)

                                                              [1962]

Strauss, Stravinsky, and Mozart

Among the many gems in Robert Craft's *Conversations with Igor Stravinsky* is the following. Craft: 'Do you now admit any of the operas of Richard Strauss?' Stravinsky: 'I would like to admit all Strauss's operas to whichever purgatory punishes triumphant banality. Their musical substance is cheap and poor; it cannot interest a musician today. That now so ascendant *Ariadne*? I cannot bear Strauss's six-four chords: *Ariadne* makes me want to scream'.

Unfortunately, such comical splenetic outbursts, coming from a distinguished composer of our time, are accepted unthinkingly in some quarters as valid judgments. Yet the odd fact here is that the technique-bound Stravinsky offers no technical criticism of Strauss whatsoever but only a furious moral indictment of his style. But to castigate a composer's style is merely to enter the quicksands of personal taste, since there is no critical tool for assessing objectively the quality of musical material. Stravinsky, like the rest of us, is only saying 'I know what I don't like'—in his case German romanticism, which offends his puritanical temperament. The 'musician today' whom Strauss's material 'cannot interest' is Stravinsky and anyone who feels like him; many first-rate musicians find it inexhaustibly fascinating. For some, Strauss's material is nectar, for others it is poison; is there anything else to be said? It is obviously useless to pick out Strauss's fondness for the six-four; as well object to Bach's ubiquitous dominant sevenths in his Passions. The six-four is no more sinful than any other chord; in fact it is the basis of many of Strauss's indisputably great moments, such as those two dazzling F sharp major inspirations, the 'vigil scene' in *Don Quixote* and the 'Presentation of the Rose' in *Der Rosenkavalier*.

But we may wonder why Stravinsky should be so particularly

repelled by *Ariadne auf Naxos* as to fall into the untenable position
of lumping together all Strauss's operas as banal—the astoundingly
original *Salome* and *Elektra* with the self-repeating *Frau ohne
Schatten*, the inspired *Rosenkavalier* with the routine *Die Liebe der
Danae*. Could it be that *Ariadne* forestalled Stravinsky in his own
field of neo-classicism, and that after being written off for decades
it is now indeed ascendant, having achieved as wide a popularity as
his own *Rake's Progress*? For in composing *Ariadne*, in 1911,
Strauss gave musical actuality to the neo-classical concept of opera
while it was still an idea in Busoni's brain, and while Stravinsky was
still working with nationalist and impressionistic techniques.

After his purely Wagnerian *Guntram* of 1894, Strauss was the
first to begin breaking away from the continuous leitmotivic construction of music-drama towards a new classical conception.
Feuersnot (1901) was only a hint, but after *Salome* and *Elektra* he
turned further towards classical opera in *Der Rosenkavalier* (1910),
which, despite its reliance on leitmotif and its continuously woven
texture, introduced several Mozartian elements—a simple diatoni-
cism, the use of set numbers, and (in places) a slimming-down of
the huge romantic orchestra. And in *Ariadne* these tendencies cry-
stallized into a comprehensive inauguration of a new type of neo-
classical stage-work: a short, consciously artificial opera on a
Greek classical subject, shunning musico-dramatic profundity in
favour of sophisticated entertainment, including elements of the
commedia dell' arte, and using a chamber orchestra, set numbers in
classical forms, secco recitative, and vocal lyricism and virtuosity.

Yet clearly the later neo-classics owed nothing to *Ariadne*: neo-
classicism took quite a different path during the twenties, in the
music of Stravinsky and others. We are faced with two totally different conceptions: in attempting to go 'back to Mozart', or to
anyone else (an utterly unreal quest, in any case), there were two
possible approaches—the letter and the spirit. Stravinsky recap-
tured something of the letter, Strauss something of the spirit, and
both inevitably subjected their discoveries to extreme personal dis-
tortion. Whereas Stravinsky approached Mozart externally, using
what he considered to be his 'structural principles' in an entirely
cool way of his own (and occasionally making a dehydrated
pastiche of his style), Strauss, being in the great German line, inherited Mozart's legacy on the deeper level of musical language; he
drew to the full on two essential expressive elements ignored by

Stravinsky—the haunting symmetrical tune and the warmly emotional harmony. But these features had found a natural historical continuation in certain aspects of Germanic romanticism, and so Strauss's image of Mozart was essentially a national and romantic one, seen through the eyes of Schubert, Wagner, Brahms, Wolf, and even Johann Strauss.

It is this, of course, which makes Strauss's neo-classicism so unpalatable to Stravinsky—the incorrigibly romantic character of the actual style. The trouble was that in *Ariadne* Strauss was unable to go the whole neo-classical way, because of his ineradicable Wagnerian inheritance. Not only did he magically romanticize Mozart for the lyrical music, and Viennese operetta for the *commedia dell' arte* characters, but he often fell back on his own complex and Wagnerianly violent romantic idiom for forceful purposes, and he made pervasive use of a typically Wagnerian leitmotif—a powerful rising arpeggio-figure—to bind the whole structure together.

The resulting intensity of the material had its effect on the orchestration. Strauss innocently began with the ultra-classical idea of 'chamber music' for 'fifteen to twenty players in all'—single wind and strings, one or two horns, 'possibly a trumpet', harpsichord, harp, celesta, harmonium, and percussion—but this was clearly unrealistic for any operatic score which he could write. He eventually used an orchestra of thirty-six—double wind, sixteen strings, two horns, trumpet, trombone, two harps, celesta, and percussion; the harpsichord ominously gave way to a piano, and the harmonium remained, to be used sometimes with felicitous imagination but more often to thicken the texture unduly. This is still a chamber orchestra, of course, and indeed it is used with the most fastidious delicacy for many numbers; but Strauss, with his fantastic orchestral technique, was able to blow up its sonority, when he needed, into something which was hardly distinguishable from his rich and weighty full orchestral style. He could never have done this with the smaller group.

The work is a fascinating hybrid, then—and also very uneven in quality. Strauss's fatal lack of self-criticism, his acceptance of inferior inspiration and his facile development of it, spoils at least a third of the score. The prologue, set outside the opera itself in the eighteenth century, is a masterly piece of Straussian social comedy, and the delicate music of Ariadne herself and the three nymphs is exquisite almost throughout; but the *commedia dell' arte* characters, after a delightful start with their operetta-type polka, soon begin spinning out second-rate material at length. The big coloratura aria of Zebinetta, who is so excellent in the Prologue, unhappily revives the most regrettable features of the old display aria; and Bacchus enters like a god only to degenerate into a stock Italian tenor—sometimes into Strauss's own sticky parody of that type in the weakest spot of *Der Rosenkavalier*.

So, like Stravinsky, one enters the quicksands of personal taste, though less recklessly, to suggest that when Strauss is bad—which is only in certain parts of his *oeuvre*—his failure is indeed due to an undiscriminating use of cheap and poor material. Such intermittent lapses in *Ariadne* may well cause it to fall somewhat from its present ascendancy. As for *The Rake's Progress*, which is still much too new for any balanced critical assessment, one wonders what posterity's verdict will be. Perhaps it will ratify that, between the frequently over-heated Strauss and the often refrigerated Stravinsky, there was and always will be the classical golden mean—the sane, human warmth that Mozart defined so precisely.

[1961]

Shakespeare Into Music

Modern literary theory holds that a literary work exists entirely in its words: conceptions such as its 'ideas' or 'characters' cannot exist independently of the text. Likewise, modern musical theory declares that a musical work exists entirely in its notes; and further, that when words are set to music, or taken as 'inspiration' for a purely instrumental work, they lose all rights of their own and become complete slaves to musical considerations. How, then, can we establish any connection between Shakespeare's plays and the music ostensibly inspired by them?

We may begin by recognizing that certain important moments in the verbal texts are themselves musical. It is unthinkable, for instance, that *Othello* should ever be performed with the 'song of willow' *spoken*. As a late culmination of poetic-tragic tension, Desdemona's 'Sing willow, willow, willow' is as indispensable as Macbeth's 'Tomorrow and tomorrow and tomorrow', but it belongs to quite a different order of poetry. It is a 'lyric'—which is dramatically nothing without a musical setting. Thus Shakespeare himself turned to words-plus-music for a peculiar type of dramatic effect, even to the extent of appropriating, as here, an already existing ballad, lyric as well as tune. But this dramatic use of words-plus-music was only possible because, when a Shakespearean lyric (whether by him or not) is coupled with a simple tune, neither poetry nor music dominates. Simultaneously, the lyric gives verbal sense and sound and feeling, and the tune gives musical sense and sound and feeling, the two fusing into a single dramatic effect which is neither words nor notes, but song. This is the true Shakespearean music, as deeply moving in its dramatic context as any in existence.

But the lyric's integrity must be left inviolate by a tune which fits the verse's rhythmic dance exactly and provides only one note (or two slurred together) per syllable, so that the words retain all their intelligibility and 'verbal music'. That was the Elizabethan way; but when, with Purcell, we 'come unto these ye-he-he . . . hellow sands' or, with Dr Arne, 'on a bat's back we do fly-y-y . . . y', music is flaunting itself at the expense of the lyric, and the dramatic effect of song is impaired. Fine though such creations are as art-songs, the syllabic Elizabethan tunes are best for the lyrics in performances of the plays. Yet of the many composers who, since the romantics' rediscovery of Shakespeare, have set the lyrics as independent art-songs, most have intuitively grasped the syllabic trick, from Schubert in 'Hark hark the lark' to Quilter in 'O mistress mine' and Finzi in 'Come away death'. Such as these are still true Shakespearean music.

When it comes to setting Shakespeare's dramatic blank verse as opera, however, the true Shakespeare-lover can only admit that here modern literary and musical theory is right. The whole main essence of Shakespeare's art does exist in the incomparable poetic music-plus-meaning of his dialogue, and this has everything to lose and nothing to gain by being stretched on the rack of an operatic vocal line, which must distort it entirely in the interests of musico-dramatic effect. Opera is the composer's art: he must completely dominate his libretto—which, for a 'Shakespeare' opera, can only be made by cutting and re-shaping the original play into operatic form. But who would dare treat Shakespeare like this as a mere servant? English composers have almost unanimously avoided the plays. If we mercifully forget all about those misbegotten Restoration 'musicals', like *The Fairy Queen* ('after' *A Midsummer Night's Dream*), in which so much of Purcell's finest music lies virtually buried, then three little-prized works—Stanford's *Much Ado,* Holst's *At the Boar's Head,* and Vaughan Williams's *Sir John in Love*—exhaust the list of English 'Shakespeare' operas by reputable names. Except, that is, for Britten's *A Midsummer Night's Dream,* but even here the general rule holds good. Only the lyrics, like 'You spotted snakes' (superb syllabic settings), are true Shakespearean music; the remainder may be delectable Britten—but for the very reason that it is no longer Shakespeare. Anyone with a love of great poetry must continually wince at Britten's bullying of Shakespeare's dramatic verse into the service of his own dramatic music.

The amazingly long list of 'Shakespeare' operas, then, is almost entirely by foreign composers—who indeed have the advantage. Since they are dealing with translations, Shakespeare's poetic music-plus-meaning has yielded to something vastly inferior, which can be used without fear of sacrilege as verbal dross for transformation into musical gold. When even Boito's superb libretto for Verdi's *Otello* opens with the drunken brawl from Shakespeare's Act 2 Scene 3, set amid the storm of Act 2 Scene 1, and Othello enters with his 'Keep up your bright swords, for the dew will rust them' from Act 1 Scene 2, transformed into the peremptory command *'Abbasso le spade'* ('Down with your swords')—then clearly the textual Shakespeare has vanished ultimately. All that counts now is the spirit—Verdi's musico-dramatic presentation of Othello's commanding authority by that high tenor ejaculation which switches the tonality with shattering abruptness from the long noisy B minor of the brawl to his own immediate calm C minor of order restored. For we must insist, against the literary theorists, that there is, in one sense, a Shakespearean spirit independent of the original text. The characters, ideas, feelings, and events of the dramas have some general existence which survives translation, and so the foreign composer is free to create a completely new work enshrining the spirit of the original in purely operatic terms (a feat one could credit Britten with, were it not for the warring of two simultaneous spirits—the original poetic one, crippled, and the proxy musical one, soaring).

Yet how few successes there are in that seemingly endless list! Looking down it, one stares incredulously at unlikely shots such as Ambroise Thomas's *Hamlet* (what a thought!), at obvious outsiders like Ghislanzoni's *Re Lear,* and at such bewildering titles as Domenico Scarlatti's *Ambleto,* Otto Taubmann's *Porzia,* and even a *Dinah* by Edmond Missa (how far 'after' *Cymbeline* can that be?). The only possible reaction is a Paul Jennings outburst: 'Who *are* these people?—I see Ambleto, a hunch-backed Neapolitan pretender with an undershot jaw; Porzia, a portly pink-cheeked *Mädchen* sweeping into the Berlin *Gerichtshof* fresh from preparing a tasty *Bratwurst . . .*'. Whoever they may be, these people are hardly, one imagines, Shakespeare's characters. In the end, after pushing past reputable failures like Berlioz's *Béatrice et Bénédict,* once-popular misconceptions like Rossini's *Otello,* and modest successes like Nicolai's *Lustigen Weiber von Windsor,* we find ourselves alone with Verdi, who composed the only two great operas inspired by Shakespeare.

Two, and not three. Only during the present Verdi craze could his *Macbeth* be seriously set beside its tremendous original. What can we make of a Macbeth who pursues his fatal vision through a musical desert of the old fustian recitative, or a Lady Macbeth whose prayer to be unsexed is a barn-storming martial *cabaletta*? In the *Gran scena di sonnambulismo,* admittedly, Verdi did so magically stroke the big strumming guitar of his orchestra, and so chasten the vocal pride of Italian *bel canto,* as to foreshadow his achievements of some forty years later. *Otello* and *Falstaff,* those two towering masterpieces, were of course made possible by the librettos so selflessly prepared by his intellectual fellow-composer Boito (who in *Falstaff* even 'improved' on Shakespeare by convincingly weaving the best Falstaffian moments from the *Henry IV* plays into a taut recasting of *The Merry Wives*). But the glory, as always, goes entirely to the composer: Verdi alone—the old Verdi—could have transformed those clever scenarios into musical dramas filled with the true spirit of Shakespeare. Even if his lack of the hilarious comic touch of a Rossini meant the absence of a real sense of the uproarious in *Falstaff,* and operatic explicitness required Iago to declare his hand openly (and magnificently) to the audience as an atheistic nihilist, these are slight question-marks to set against two musical dramas which so superlatively recreate the profound human realities of the originals.

But it is significant that the only one of the great tragedies that has proved operatically tractable is the one which lacks the universal, metaphysical dimension. What could Verdi have made of the *King Lear* he planned? Indeed, could any composer operatically recreate this drama, or *Hamlet,* or *Macbeth,* or *Antony and Cleopatra*? It is tempting to imagine Wagner returning to Shakespeare, long after the Donizettified travesty of *Measure for Measure* of his youth that he called *Das Liebesverbot—The Ban on Love.* He alone among composers commanded a musical language commensurate with Shakespeare's poetic language, in its tremendous rhetorical sweep, its many-faceted symbolism, and its richness of interlocked imagery. *Die Meistersinger,* in fact, is a curiously Shakespearean comedy, in a *Twelfth Night* sense, both mellower and more richly comic than Verdi's *Falstaff.* But except in this comic vein, Wagner could hardly have handled Shakespeare's multiplicity of incident, since his own normal dramatic method in tragedy—moving each act imperceptibly forward to one single crucial event—goes back to the *Oresteia*. He was surely wise to avoid Shakespeare and become himself the only Shakespeare among opera-composers: a transformer of old legends into symbolic dramas entirely of his own creating—scenario, characters, meaning, music and all.

It might be thought an equally wise idea to ignore Shakespeare's actual texts altogether, and to transform the Shakespearean essence into pure music. Again the plays themselves offer a starting-point, for Shakespeare demanded pure music for many types of dramatic situation, from routine flourishes, through Brutus's sleeplessness, to the pitiful reunion of Lear and Cordelia. Here, for once, notes are the slaves of words, for they must not obtrude in their own right when creating the required atmosphere. Normally the composer need only follow accepted ways of writing 'mood music'; the *outré* is seldom indicated—though our avant-garde should be expert in providing Caliban's 'thousand twangling instruments'. In consequence, incidental music is rarely of enduring significance: deprived of its subsidiary place in the theatre, it cannot usually subsist in its own right. Glancing down an almost infinite list, one's eye stops occasionally with a gleam of admiring recognition (Berlioz's *Marche funèbre* for *Hamlet*) or curiosity (Shostakovich's music for *Othello, Hamlet,* and *King Lear*)—till suddenly it lights on the name of Mendelssohn, the fantastic exception which proves the rule.

And yet is it an exception? Certainly the main movements of the *Midsummer Night's Dream* music—the Overture, Nocturne, Scherzo, and Wedding March—stand magnificently in their own right as a concert suite; but for this very reason they seem uncomfortable in the theatre (the smaller items less so, especially the exquisite syllabic setting of the lyric 'You spotted snakes'). Even if one does not find, as some do, a fatal clash between the two different romanticisms of Elizabethan England and early nineteenth-century Germany, the effort of absorbing Shakespeare's poetry and Mendelssohn's music side by side can cause cultural indigestion. Most people prefer the music on the concert platform. But can it there, all alone, evoke the spirit of Shakespeare's play? The answer is simply 'as you like it, or what you will'. If you choose, you may let the fluttering strings conjure up Shakespeare's fairies, and even identify Cobweb, Pease-Blossom, and Mustard-Seed severally; likewise with the hee-hawing ninths and the ass's head, and all the rest. No one will either prevent you or force you.

And so it is with the many attempts to evoke a Shakespeare play in purely instrumental forms. Both Tchaikovsky, in his great fantasy-overture, and Berlioz, in his intermittently great 'dramatic symphony', place in opposition purely symphonic portrayals of the violence of armed conflict and the transports of youthful love— Tchaikovsky infusing the latter with a sense of inescapable doom, and Berlioz giving a further hint with a feathery fairy scherzo; yet neither can make explicit that the love is that of Shakespeare's Romeo and Juliet. (It is charitable to ignore the curious vocal part of Berlioz's work, since while one can let the symphonic music evoke the brawls and the lovers, if one wishes, one can hardly accept a *Romeo and Juliet* which consists dramatically of only Mercutio and Friar Lawrence, and those in evening dress, usually singing from an open vocal score, as in oratorio.) The same option is there with the only other great symphonic music inspired by Shakespeare: one may interpret Elgar's rich symphonic study, redolent of English humours and martial scenes amid the English countryside, as telling the story of Falstaff—if one so desires. In this, as in every other symphonic case, it is up to the listener to accept or reject the 'local habitation and a name' given by the composer to his pure music.

Again, as with Wagner and the operatic field, one likes to imagine Richard Strauss returning to Shakespeare some time after his not quite mature *Macbeth*. A *Falstaff* by him, composed before his decline, could have been the most vivid of Shakespearean symphonic poems, if he had brought to it all the salty humour, the prodigious fantasy, and the unique gift for making the listener 'see with his ears', that he had displayed so supremely in his *Don Quixote*. But perhaps he too became wise in his maturity. He was certainly well-advised not to touch the great tragedies, as others had done and failed. No doubt he was realist enough to see that, even if it might just be possible that a great opera could be made out of *King Lear, Hamlet, Macbeth,* or *Antony and Cleopatra*, any composer attempting to transform one of them into pure music would be chasing as wild a goose as he who should try to transform Beethoven's Fifth Symphony into pure poetry.

[1964]

Reading and Re-reading
Wuthering Heights

When I was a boy, in the nineteen-twenties, our solitary bookcase at home had one shelf which was still a common feature of many a household at that time. It contained a row of old novels, all in the same cheap binding—one of the many popular collected editions of famous Victorian best-sellers. Some of them had mysterious sounding place names for titles—*The Mill on the Floss, East Lynne*; others had women's names—*Jane Eyre, Lorna Doone*; several of them were written by women. To me, as a boy, the whole atmosphere surrounding them, even before I opened one of them, was romantic. And there with the rest was *Wuthering Heights* by Emily Brontë.

Later, of course, I discovered that these novels, though they were all romantic, varied considerably in artistic quality; and when I came to read *Wuthering Heights* I wondered what it was doing on that shelf at all. Its companions, on their various levels, had seemed romantic in a rather old-fashioned, stilted way; but this novel was romantic and vividly real at the same time. I couldn't put it down: I read on, gripped, enthralled, and frequently appalled. Since then I've gone back to it many times, and every re-reading has confirmed my opinion that it's one of the greatest novels ever written, as well as being one of the most easily readable.

But I think the aura of that old type of bookshelf still lingers on for many people today. For those who haven't read *Wuthering Heights*, I'm sure, a vague impression of old-fashioned feminine romanticism must cling to the title; and anyone who has seen the famous film of it, with the young Laurence Olivier and Merle Oberon, will have had this impression only too plausibly confirmed, since it watered the novel down into a sentimental novelette.

Even people with a vague memory of the novel will hardly have noticed the difference. Literature, like history in *1066 and All That*, is what people remember; and what everybody remembers about *Wuthering Heights* is the passionate love between an outcast, gypsy-type hero, Heathcliff, and a high-spirited farmer's daughter of a heroine, Cathy, set against the background of the Yorkshire moors. These sound like the stock properties of romance, and the film treated them as such; but once we return to the novel itself, we find any idea of romance blown to the winds by a ruthless realism.

I may seem to be contradicting myself, since I've said that the novel is both real and romantic. In fact, like all great works of art, *Wuthering Heights* moves on several different levels at the same time, and one of these levels is romantic—but in the true, fundamental sense of the word, which has nothing to do with conventional romance. I'll explain later what I mean by this; but I'd like to concentrate mainly on the basic level, which is all too often forgotten—the level of realism.

Any discussion of *Wuthering Heights* should start from the plain fact that it can be read quite simply as an exciting and moving story about true-to-life people in true-to-life situations. The Yorkshire moors don't feature as a romantic backcloth, but as the perfectly natural setting of the story; and the house Wuthering Heights itself, in spite of its romantic-sounding name, is a solid old Yorkshire farmhouse, which is described in the most meticulously realistic detail. Some of the main characters are certainly passionate, violent, and even brutal; but they behave as such people would in real life, not like vague figments of the imagination. Even Charlotte Brontë, who made no secret of her distaste for sister Emily's novel, because it was so brutal, took it for granted that it was true to the life of the locality where they lived, in its darker aspects.

Let's start by considering the hero of the novel, Heathcliff. In a typical romance, the outcast type of hero is an idealized, glamourized figure. An aura of mystery surrounds him, and, however dubious his actions may be, he seems somehow well-intentioned, perhaps misguided, likeable enough to retain our sympathy, and ultimately redeemable. But Emily Brontë portrays Heathcliff in such a down-to-earth way as a hard, vindictive, unforgiving nature, that he forfeits any sympathy we might have had for him; in fact he figures as an anti-hero, in the modern sense.

The only mystery about Heathcliff is his origin; but this is merely mysterious in the sense that a person's origin may be obscure in real life. The master of Wuthering Heights, old Mr. Earnshaw, finds one day, on a visit to Liverpool, a dirty, ragged, dark-haired waif, who speaks some incomprehensible language—probably a gypsy's child, or a Lascar's. He takes him home to Wuthering Heights, christens him Heathcliff, and brings him up with his own children—Cathy, about the same age, and Hindley, seven years older; and this soon causes trouble in the Earnshaw household. The old man makes a favourite of Heathcliff, with the result that Hindley comes to hate the boy, and bullies him; nobody is kind to him except the old man and Cathy, who takes his part against Hindley.

At the start, then, we are apparently expected to feel a strong sympathy for Heathcliff. But our sympathy is soon counteracted when we find that he is neither grateful for his benefactor's kindness, nor hurt by anybody's ill-treatment: he is simply concerned with turning both to his own account, with iron determination. We learn this from a scene between the two boys not long after Heathcliff's arrival; it's related to us by the servant Ellen Dean, the main narrator of the story:

> I remember Mr. Earnshaw once bought a couple of colts at the parish fair, and gave the lads each one. Heathcliff took the handsomest, but it soon fell lame, and when he discovered it, he said to Hindley—
> "You must exchange horses with me: I don't like mine; and if you won't I shall tell your father of the three thrashings you've given me this week, and show him my arm, which is black to the shoulder." Hindley put out his tongue and cuffed him over the ears. "You'd better do it at once," he persisted, escaping to the porch (they were in the stable): "you will have to; and if I speak of these blows, you'll get them again with interest." "Off, dog!" cried Hindley, threatening him with an iron weight used for weighing potatoes and hay. "Throw it," he replied, standing still, "and then I'll tell how you boasted that you would turn me out of doors as soon as he died, and see whether he will not turn you out directly." Hindley threw it, hitting him on the breast, and down he fell, but staggered up immediately, breathless and white; and, had not I prevented it, he would have gone just so to the master, and got full

revenge by letting his condition plead for him, intimating who had caused it. "Take my colt, gipsy, then!" said young Earnshaw. "And I pray that he may break your neck: take him, and be damned, you beggarly interloper! and wheedle my father out of all he has: only afterwards show him what you are, imp of Satan.—And take that, I hope he'll kick out your brains!"

Heathcliff had gone to loose the beast, and shift it to his own stall; he was passing behind it, when Hindley finished his speech by knocking him under its feet, and without stopping to examine whether his hopes were fulfilled, ran away as fast as he could. I was surprised to witness how coolly the child gathered himself up, and went on with his intention; exchanging saddles and all, and then sitting down on a bundle of hay to overcome the qualm which the violent blow occasioned, before he entered the house. I persuaded him easily to let me lay the blame of his bruises on the horse: he minded little what tale was told since he had what he wanted.

This scene typifies the realism of the novel—the way passion arises out of practical everyday affairs and culminates in crude physical violence. Now we might perhaps expect that Heathcliff's relationship with Cathy will be set in contrast with this, showing him in a more idealized and sympathetic light, and providing the 'love-interest' of the novel. But the love between Heathcliff and Cathy isn't romantic love at all, in the usual sense of the word, and neither of them is idealized in the slightest.

Their relationship begins, as I've said, when they are children, and Cathy takes Heathcliff's side against the bullying Hindley. When old Mr. Earnshaw dies, Hindley marries and becomes master of Wuthering Heights; he takes the opportunity to tyrannize over Heathcliff and Cathy, and further, he degrades Heathcliff to the position of a farm-labourer. As he also neglects their upbringing, and ill-treats both of them, Cathy as well as Heathcliff, the union-in-rebellion of the two young people grows stronger during their teens, and they grow up tough and wild.

But Cathy eventually makes friends with the son and daughter of the refined Linton family, who live four miles away, at Thrushcross Grange; and here she finds a world of civilized comfort and good manners which is quite new to her. Under their influence, she begins to become quite a little lady, and as a result, she soon finds herself torn between the dark, unkempt, savage Heathcliff, the inseparable companion of her unhappy childhood, and the fair, well-groomed, gentlemanly Edgar, for whom she begins to feel a youthful infatuation.

The outcome, naturally, is a sequence of furious quarrels. But these aren't romantic scenes played out by idealized lovers with the moors as a background: they are true-to-life family scenes, played out by very real adolescents in the main room of Wuthering Heights; and again they involve practical everyday activities, and culminate in physical violence. Heathcliff and Edgar Linton inevitably come into conflict. Edgar and Isabella are invited to Wuthering Heights for Christmas Eve; and Ellen Dean manages to persuade Heathcliff to spruce himself up so as to be able to join the company and not be outshone by Edgar. The moment Edgar arrives, the trouble begins; it's set off by the tyrannical Hindley, who won't have Heathcliff with the rest of the company at any price:

> "He shall have his share of my hand, if I catch him downstairs till dark," cried Hindley. "Begone, you vagabond! What! you are attempting the coxcomb, are you? Wait till I get hold of those elegant locks—see if I won't pull them a bit longer."
>
> "They are long enough, already," observed Master Linton, peeping from the doorway; "I wonder they don't make his head ache. It's like a colt's mane over his eyes!"
>
> He ventured this remark without any intention to insult; but Heathcliff's violent nature was not prepared to endure the appearance of impertinence from one whom he seemed to hate, even then, as a rival. He seized a tureen of hot apple sauce (the first thing that came under his gripe) and dashed it full against the speaker's face and neck; who instantly commenced a lament that brought Isabella and Catherine hurrying to the place. Mr. Earnshaw snatched up the culprit directly and conveyed him to his chamber; where, doubtless, he administered a rough remedy to cool the fit of passion, for he appeared red and breathless.

Again, we're inclined to feel sympathy for Heathcliff, but we're not allowed to forget what he is really like. When Ellen Dean tries

to console him, we find that he is more than a match for Hindley in
implacable malevolence:

> I set him a stool by the fire, and offered him a quantity of good
> things; but he was sick and could eat little, and my attempts to
> entertain him were thrown away. He leant his two elbows on
> his knees, and his chin on his hands, and remained wrapt in
> dumb meditation. On my inquiring the subject of his thoughts,
> he answered gravely:
>
> "I'm trying to settle how I shall pay Hindley back. I don't
> care how long I wait, if I can only do it at last. I hope he will not
> die before I do!"
>
> "For shame, Heathcliff!" said I. "It is for God to punish
> wicked people; we should learn to forgive."
>
> "No, God won't have the satisfaction that I shall," he
> returned. "I only wish I knew the best way! Let me alone, and
> I'll plan it out: while I'm thinking of that I don't feel pain."

Cathy is no more idealized than Heathcliff. The next scene,
though it marks a crucial stage in her relationship with Edgar,
actually reveals the essential unity between her passionate, violent
temperament and Heathcliff's as opposed to Edgar's mild and
inoffensive nature. It comes about because Ellen, on Hindley's
instructions, stays in the room dusting the plate, so as not to leave
Cathy and Edgar alone together. Cathy tries to get her to leave;
and when Ellen refuses, she flies into a rage, which not only falls on
Ellen, but on Hindley's two-year-old son Hareton, and even on
Edgar himself:

> She, supposing Edgar could not see her, snatched the cloth
> from my hand, and pinched me, with a prolonged wrench,
> very spitefully on the arm. I've said I did not love her, and
> rather relished mortifying her vanity now and then: besides,
> she hurt me extremely; so I started up from my knees, and
> screamed out, "Oh, miss, that's a nasty trick! You have no
> right to nip me, and I'm not going to bear it."
>
> "I didn't touch you, you lying creature!" cried she, her
> fingers tingling to repeat the act, and her ears red with rage.
> She never had power to conceal her passion, it always set her
> whole complexion in a blaze.
>
> "What's that, then?" I retorted, showing a decided purple

witness to refute her.

She stamped her foot, wavered a moment, and then irresistibly impelled by the naughty spirit within her, slapped me on the cheek: a stinging blow that filled both eyes with water.

"Catherine, love! Catherine!" interposed Linton, greatly shocked at the double fault of falsehood and violence which his idol had committed.

"Leave the room, Ellen!" she repeated, trembling all over.

Little Hareton, who followed me everywhere, and was sitting near me on the floor, at seeing my tears commenced crying himself, and sobbed out complaints against "wicked aunt Cathy," which drew her fury on to his unlucky head: she seized his shoulders, and shook him till the poor child waxed livid, and Edgar thoughtlessly laid hold of her hands to deliver him. In an instant one was wrung free, and the astonished young man felt it applied over his own ear in a way that could not be mistaken for jest. He drew back in consternation. I lifted Hareton in my arms, and walked off to the kitchen with him, leaving the door of communication open, for I was curious to watch how they would settle their disagreement.

They settle it, eventually, by confessing their love for each other; and in so far as there is any 'love-interest' in the novel, it is between Cathy and Edgar. But this 'love-interest' is actually a realistic portrayal of the kind of childish infatuation we might expect from a very young girl—Cathy is fifteen at the time; and it is set off against the central relationship of the novel—that between Cathy and Heathcliff. This love-relationship involves no 'falling in love': it's more like the indissoluble bond of a deep and passionate friendship between two people who feel themselves as one indivisible unity. When Cathy, soon afterwards, accepts Edgar's proposal of marriage, and thus separates herself from Heathcliff, she knows she is going against her own deepest nature: after telling Ellen she intends to marry Edgar, she goes on to confess the bedrock nature of her love for Heathcliff:

"It would degrade me to marry Heathcliff now; so he shall never know how I love him: and that, not because he's handsome, Nelly, but because he's more myself than I am. Whatever our souls are made of, his and mine are the same;

and Linton's is as different as a moonbeam from lightning, or frost from fire.... My great miseries in this world have been Heathcliff's miseries, and I watched and felt each from the beginning: my great thought in living is himself. If all else perished and *he* remained, *I* should still continue to be; and if all else remained, and he were annihilated, the universe would turn to a mighty stranger: I should not seem a part of it. My love for Linton is like the foliage in the woods: time will change it, I'm well aware, as winter changes the trees. My love for Heathcliff resembles the eternal rocks beneath: a source of little visible delight, but necessary. Nelly, I *am* Heathcliff! He's always, always in my mind: not as a pleasure, any more than I am always a pleasure to myself, but as my own being."

It's unfortunate that Heathcliff happens to overhear Cathy talking to Ellen about her intention to marry Edgar, as far as her remark that it would degrade her to marry him, and that he immediately steals away in despair without waiting to hear any more, and runs away from Wuthering Heights. Cathy, when she discovers this, falls into a prolonged paroxysm of inconsolable grief which weakens her constitution; but after three years have passed, and it seems that Heathcliff has gone for good, she marries Edgar. Edgar's parents have died in the meantime, and so he and Cathy become master and mistress of Thrushcross Grange, with Ellen as their maid.

At this point, our sympathy has certainly been reawakened for Heathcliff, in spite of his bad nature; but when he returns, very soon after the marriage, it vanishes once and for all. We soon find that his threats of vengeance as a boy were no passing moods.

He's better-off, better-spoken, better-educated—superficially a gentleman: these are the weapons he has provided himself with, to get even with the world. His frustrated love for Cathy is still a main theme; but it gradually gives way to the other main theme—that of his revenge—which dominates the whole second half of the novel, continuing after Cathy's death to involve a completely new generation.

Heathcliff's revenge, which I can only summarize, is a merciless dispossession of his former enemies, Hindley and Edgar. Hindley, after his wife's death, has become a drunkard and a gambler, and Heathcliff gambles him out of house and home, and into the grave;

and having thus become master of Wuthering Heights, he degrades Hindley's young son Hareton as Hindley had degraded him. His persistent visits to Thrushcross Grange, which the hapless Edgar has to allow to placate Cathy, inevitably lead to conflict; she is torn once more between the two men, and this brings on a breakdown which affects her mind and causes her death in giving birth to a daughter, Catherine.

Although stunned by her death, Heathcliff continues with his plans. Isabella has entertained a foolish infatuation for him, in spite of Cathy's warnings; and although he hates her as much as he hates Edgar, he elopes with her, with the set purpose of becoming the heir to Thrushcross Grange through her right. Edgar disinherits his sister, and later she bears Heathcliff a sickly son, Linton. Linton dies when he is only seventeen; but just before he dies, Heathcliff abducts Catherine and bullies the boy into a forced marriage with her, so as to become heir to Thrushcross Grange by his son's right. Edgar and Isabella, broken by their experiences, both die early; and so Heathcliff, with all his childhood associates dead, lives at Wuthering Heights as master of both houses, tyrannizing over the two dispossessed young heirs, the innocent Catherine and Hareton, who are utterly dependent on him.

Heathcliff's revenge is so realistically effected, through mortgages, marriage-settlements and wills, that some critics have gone as far as to describe the novel as basically one of social protest—the expropriation of the expropriators by the expropriated. There's certainly much truth in this view: Heathcliff's severely materialistic conception of vengeance has already been revealed by the childhood incident when he gets possession of Hindley's colt; and it's now openly avowed by him when he makes clear to Ellen that he looks on his sickly son Linton merely as a tool to serve his own ends:

> "Well," replied I, "I hope you'll be kind to the boy, Mr. Heathcliff, or you'll not keep him long; and he's all you have akin in the wide world, that you will ever know—remember."
>
> "I'll be *very* kind to him, you needn't fear," he said, laughing. "Only nobody else must be kind to him: I'm jealous of monopolising his affection. And, to begin my kindness, Joseph, bring the lad some breakfast. Hareton, you infernal calf, begone to your work. Yes, Nell," he added, when they

had departed, "my son is prospective owner of your place, and I should not wish him to die till I was certain of being his successor. Besides, he's *mine*, and I want the triumph of seeing *my* descendant fairly lord of their estates: my child hiring their children to till their father's lands for wages. That is the sole consideration which can make me endure the whelp: I depise him for himself, and hate him for the memories he revives!

The extra realistic element of physical violence also continues, and now it moves more and more on to the plane of gratuitous cruelty, as when Heathcliff hangs Isabella's pet dog at the very moment he elopes with her. Cathy, too, in spite of her respectable position as Mrs. Edgar Linton, is still involved in physical violence, owing to Heathcliff's presence. To take only one instance, she brings Isabella before Heathcliff, on one of his visits to Thrushcross Grange, and tells him of her infatuation for him, holding her there by force while she does so, to endure his contempt:

> And he stared hard at the object of discourse, as one might do at a strange repulsive animal: a centipede from the Indies, for instance, which curiosity leads one to examine in spite of the aversion it raises. The poor thing couldn't bear that: she grew white and red in rapid succession, and, while tears beaded her lashes, bent the strength of her small fingers to loosen the firm clutch of Catherine; and perceiving that as fast as she raised one finger off her arm another closed down, and she could not remove the whole together, she began to make use of her nails; and their sharpness presently ornamented the detainer's with crescents of red.
>
> "There's a tigress!" exclaimed Mrs. Linton, setting her free, and shaking her head with pain. "Begone, for God's sake, and hide your vixen face! How foolish to reveal those talons to *him*. Can't you fancy the conclusions he'll draw? Look, Heathcliff! they are instruments that will do execution—you must beware of your eyes."
>
> "I'd wrench them off her fingers, if they ever menaced me," he answered brutally, when the door had closed after her.

The relationship between Heathcliff and Cathy moves further away than ever from any possible idealization. Cathy knows exactly what Heathcliff is, and doesn't expect him to be otherwise;

yet she is still just as inseparable from him in spirit. She reveals this, a little before the scene just quoted from, when she warns Isabella against Heathcliff, and gives her a most exact and unflattering character-sketch of him:

> Pray, don't imagine that he conceals depths of benevolence and affection beneath a stern exterior! He's not a rough diamond—a pearl-containing oyster of a rustic: he's a fierce, pitiless, wolfish man. I never say to him, 'Let this or that enemy alone, because it would be ungenerous or cruel to harm them;' I say, 'Let them alone, because *I* should hate them to be wronged:' and he'd crush you like a sparrow's egg, Isabella, if he found you a troublesome charge. I know he couldn't love a Linton; and yet he'd be quite capable of marrying your fortune and expectations! avarice is growing with him a besetting sin. There's my picture: and I'm his friend—so much so, that had he thought seriously to catch you, I should, perhaps, have held my tongue, and let you fall into his trap."

Heathcliff, too, has no illusions about Cathy, though he wishes she could have been otherwise and stayed faithful to him. In the only scene between them which can be regarded as in any way a love-scene—when Heathcliff comes to Thrushcross Grange in Edgar's absence to find Cathy near to death, and they fiercely embrace and kiss for the first time—he reproaches her bitterly for betraying their bond, without attempting to deceive her or himself, and yet he ends by disavowing any desire to live on without her:

> "You teach me now how cruel you've been—cruel and false. *Why* did you despise me? *Why* did you betray your own heart, Cathy? I have not one word of comfort. You deserve this. You have killed yourself. Yes, you may kiss me, and cry; and ring out my kisses and tears: they'll blight you—they'll damn you. You loved me—then what *right* had you to leave me? What right—answer me—for the poor fancy you felt for Linton? Because misery and degradation, and death, and nothing that God or Satan could inflict would have parted us, *you*, of your own will, did it. I have not broken your heart— *you* have broken it; and in breaking it, you have broken mine. So much the worse for me, that I am strong. Do I want to live? What kind of living will it be when you—oh, God! would *you*

like to live with your soul in the grave?''

If, as I have tried to show, *Wuthering Heights* is basically a realistic novel, concerned with unidealized, true-to-life characters of an unsympathetic kind, where does the genuine romanticism come in, which I mentioned at the beginning?

True romanticism is the artistic impulse which insists on bringing up to the surface the raw, primitive, unmoral force of life which lies submerged and tamed beneath the essentially classical order of civilized society; and Heathcliff and Cathy are a magnificent expression of this force. The truth is, strangely enough, that while we read the complete novel, something inside us does sympathize with them, or rather, it identifies itself with them, as against the debilitated civilized conformity of Edgar and Isabella Linton, who do nobody any harm. It's the same response we have to other great romantic figures whose behaviour is socially destructive, such as Don Juan and Faust. But figures like these are purely symbolic: the achievement of that strange woman Emily Brontë was to make use of her knowledge of certain aspects of the only partly civilized community in which she lived, to evoke the same response through true-to-life characters acting realistically in a real world. We identify ourselves with the life-force in Heathcliff and Cathy, however horrified we may be at the distorted form forced on it by the injustices of an inequitable society; we even identify ourselves with it in Heathcliff alone, as it avenges itself viciously on that society by destroying the pillars of it. The life-force is the whole romantic essence of the novel, even when the final release of tension turns the darkness to dawn. This only happens when the two dispossessed young heirs, Hareton and Catherine, who are both vital and likeable young people, join forces to defy Heathcliff and demand their rights: it's when he recognizes in them something of his own tremendous strength beginning to operate with a reconstructive purpose, that he is content to relinquish his hollow victory, and to join Cathy in the grave.

The life-force, in both Heathcliff and Cathy, is conveyed at its highest through a non-realistic means—through the heightened poetic language which is superimposed at times on their real feelings, especially in their expression of their unity with one another, as we have seen. It is also conveyed by one other non-realistic feature—the haunting of Heathcliff by Cathy's ghost, and the appearance of both of them as ghosts at the end of the novel. But even these supernatural elements are anything but the trappings of romance. They are tied firmly to the realistic level by being represented as dreams, hallucinations, and superstition; and they are there for the fundamental romantic purpose of suggesting the indestructibility of the life-force that Heathcliff and Cathy represent—its survival in spite of death.

Survival of the life-force, but not of the individual life, in the form of a disembodied phantom existence, as Emily Brontë is careful to make clear. At the very end, Mr. Lockwood—a stranger to the district, to whom Ellen Dean has been telling the whole story—walks away to the churchyard to see the graves of Heathcliff, Cathy, and Edgar. He remembers that a little shepherd lad recently came crying in terror to Ellen one night, saying he had seen the ghosts of Heathcliff and Cathy walking the moors. But he dismisses the fancy in a final benediction which brings the terrible story to a beautifully quiet ending, by suggesting the absorption back into nature of the dynamic human vitality which it continually brings forth:

> I sought, and soon discovered, the three head-stones on the slope next the moor: the middle one grey, and half buried in heath: Edgar Linton's only harmonised by the turf and moss creeping up its foot: Heathcliff's still bare.
>
> I lingered round them, under that benign sky; watched the moths fluttering among the heath and harebells, listened to the soft wind breathing through the grass, and wondered how any one could ever imagine unquiet slumbers for the sleepers in that quiet earth.

[1965]

Reactionary

Writing about the new music—post-Schoenberg music—is a futile occupation for a reactionary: everything you write implies that you wish music had followed a different path in this century, but you can't roll back history. So I'm giving it up altogether; but before I sign off, I'd like to explain briefly what makes me a reactionary. It's a simple fundamental fact which lies unacknowledged beneath all the technical surface talk of atonality, dodecaphony, serialism, and what have you: the really crucial thing that happened to music in Schoenberg's hands was that it completely severed contact with the musical vernacular, in which it had always been rooted.

This statement itself sounds technical—but don't stop reading, even if you have no technical knowledge and can't read music. I can explain. Find a piano, and look, near the centre of the keyboard, at one of the groups of three black keys (as opposed to the groups of two): strike the white key between the left and centre black keys, then the next but one white key to the right of it, and then the next but one white key to the right of that. Technically speaking, these are the first, third, and fifth degrees of the major scale; but ages before this analytical description was thought up, the complete sequence of three sounds was used instinctively as one of the basic terms of the musical vernacular, and it's been used ever since, in folk, traditional and popular music alike. To mention only three examples through the ages, it's the starting point of the 'Eriskay Love Lilt', the German chorale 'Sleepers Wake' and 'The Blue Danube'. Try it and hear.

This bright, confident phrase—together with its many fellow-terms, which cover a wide range of human feelings—was taken over from the vernacular by art-composers and used likewise by them as the basis of their music. Again, taking only three instances, our term begins Bach's E major Violin Concerto, the finale of

Beethoven's Fifth Symphony and the finale of Dvorak's Fourth. Once more, try it and hear. But with Schoenberg, from about 1908 onwards, this and every other term of the musical vernacular vanished, and remained absent from all the new music—Webern, Boulez, Stockhausen and the rest. The vernacular itself, of course, remains as securely founded on these terms as it ever was (our particularly cheerful term is the basis of that cracking Beatle tune 'Can't buy me love'); and they're still the basis of music by composers who haven't followed Schoenberg (Britten used our term, with superb tragic irony, for the 'Bugles sang' section of his *War Requiem*).

But so what? Isn't it a great step forward to cut adrift from the vernacular and evolve a completely new musical language altogether? Perhaps, for some people; but it's as though the whole main modern school of literature had taken Joyce's *Finnegans Wake* as its starting-point. No doubt there are *littérateurs* who wish that this had happened; if so, they should change over to music, where its equivalent has actually taken place. I know that I, like almost everybody, can't *live* with *Finnegans Wake*; and if modern literature had followed that path, few of us would still be reading it. I enjoy Sterne, Melville or Graham Greene for the expressive miracles they achieve with the immediately intelligible vernacular; and that's what I enjoy in Bach, Wagner or Britten. When I read *Finnegans Wake*, I can only goggle at an artist achieving a well-nigh incomprehensible miracle with a private language of his own; and the same applies to listening to Schoenberg. Briefly, 'music', for me, means what it always used to mean—music based on the common musical language, the vernacular. So I shall just have to go on concerning myself with that, and ignore the other 'music'—the sort based on one man's private language.

[1967]

The Lennon–McCartney Songs

My recent confession that I'd finished with post-Schoenberg music, because it had rejected the musical vernacular, was apparently taken in some quarters as an attack on Schoenberg himself, and a call for a return to musical 'sanity'. In fact, it was neither. It was a statement of a personal dilemma, which seemed worth making since it's clearly the dilemma of others as well.

No musician likes living entirely in the past. He wants to follow the development of present-day music towards the future; and I've no quarrel with genuine followers of the Schoenberg-to-Stockhausen line. It's just that I can't breathe in a world where the common musical language evolved by humanity at large has been abandoned for the private language invented by a single individual. So I follow the development of the vernacular by composers like Britten and Shostakovich—but this hardly leads to the future, since young composers everywhere dismiss the vernacular as 'exhausted', and follow the non-vernacular path. At which point I face a cul-de-sac—or I would do if I weren't aware that all music is music, not just the 'serious' kind, and that the vernacular is still far from exhausted—self-renewing, rather—in the world of popular music which gave it birth.

Of course, in turning to popular music, one risks reproach from colleagues for debasing standards. But the only realistic standard is the one which operates on all levels—that of creative genius, manifest in ultimate durability. The only English Victorian composer still alive today is Sullivan; the only Austrian one, except Bruckner, is Johann Strauss; Gershwin seems certain to outlive his 'serious' American contemporaries. And my guess is that Lennon and McCartney will still be remembered when most of our 'modern composers' are forgotten by everybody except musical historians.

Some 'serious' musicians have already acclaimed these songwriters—notably Hans Keller, William Mann and Wilfrid Mellers. But Keller apart (in television appearances), they haven't explained what is so special about them. There has been too much concentration on harmony, following Mann's original dovecot-fluttering *Times* article of 1963, with its references to 'pandiatonic clusters' and 'flat-submediant key-switches'. A purely harmonic analysis is misleading, and only invites misleading retorts: Sir Jack Westrup, damning all pop music in the current *Music and Letters*, talks of 'harmonic ingenuities which serious critics mistakenly attribute to the singers instead of the expert musicians who write the "backing"'. Actually, this cannot apply to Lennon and McCartney, whose harmonic originality is evident in several songs written before they entered the commercial pop world, but it's irrelevant anyway, since an outstanding pop song is a structural fusion of harmonic, rhythmic and melodic originality, like any other outstanding piece of music.

Still, Mann was accurate; others have since fared worse. Glenn Gould, writing in the November 1967 *High Fidelity*, attributes the appeal of the Lennon-McCartney songs to a 'happy, cocky, belligerently resourceless brand of harmonic primitivism'. According to him, 'the chromatic bent that infiltrated big-band arrangements in the Thirties and Forties ran its course' and the reason for Lennon and McCartney's success is 'our need of the common chord as purgative'; however, they themselves are 'entirely incidental' in this situation, since 'almost all pop music today is relentlessly diatonic.' He then compares their songs unfavourably with four by Tony Hatch—'Down Town', 'Sign of the Times', 'My Love' and 'Who am I'—saying that although in these 'the harmonic attitude is relentlessly diatonic,' nevertheless 'for Tony Hatch tonality is not a worked-out lode.'

Which only shows how far astray a general harmonic approach can lead. The big-band arrangement is in an entirely different category from the popular song, which has always been relentlessly diatonic and based on common chords; but Lennon and McCartney continually juxtapose these chords, and others, in surprising new relationships, mingling major, minor, Dorian, Aeolian, Lydian and Blues progressions in unprecedented ways. It's for them that tonality isn't a worked-out lode, and it's Hatch who is harmonically resourceless and primitive, since he uses little but the most conventional major progressions.

What his songs do have is appealing tunes—and that is the crux of the matter, since a popular song is primarily an appealing tune. Melodic appeal is impossible to analyse, but it's easy to identify, since any song which has it catches on, however banal its rhythm and harmony, whereas the most ingenious rhythm and harmony can't save a tune which lacks it. Even so, an appealing tune which has no rhythmic or harmonic originality soon wears out. The four Hatch songs mentioned have neither, except for 'Down Town', with its tense syncopated approach to its climax—and in fact this song is wearing best. But an appealing tune which does have rhythmic or harmonic originality lasts infinitely: the characteristic Lennon-McCartney song has so much of both as to need a few hearings for its appeal to register, but then it survives any number of hearings.

Rhythmic originality is the most important, especially as regards bar-periods, since popular song has long been confined to an appalling eight-bar monotony. An eight-bar section, repeated; a 'middle eight' and the first eight again: only the finest songs have overcome this crippling restriction, by sheer melodic and harmonic inspiration. One or two nearly escaped, without realising it: 'Stormy Weather' has a genuine seven-bar first section, spoiled by Harold Arlen's mechanical addition of an unnecessary instrumental bar to make up the eight. But Lennon and McCartney have broken completely free: sections of five, seven, nine, 11 and 13 bars are nothing to them. Particularly remarkable, as Keller pointed out, is 'Strawberry Fields', with its nine-bar first section divided into 1½, 2, 2, 1½ and 2, the penultimate bar being in 6/8 instead of 4/4, quaver equalling quaver. Of course, it's the individual melody and harmony which determines these irregular bar-periods, creating the structural fusion of harmonic, rhythmic and melodic originality I mentioned above. Here, after a delaying six-beat major phrase harmonised by the tonic chord ('Let me take you down 'cos I'm going'), the tune plunges fiercely on to the flat seventh, harmonized by the minor seventh on the dominant, for a solidly rhythmic eight-beat phrase ('*to* Strawberry Fields').

Equally subtle is the poignant 'Yesterday'. The seven-bar first section divides into 1 ('Yesterday'), 2 ('all my troubles seemed so / far away'), 2 (Now it looks as if they're / here to stay'), and 2 ('O I believe in / yesterday'). The first bar sounds isolated—it's more like an end than a beginning, being a cadential appoggiatura (G-F-F over the tonic F major chord). But the following pair of two-bar phrases (D minor, F major again) innocently assume complete regularity as if a bar had just been mislaid somewhere at the beginning; and bar six ends with a dominant seventh on G, ready to cadence conventionally on the dominant, C, in bar seven. We expect the final 'yesterday' will be something like F-E-E over a C major chord; and since the previous two-bar phrases haven't entirely erased the feeling of being one bar short, we also expect an eighth (instrumental) bar, probably echoing the voice with D-C-C over a dominant seventh on C, ready to go back to the beginning. But the dominant expectations of bar six are rudely disappointed: bar seven contradicts the G dominant seventh with its complete opposite, the subdominant chord of B flat major, which cadences immediately on the tonic F major. Very strange—and even stranger, the tune doesn't cadence at all: it rises expectantly F-A-A—with no eighth bar to follow. Or rather, amazingly, the missing bar is discovered the moment the repeat begins. That first isolated bar now reveals the point of its cadential character, acting as the final eighth bar of the first statement—yet of course simultaneously as the opening bar of the repeat. More amazing still, bar seven of the first statement is now felt to be absorbed by the repeat to supply the bar missing at the beginning.

Yet when the repeat is over, the missing-bar effect still remains, naturally, and so the situation continues into the 'middle eight'. This is ostensibly orthodox, with two nearly identical four-bar phrases, each moving from D minor to F major. But since it promptly loans its first up-beat bar ('Why she') to the first section, to supply the missing bar, it really starts with its second bar. And so the periods become four bars ('had to go I don't / know, she wouldn't / say; / I said') and three bars ('something wrong, now I / long for yester / day'). Again a tonic cadence is reached on the word 'yesterday', and again a bar is missing. Inevitably, with the return to the beginning, the first bar of all supplies the need once more. But when the final repeat of the first section is over, and the song ends, the bar is still missing. Bars have been loaned backwards and forwards, but one is continually and finally lost, like the obsessive 'yesterday' of the lyric.

Lennon and McCartney are genuine creators of a 'new music'. Strangely enough, a few 'serious' composers of 'new music' admire them, and some will say it shows you can enjoy the best of both worlds. Others will maintain it only shows that both types of music are rubbish. I wonder myself whether it isn't that the avant-garde are fascinated to find mere pop composers doing such creative things with the 'exhausted' vernacular.

[1968]

The Futility of Music Criticism

It is fatuous to condemn that as deficient in art which has been so full of art as to captivate all men. If the thing be done which was the aim of the artist—fully done—done beyond the power of other artists to accomplish—the time for criticizing the mode of doing it is gone by.—Anthony Trollope, obituary article on Dickens in *St. Paul's Magazine,* July 1870.

In reality there is no kind of evidence or argument by which one can show that Shakespeare, or any other writer, is 'good'. Nor is there any way of proving that—for instance—Warwick Deeping is 'bad'. Ultimately there is no test of literary merit except survival, which is itself an index to majority opinion.—George Orwell, 'Lear, Tolstoy and the Fool.' in *Collected Essays.*

Why is classical and folk music considered good music? Because that music has stood the test of time, has lived for tens and even hundreds of years, and still gives pleasure.—Prokofiev, *Pioneer,* 1939.

It was Sibelius who pointed out that no one has ever raised a statue to a music critic—and the reason is obvious. Statues of musicians are raised to those who live on in what they have created after their deaths; music critics, creating nothing, are forgotten when they die. But many of them have at least compensated themselves in advance, by setting themselves on pedestals in their own lifetimes, from which they have looked down on creative musicians as their inferiors. Hanslick's watchword, for example, was 'Those whom I wish to destroy, I destroy!' Well, among those he wished to destroy, was Bruckner, but Bruckner has the statues and Hanslick has none—even if the creative Wagner's caricature of him as Beckmesser in *Die Meistersinger* has prevented him from being entirely forgotten.

Hanslick, however, did at least make his monumental *gaffes* about the modern music of his own contemporaries. Today, with the new availability of the music of the past, we are faced with a far more extraordinary spectacle: that of living critics setting themselves on even loftier pedestals, from which they bend down and chip away at the statues of the dead masters beneath them. I have seen both Schubert's G major Quartet and Tchaikovsky's Fourth Symphony described as 'magnificent failures' by writers who, being unable to achieve such 'failures' themselves, can have no conception of what kind of 'magnificent successes' these works could have been. I have also seen the Pastoral Symphony described as 'one of the least flawed of Beethoven's symphonies'; and there is always Joseph Kerman to point out to us the shortcomings of the late Beethoven quartets.

At this juncture, a familiar objection is bound to be raised: one doesn't have to be a chef to criticize an omelette. But the analogy is a fallacy. Since omelettes have to be successful over and over again in the same way, experience of a few successes provides the gastronome with a single criterion against which to judge failures; but since each musical work has to be successful in an entirely different way, experience of any number of successes provides the music critic with no criterion at all. In any case, I am not suggesting that the music critic should be a composer; composers have been no better critics than the critics (see Stravinsky on Beethoven). What I do suggest is that we give up criticism of the dead masters altogether, for three reasons: it cannot establish the objective standards it hopes to; it is overridden in this respect by the majority opinion of performers and audiences, which is the only valid criterion; and it is bad for the soul, since it encourages pride, in the form of petty self-esteem.

To deal with objective standards first, let us consider the question of that controversial composer, Mahler. After his music had been largely written off, for something like fifty years after his death, the sixties brought a Mahler 'craze', which is still with us today. Now the critic intent on objective standards has to decide which of the three possible explanations of this strange fact is the correct one:

(1) Mahler is a truly great composer, who is at last coming into his own.

(2) Mahler is a remarkable but uneven composer, who is being granted more than his fair share of recognition as a natural consequence of undue neglect.

(3) Mahler is a bad composer, whose sound and fury have at last deceived many gullible people into mistaking them for great music.

Plenty of people support each of these three views, and it would certainly be nice to think we could decide objectively which of them is right. But such an objective decision is impossible, since different musicians will decide differently, and no general agreement can be reached. If a critic writes an article claiming to show that Mahler was, say, a bad composer, his judgement cannot bear any weight, because it must entail that those who believe Mahler to be a great composer are either unintelligent, or insensitive, or perhaps even insincere or self-deluded—and this must therefore apply to musicians like Walter, Klemperer, Bernstein, Schoenberg, Shostakovich, Britten, Henze and Berio to name only a few. To put it like this is to see immediately that the critic's supposed judgement is no more than an opinion, backed by rationalization of his own distaste for the music. He is naturally entitled to publish that opinion, provided he makes clear that he claims it to be no *more* than that. But then the question arises, what is the value of such negative opinions?

Hans Keller has a nice term for them: he calls them 'autobiographical'. He once referred to 'Joseph Kerman's autobiography on the Beethoven quartets'—and one sees what he means. On many a page of Kerman's book one encounters criticism of 'weaknesses' in the quartets, which strikes one as merely curious, since nobody had noticed these weaknesses before, and one cannot now see them oneself. Obviously, one realizes, they can be no more than illusions produced by Kerman's negative personal reaction to certain elements in Beethoven; and the expression of them does in fact strike one as being autobiographical without the writer realizing it.

The same may be said of Stravinsky's description of the Cavatina of the late B flat major Quartet as 'pedestrian'; and we are all, of course, guilty of such autobiography in conversation. For example, my own reaction to the theme of the slow movement of Beethoven's Fifth Symphony is amazement that he should have used such a poor melody, and I have occasionally been fool enough to say so in private. Not surprisingly, I have been greeted with surprise, amusement, and even commiseration, and no one has ever agreed with me. Any such negative reaction (given that the composer is widely admired, and that practically no one else shares that reaction) is obviously a 'blind spot'; and one should surely regard a blind spot as a misfortune rather than as something to blazon abroad. To a vast majority of people the slow movement of Beethoven's Fifth conveys something quite wonderful; what a pity that to me it is a closed book!

But if criticism cannot establish objective standards, how is it that certain standards do exist, in that we recognize the supreme quality of Bach and Beethoven, for example, and the much inferior quality of Johann Froberger and Johann Albrechstberger? Here we come to the second reason for doing away with criticism: these standards have not been created by criticism but by informed majority opinion. If enough intelligent and sensitive artists want to perform a composer's music and go on performing it, and if enough intelligent and sensitive listeners want to hear it and go on hearing it—then that music has to be regarded as being of the finest.

This may seem a peculiar statement, but after all, it is these two factors which have kept, say, Beethoven right at the centre of our musical experience, and have led us to regard him as great. Nobody can *prove* he is great; nobody *has* ever proved it. He remains great because everyone *believes* he is great—everybody *knows* he is great, one might say—and no music critic is needed to confirm the fact.

There is, of course, a sliding scale. With Beethoven, informed majority opinion is so nearly a hundred per cent as to place him right at the centre, but with Wagner, for instance, there is perhaps only a ninety per cent majority—one can still find people who reject his music as some kind of confidence trick. What can be said in such a case? The Wagnerian will say that those who deny Wagner's greatness are unintelligent or insensitive; the anti-Wagnerian will say that those who think Wagner great are taken in by their own exessive emotional response to the music. The two arguments cannot be brought to an objective conclusion—i.e., one that will satisfy everybody. In consequence, only one objective statement seems possible: Wagner is a great composer for about ninety per cent of intelligent musicians and music-lovers, but not for the other ten per cent.

This will no doubt seem an even more peculiar statement, but in fact it is a straightforward pragmatic one. Only because of this ninety per cent consensus does Wagner stand near the centre of our musical experience: if it should one day shrink drastically, he would move to the edge, to join Meyerbeer; if it should increase to practically a hundred per cent, he would move to the very centre, to join Beethoven. The same applies to Mahler, where the percentage seems more like fifty-fifty. His position will be decided, not by criticism, but by the eventual stabilizing of informed majority opinion.

The process happens quite independently of criticism, and can even survive the most concentrated barrage of *negative* criticism. The continued enthusiasm of performers and listeners has kept both Puccini and Rachmaninov well within the edge, despite a persistent critical campaign to push them over it. Wagner stayed near the centre all through the twenties, when anti-Wagnerian criticism was at its height; and Mahler, although his name was anathema to the critics, was brought swiftly towards the centre in the sixties by the belief of certain conductors and the response of the public.

The truth is that vast amounts of hot air could be dispensed with if only we could accept the obvious fact that some composers are great for you and not for me, and others are great for me and not for you. What I am suggesting is that when a composer has an impressive following, and one's own view is that he is no good, one should realize that this view is conditioned by one's own personal taste, and that the other side is just as entitled to its *positive* view, which is certainly conditioned by *its* personal taste. In other words, a policy of live and let live, instead of a holy crusade against music alien to one's own taste, in the interests of 'objective standards' which can never exist.

Perhaps it is asking too much of sinful humanity to expect people to admit the validity of contrary opinions, even in a field where there is no possibility of establishing objective standards. What *can* be asked, I think, and very much needs to be asked, is that we should stop trying to pick holes in works which are acknowledged by a very large consensus to be masterpieces.

Supposing a critic could find a flaw in the Eroica—though it seems more realistic to think that Beethoven alone could think on that level—would it really matter? I have myself—to indulge in 'autobiography' again, or perhaps 'confession' would be a better word—a slightly negative reaction to the work's last two movements. Superb though they are, I cannot feel that they maintain the supreme quality of the first two. Yes, I could give reasons—but can anyone want to listen to me, or should I expect them to? Who am I to start belittling one of the greatest achievements of the human mind?

So we arrive at the final reason for doing away with criticism—the moral one, which has to do with pride and humanity. The great composers, whatever else they may or may not have been, were the supreme musical minds in history. As such, they deserve nothing but our gratitude and admiration for what they have bequeathed us. The spectacle of a far lesser musical mind censuring one of them for supposed 'weaknesses', which are in fact illusions produced by blind spots, is quite ludicrous. And when, as so often, the censure is put forward in an arrogant, self-regarding, self-advertising way, the result is enough to make the angels weep. We have all been guilty of this, to some extent. I remember one article of my own—a wholesale attempt to write off Stravinsky's *Rake's Progress*—the thought of which now makes me shudder. Humility—the realistic recognition of one's own musical littleness, compared with the masters, is the very first requisite of any writer on music. And even if the writer is a composer of the stature of Stravinsky himself, he should still show the humility due to another master of equal stature.

Far more valuable than any criticism I have ever read is the expository writing of Tovey, who meekly accepted the supremacy of the masters, and tried to elucidate the secrets of their art. There has been far too little of this expository kind of writing. Kerman certainly attempted something of the kind in his book on the Beethoven quartets, but his blind spots, coupled with his illusory view of them as objective reality, made it impossible for him to succeed. And many other writers (Elliott Zuckerman in his *100 Years of Tristan*, for instance) make no attempt to increase understanding, but use their blind spots as a basis for wholesale denigration. Rather than try to find out what is wrong with works that have stood the test of time—which is nothing that matters—we should try to understand more deeply what is right about them—which is everything that matters.

[1972]

The Future of Musical Language

The analysis of musical language in my book, *The Language of Music*, was confined entirely to tonal music; but since about 1910, many composers have abandoned the tonal system altogether, and used a quite different means of expression—either free atonality or the twelve-note system. Naturally, the expressive laws of tonality, like its technical laws, do not apply to this music; and since there is a strong feeling that tonality will eventually give up the field entirely to atonality, the question arises 'What will be the future of music as a language?'

The first point to get clear is that the atonal revolution is something quite extraordinary. Although text-books may talk of several revolutions in musical history—the change from polyphony to monophony, the advent of the figured bass, the change from fugue to sonata-form, the romantic revolution,—these were only minor *coups d'état*. There have only ever been two real revolutions in music: the discovery of harmony and the tonal system (ninth century) and the discovery of atonality and the twelve-note system (twentieth century). The tonal system, after uncertain beginnings, has reigned for something like seven hundred years, and even now clings desperately to its dominion. We have seen [in *The Language of Music*] how the major 1-3-5-6-5 phrase could be used by a *trouvère* of the thirteenth century and the 'modernist' twentieth-century composer Busoni, in exactly the same sense; and how Bartók, in 1930, could still use the minor 6–5 for the anguish of the father in his *Cantata Profana*, which Arnold de Lantins had used for a lover's anguish about 530 years earlier. But neither of these terms, nor any of the others in the tonal system, exists in the new music.

The fundamental law of the expressive language of the tonal system is 'the more painful the emotion, the more painful the dissonance'. Through the centuries, composers have exploited dissonance to express painful emotions; but the new school has 'emancipated the dissonance'. Intermittent chromatic dissonance was used by Gesualdo, Dowland, Purcell, Bach, Mozart, Wagner, and Mahler, to express a strong feeling of anguish, but the new music avails itself of 'pan-chromaticism'. Atonal music is in fact full of dissonance, looking at it from the tonal point of view; from its own point of view there is no longer any such thing as dissonance, because the old laws have vanished, and any combination of notes is now as consonant as any other. Only it does not use the triads of the tonal system, since they would re-introduce the laws of tonality: in other words, from the tonal point of view, dissonance is omnipresent in atonal music.

The argument of the new school is that dissonance is 'relative'. Chords in the tonal system which were at first thought 'modern' and 'ugly' were soon accepted as quite normal and used freely; and the same evolutionary process will finally make twelve-note music sound perfectly straightforward. According to this theory, it is only a matter of 'advancing your norm of dissonance', or in vulgar parlance 'stretching your ears'. Technically speaking, this is unanswerable; many people have already succeeded in getting used to atonal harmony, and no doubt in time twelve-note music will become widely intelligible, at least to musicians. But the fact remains that the most chromatically dissonant harmonies of the tonal system were discovered and exploited by the late romantics, *to express more and more painful emotions*, and however 'normal' they have become, aurally speaking, *they still express those same emotions*—just as the minor 6-5 *appoggiatura* could still express anguish, in 1930, in the *Cantata Profana* of that master of semitonal dissonance, Bartok. 'Getting used to' a chord means nothing more than getting to understand it, and once we understand it, it doesn't lose its emotive power. The freely chromatic madrigals of Gesualdo sound just as full of anguish today as they ever did.

Here are three dissonant chords discovered by the romantics:

Ex. 1

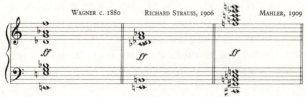

All three are connected with the most painful emotions. The first was used by Wagner to express the chronic hysteria of the accursed woman Kundry in *Parsifal*; the second by Richard Strauss to express Elektra's hysterical bitterness and hatred in the opera which bears her name; the third was placed by Mahler at the climax of the Adagio which was all that he completed of his Tenth Symphony (the manuscript is scrawled with pitiful *cris de coeur* which betray a mind near to its breaking-point). These chords still express these very feelings when we hear them today. It is pointless to say that we 'put ourselves back in the period' and 'accept their terms of reference': there is no need for mental readjustment, for they strike us like a blow. And so do the chords of atonal music.

Some modern composers have in fact openly regarded atonality as a system of total dissonance, appropriate for the expression of total anguish; Alban Berg in *Wozzeck*, for example, and Luigi Dallapiccola in *Il Prigioniero*. Berg, in his opera based on Büchner's grim, pathetic, sordid and terribly depressing play, used atonality throughout, though with one or two exceptions. The triad of C major suddenly enters like a ray of light when the poor soldier Wozzeck gives his pitiful wages to his mistress, Marie. It is said that Berg used it to convey the utterly commonplace notion of money, but we know that music cannot express abstract ideas. Berg may have explained the triad in this way afterwards, in a sardonic mood, but surely C major expresses here what it always did—the simple, common joy of life (for which the poor are dependent on money). Another striking use of tonality in this opera is the final interlude after the penultimate scene: Wozzeck has killed Marie and drowned himself, and the music suddenly slips surely and deliberately into D minor, the better to build up a powerful, ferocious indictment of the world in which such things can happen. The other interesting case is the end of the opera. The last act has begun in G minor (Mozart's 'anxiety' key) for the scene in which Marie writhes in remorse at having been unfaithful to Wozzeck; and at the end of the opera the key of G seems likely to return. The children are playing in the street, and suddenly, being told that Marie is dead, they all run off to see the body, leaving only Marie's (and Wozzeck's) child, playing alone with his hobby-horse. The pathos is extreme: two atonal woodwind chords oscillate gently in triplets, and against these the strings play the bare fifth G and D, *pianissimo*—again *piano*—again *mezzo-piano*—and again *piano* fading to *pianissimo* and dying out, leaving the atonal chords to waver on, and finally break off in midstream without a formal ending. This deliberate refusal to realise the faint hope of a firm tonal ending is the comment of one great atonal composer on the expressive power of his chosen medium: there can be no happy ending (G major) nor unhappy ending (G minor) nor even a bare ending (fifths of G and D), but only unrelieved unhappiness continuing on into the future.

Likewise, Dallapiccola, in his opera *Il Prigioniero*, based on a harrowing tale of persecution and torture during the Spanish Inquisition, set against the atonal anguish of his desperate prisoner a chorus singing sacred words of faith and comfort, off-stage, in the key of C major.

But these are obviously composers with a 'nostalgia' for tonality: Berg confessed this in *Wozzeck* when he set the opening of the fairy-story, told by Marie to her child, in the key of F minor—'Once upon time....'. What of those composers who have no nostalgia for tonality, but are quite at home with atonality—what of Schoenberg, the master of them all?

In his early tonal works, such as the *Gurrelieder* and *Verklärte Nacht*, Schoenberg used the tonal system in the same expressive way as other late romantics. And in one twelve-note work, in which he organized his series with implications of the key of C—*A Survivor from Warsaw*, which tells of the splendours and miseries of a concentration camp—he showed that he still accepted the expressive characteristics of various tonal tensions. He made use both of the minor sixth of anguish, for the awful moment of *reveille* (bar 25), and of the minor 6–5 burst of anguish for the horrors of separation (bar 29); and the whole work ends with a 6/4 chord built out of notes 2 to 6 of his series (G, A flat, C, E natural, E flat), combining the major triad ('splendours') minor triad ('miseries') and minor sixth (anguish) into a basically tragic term containing an element of triumph. Moreover, the upper note E flat is approached melodically by way of E natural—the major third falling to the minor third. Nevertheless, the whole piece remains fairly and squarely twelve-note and atonal.

Here again, we have atonality used for total anguish, and indeed, in his early atonal works, Schoenberg used the new style for just such a purpose: *Pierrot Lunaire* has a *fin-de-siècle* text full of the most strained and disordered imaginings; and *Erwartung* is a monodrama in which the protagonist runs through the gamut of the painful emotions, fear, jealousy, horror, anguish, despair.

When we come to his absolute music, shall we find that this equation of atonality with anguish holds good? Attempts have been made by admirers of twelve-note music to deny any such connection: for example, they point to the *Serenade*, op.24, as an example of 'light' atonal music, essentially genial and cheerful. With the best will in the world, one cannot agree. The opening and closing March, with its hard, firm dissonances, and aggressive rhythms, has a grimly forceful effect; the *Ländler* is a grotesque parody of Austrian popular music—an intensification of Mahler's 'take-off' of Viennese *schmaltz*; and the *Lied* is full of romantic pathos, enhanced by the new type of dissonance. This is a Serenade 'of our time'.

Stravinsky has declared that Schoenberg belongs spiritually to the last century. Speaking of his Violin Concerto of 1936, he said: 'The pathos [in the sense of 'emotionalism'] is last century's; and since pathos is created by language, the language in essence must be last century's too;[1] harmonize the second movement in a purely Brahmsian manner—you have only to move a few notes over a bit—and the theme is happily restored to its true habitat; Schoenberg is the true evolutionary centre, but only up to a period many years before this Concerto'.

Skipping the psychological question of Stravinsky's ambivalent attitude towards Schoenberg, we shall not need to take these remarks very seriously. Given permission to 'move a few notes over a bit' in the harmony, one could guarantee to make Stravinsky's own music sound like Mahler. But one feels his main point is correct: Schoenberg's style derives ultimately from the last century, and with it of course his sense of music as a language. It seems undeniable that he used atonality to express painful emotions: there is no geniality, happiness, or tenderness in his later music, but only a fierce, unrelenting purpose, a constant sense of life's grimness, and a good deal of aching pathos. One does not deny that an aura of purely aesthetic beauty is cast over the expression, transfiguring the basically painful emotions in a strange, unearthly way, in much the same way as in Samuel Beckett's play

---

[1] It seems that Stravinsky has changed his mind about music being 'powerless to express anything at all, whether a feeling, an attitude of mind, a psychological mood. . . .'

Waiting for Godot; that the dynamic rhythms give an aggressive feeling to much of his music, saving it from the morbidity that affects most twelve-note music; and that the masterly form gives an objective counterbalance to the intensely subjective material.

It seems only natural that atonal music *should* express painful emotion since, as we have tried to show, the various harmonic tensions between notes are derived from tensions in the natural scheme of things—the harmonic series. When the augmented fourth, major seventh, and minor ninth are pretty well omnipresent, how else can we interpret them than in the way we always have? They exert the same effect on us, aurally and emotionally. The more 'used' one gets to a work by Schoenberg, the more one understands its inherent grimness: familiarity does not bring about a change in the emotional connotation of the sounds, but only a comprehension of the way in which they function as a coherent expressive whole.

Does this mean that atonality is the natural outcome of twentieth-century life, with its stresses and strains, insecurity, and continual threat of destruction? That man has discovered more and more unpleasant truths about himself through the science of psychology, and cannot ignore them when he comes to write music? That we have to live with what we have made of ourselves in the world we have created, and we cannot find a God to redeem us, and it isn't pleasant? This would seem to be the answer: the same process must be at work in music as in the explicit world of the theatre, in the pessimistic plays of Beckett and Ionesco. It seems that, as Berg so poignantly pointed out at the end of *Wozzeck*, we have come to the end of happy endings, and also of neatly tragic endings. We can't resolve our chromatic tensions into a major chord of 'transfiguration', as at the end of *Tristan*, or even into a minor chord of utter disaster, as at the end of Tchaikovsky's *Pathétique* Symphony. Life isn't as simple as that; it's more like a novel by James Joyce—no clear cut ending, but only life continuing with plenty of pain in it.

But surely life isn't entirely painful? Surely it is still possible, even in mid-twentieth century, to experience a good deal of joy? It seems reasonable that art should tell the whole truth about life, not just a part. The fathers of the medieval church insisted that life was a 'vale of tears' and consequently tried to keep the triad out of their music, preferring octaves, fifths, and fourths. The Soviet auth-

orities insist that life must be viewed as a 'bed of roses', and hold
fast to the triad, forbidding all experiments in atonality. Atonal
composers, it seems, insist that life is a 'bed of thorns', for they
refuse to admit any triads into their music, concentrating largely on
the semitone of anguish and the augmented fourth of disruption.
But perhaps the true basis of life *is* pain, to the discerning?

It cannot be as simple as this, of course. There must be another
explanation, though one does not seem to be forthcoming. When
one asks a Schoenbergian what emotions are expressed in the
music, he either hedges, or pretends not to understand the
question. Schoenberg himself made unequivocal remarks which
show that he regarded music as a language, as when he wrote that
'a tender thought can be expressed by a quick and violent theme,
because the following violence will develop from it more organi-
cally'. However, this very remark, contradicting the unwritten laws
of musical expression which have persisted for centuries, reveals
just how difficult the problem is: whatever this music expresses, it
is not the joys and sorrows of life as most of us know them. Perhaps
the answer is to be found on the metaphysical plane; indeed, the
inexplicably moving experience provided by Schoenberg's opera
Moses and Aaron would seem to suggest this. Is there not one
single dodecaphonic expert with a human heart who is not too busy
analysing intricacies of technique to give a much-needed answer to
this all-important question: what is the new music trying to say?

Perhaps no answer is yet possible. The new language of music is
surely growing up, just as the old one did, on a basis of instinct; and
it may very well remain inaccessible to the understanding for just as
long a time.

[1958?]

The Future of *The Language of Music*

It is fifteen years now since *The Language of Music* appeared, and I have been fairly disappointed with its reception. This is not because it hasn't been praised—it has been more praised than blamed, and the extent of my personal success or failure is unimportant. But I regarded it, and still regard it, as a pioneer work in a new field—a work to be either shown to be wrong or accepted as a basis to build on (or a bit of both). However, those who dismissed it didn't show it to be wrong, and those who accepted it haven't built on it. It also appears that, in university circles, the book is regarded with suspicion and indifference.

In fact, I think the book has been misunderstood. It has been seen as the expression of an extreme opinion, whereas my intention was to present a new theory, claiming to be true. Only one writer has realized this—Robert Donington, who wrote in his book *Wagner's 'Ring' and its Symbols* that 'none of the previous writers on the subject quite succeeded in arriving at Cooke's starting-point.' I quote this without false modesty, because I think it's no more than the simple truth.

Of course, the book has its faults, and I am well aware of them. If I were writing it today, I should write it differently. In the first place, the word 'language' has upset a lot of philosophers, who have gone to great lengths to show that music doesn't function like *verbal* language. Of course it doesn't: I devoted a lot of the book to saying precisely that. I used the word 'language' in its widest sense—perhaps in a metaphorical sense—to signify 'a means of communication'. But this was unfortunate, since it created a red herring for philosophers to chew over. Their excellent proofs that music isn't a language in the same way as verbal language is a language were a waste of time. The question isn't whether music is a language, but whether it conveys or communicates something to the listener.

The second fault of the book was the way I described this something which music conveys or communicates. I called it 'emotion', and thereby stirred up a philosophical hornets' nest. 'What *is* emotion? Doesn't there have to be someone to feel an emotion, and something to arouse it? How can this "someone" be the composer if the "something" remains unknown? Since we say "this piece of music is sad", doesn't music express *moods* rather than emotions?' And so on. I tried to raise and answer these questions; but since I'm no philosopher, I couldn't express myself precisely. In consequence, another red herring was there, for everyone to argue about.

The question, 'What is it exactly that music communicates?' is certainly a very important one, but not one that I was trying to answer. I was merely trying to show that music did express something which could be loosely characterised as 'emotion' or 'feeling': it's up to the philosophers, if they can, to find the right word or words to define it. My own point of view is the same as that of the man who was perhaps the greatest thinker about music of all time—Richard Wagner. In an essay written in Paris when he was twenty-eight he said:

> What music expresses is eternal, infinite and ideal. It does *not* express the passion, love or longing of this or that individual in this or that situation, but passion, love, or longing in itself; and this it presents in that unlimited variety of motivations which is the exclusive and particular characteristic of music, foreign and inexpressible in any other language.

If I had known that quotation when I wrote *The Language of Music*, I would have used it as a motto for the book.

Wagner's phrase 'inexpressible in any other language' sums up another fault of the book—or rather, not a fault but a problem. Since I was attempting to classify the vocabulary of music, I had to describe it in words—to say, for example, that this term expressed 'joy' and that term expressed 'grief'—and some people seem to have imagined that I regarded these emotive words as exact translations of music into verbal language. Of course, I imagined nothing of the kind—as I said in the book:

The words 'anguish', 'joy' and 'despair' are only hazy—but one hopes basically accurate—terms for describing the particular kind and degree of anguish, joy and despair expressed *precisely* by music. By 'basically accurate' one means that a million different types of anguish can be covered by the word 'anguish'—but not by the word 'joy'.

The fourth fault of the book—an inevitable one—was that it drastically over-simplified the whole problem. To cover it in full would have meant my devoting my whole life to it, and producing, say, a work in ten thick volumes. I decided against this, for two very good reasons—first, because I had other things as well to do with my life, and secondly, because people don't really *read* works in ten thick volumes. So the result was a severe over-simplification: in concentrating mainly on melody—which is, of course, the fundamental element—I didn't say a great deal about rhythm and harmony. Nevertheless, I felt that what I did say about them opened up the field for other investigators.

The faults that I have admitted can be summed up in one single phrase from a criticism of the book made by a philosopher: '*The Language of Music* is philosophically naive'. This is quite true. I am no philosopher, and *The Language of Music* is not in any sense a philosophical investigation of the problem of the meaning of music. It is, rather, an empirical inquiry by a musician, and from that point of view it still stands, unrefuted and unratified, because unexamined.

It is my belief that philosophers have never been able to solve the problem of music, because, not being musicians themselves, they have written in a musical vacuum. They have made statements about music which they are unable to verify because they lack the technical knowledge. Such statements can only be verified, or refuted, by a musician who has that knowledge.

For example, I have been taken to task one philosopher for ignoring the statement by Suzanne Langer that 'music has no vocabulary'. But this is not a statement of fact, it is merely an opinion. The only factual statement on this subject would be 'music has never been shown to have a vocabulary'. Since my book was an attempt to prove, by technical means, that music *does* have a vocabulary (though a very different type of vocabulary from verbal languages) I naturally regarded Miss Langer's non-factual statement as irrelevant. But the philosopher who criticised me lacked the technical knowledge to understand what I was trying to prove.

If music does have meaning, it must communicate that meaning through the way the notes are manipulated—melodically, rhythmically, harmonically, and so on. The only way to discover that meaning is to get to grips with the music itself, and not to talk about it in abstract terms. One has to examine music in minute detail, and find out how it functions from this point of view—and this is what I have done. The valid part of my book is the mass of block music examples, which show that composers through the ages, when setting verbal texts, have used the same melodic phrases or stressed the same degrees of the major and minor scale in association with the same emotions.

In this light the book might even be described as *scientific*, in the sense defined by Karl Popper, since it presents a theory so concrete and definite that it is open to disproof. If someone can find examples of melodic phrases being used, and degrees of the scale being stressed, in association with other emotions than the ones I have shown, then my theory will be proved wrong, and will have to be either corrected, or drastically reformulated, or abandoned altogether.

Unfortunately, no one has attempted to do this. A colleague of mine—a music critic—did once say to me personally that he was sure that he could find plenty of contradictory examples; and I eagerly encouraged him to try, and to send me his findings, but I heard no more of the matter. I am not suggesting that he couldn't find any—I'm certain that he never looked, because, since he didn't agree with my theory, he was sure that it was wrong, and that was enough for him. In the same way, everybody, whether they agreed or disagreed with my theory, has treated it as *opinion* not as theory claiming to be fact.

To demonstrate the working of the theory briefly, we will examine one small facet of it. The beginning of the slow introduction to the finale of Mozart's G minor String Quintet, K.516, is a piece of absolute music: it has no programme, it doesn't tell a story, and Mozart didn't leave on record what he intended it to communicate to the listener. Prior to *The Language of Music* there could be no attempt at an answer to the question 'What does it communicate?', yet practically all the commentators, writing about the quintet, describe this part of it as expressing melancholy, sadness, grief, or despair. There was no proof of this: it simply made them feel very sad. The philosophers were quite unable to solve the problem, since they rarely discussed specific pieces of music. To say that the music was so sad because it was in a minor key was no proof, since there is plenty of music in a minor key which isn't sad at all.

So the supposed sadness of the music remained a matter of opinion, as did the supposed emotional expression of any piece of music. The way was open for one school of thought—pursued by Hanslick, Hindemith and Stravinsky, amongst others—to offer the opposite opinion: music didn't express anything at all—it was pure form, pure beauty, pure abstraction, and so on. Since I felt the emotion in music very strongly, I wanted to find a proof that music was expressive of emotion. I had noticed that certain melodic phrases recurred throughout music—in music of different periods by different composers—and always in association with certain emotions. So I began collecting examples until I had quite a large number.

Let us now examine the first phrase from the Mozart Quintet (Ex. 1).

Ex. 1

There is a great similarity between this phrase and the beginning of the finale of Tchaikovsky's *Pathétique* Symphony (Ex. 2—here transposed into G minor).

Ex. 2

The last note is different in the melody, but is present in the harmony, and Tchaikovsky *did* leave on record what he intended to communicate: he marked it 'Adagio Lamentoso'. The theme also occurs in Beethoven's A flat major Piano Sonata, op. 110, slightly more ornamented, but with the same basic notes as the Mozart (Ex. 3—also transposed).

Ex. 3

Beethoven wrote against this phrase 'klagender Gesang'—'Song of lamentation'.

The fourth example is one of the great moments in Bach's music: the aria 'It is finished' which follows the death of Jesus in the St John Passion. The aria is accompanied by a viola de gamba obbligato which begins like this:

Ex. 4

It is almost exactly the same as the Beethoven and here too Bach left on record what he intended the phrase to communicate, by using it in a lament for the death of Jesus.

The second phrase of Mozart's theme (Ex. 5) is a kind of imprecise echo of the first—a modified repetition of it, adding

Ex. 5

nothing new, but reinforcing the feeling of lament. This is achieved partly by ornamenting the last note by 'leaning' on to it, as in the Beethoven and Bach phrases.

The third and fourth phrases of the theme are exactly the same as the first and second, but a note higher. The parallel with this is also to be found in the St John Passion, where, just before the aria quoted above, Jesus' dying words 'It is finished' are sung at the pitch of Mozart's third phrase. Then the viola da gamba takes it up a note lower, playing the phrase which compares with Mozart's first phrase. Other parallels with Mozart's third phrase are to be found in Bach's cantata *Es ist genug*, in which the Christian soul bids farewell to the world as it dies; and in Wagner's *Parsifal*, where the phrase is hammered out over and over again in the funeral march for Titurel.

The fourth phrase is the same kind of echo of the third as the second phrase was of the first, so needs no explaining. The fifth and final phrase,

Ex. 6a

reduced to its essentials, without ornamentation, becomes

Ex. 6b

We have heard this elsewhere in Tchaikovsky's *Pathétique* Symphony (Ex 7a—*Adagio Lamentoso* again), in Bach's song 'Come, soothing death' (Ex. 7b), and in John Dowland's *Lachrymae*, which begins 'Flow my tears, flow from your spring' (Ex. 7c), to take only three examples.

Ex. 7a   Ex. 7b   Ex. 7c

I have offered enough evidence here to prove that this melody of Mozart's cannot be anything but a lament. In *The Language of Music* there is much more evidence, to show that other melodies cannot be anything but a paean of joy, or an assertion of courage, or an expression of innocence, and so on. I systematized the knowledge gained from such comparisons into what I believe to be incontrovertible technical facts. The one which applies to the examples given above is as follows: any melody in a minor key, which is slow, and which is made up of descending phrases, especially those built around the eighth, seventh, sixth and fifth degrees of the minor scale, and the fifth, fourth, third, second and first degrees of that scale, expresses feelings that can be characterized by words like melancholy, sadness or grief.

Such technical facts, at the opposite pole from philosophizing about music, are the pioneer work achieved by *The Language of Music*. If they are not facts, then someone with equal technical knowledge should prove they are not, by showing, for example, some minor melodies made up of descending phrases of the kind I've specified, which have been used by composers in association with feelings of joy, or courage, or innocence. If anyone can do so, I shall be delighted, because it will mean that we shall have advanced a little towards the truth: my theory will have been proved wrong, and we shall have to start building a new one. But we shall never get near the truth by philosophizing about music, without actually examining it in all its multifarious detail. In the absence of such examination, philosophy can offer nothing more than a mass of unfounded and conflicting opinions.

[1974]

Index